D1121693

FICTION SETS YOU FREE

FICTION SETS YOU FREE

LITERATURE, LIBERTY, AND WESTERN CULTURE

Russell A. Berman

University of Iowa Press | Iowa City

University of Iowa Press, Iowa City 52242

www.uiowapress.org

Copyright © 2007 by the University of Iowa Press

All rights reserved

Printed in the United States of America

Design by April Leidig-Higgins

The University of Iowa Press is a member of Green Press
Initiative and is committed to preserving natural resources.

Printed on acid-free paper

ISBN-13: 978-1-58729-604-8

ISBN-10: 1-58729-604-7

LCCN: 2007923927

07 08 09 10 11 C 5 4 3 2 1

For Aniko and Max

CONTENTS

ACKNOWLEDGMENTS

NUMEROUS COLLEAGUES and friends have been generous with their time and wisdom, providing me with valuable suggestions, not to mention appropriate words of caution, as I undertook this project. I am grateful to them all and wish to express my particular gratitude to Stephen Haber and Barry Weingast for crucial conversations about culture and social institutions; to Andrea Lundsford for guidance in the field of literacy; to Catherine Pickstock for insights on Plato and on religion; and to David Gross, John Meyer, and Vincent Pecora for comments on versions of the manuscript. I also want to thank the following for productive suggestions: Theodore Andersson, Charlotte Fronrobert, Pierre Furlan, Ian Hodder, Henry Lowood, Ian Morris, Susan Stephens, and John Wang. Their pointers helped me along; the limitations of the book are my own fault.

Portions of chapter 1 appeared previously in *Modern Language Quarterly* 62 (2001): 317–30.

The Bertolt Brecht poem "Hollywood Quatrain" is from *Gesammelte Werke* (Frankfurt am Main: Suhrkamp Verlag, 1967), English edition translated and copyrighted by Stefan Brecht, all rights reserved by Suhrkamp Verlag Frankfurt am Main.

WHY LITERATURE MATTERS

THIS BOOK EXAMINES the distinctiveness of imaginative literature, how it emerged historically, and what it has contributed to the development of civilization. Why does literature command our attention at all? What is the advantage to society to cultivate a sphere of activity devoted to the counter-factuals of literary fiction? After all, it is surely curious that society devotes any resources to the circulation of mere fictions. There is nothing obvious about this constant habit of telling tales whose essential nature is precisely their lack of empirical truth or informational content. Yet this faith in fiction involves much more than a promulgation of falsehoods or the distribution of ideology. On the contrary, literature matters because, through its fiction-ality, it contributes integrally to the dynamism of society. The untruths of the literary imagination enable our imagination to surpass the empirical constraints that surround us. Fictions—and the cultivation of a sensibility enriched by imaginative prowess—can set us free.

The autonomy of literature, its fundamental independence from its con-text, models the independence of individuals. Against the various academic delimitations of autonomy to a modern or romantic and postromantic pe-riod of literature, this book claims a much longer trajectory of literary his-tory. Literary autonomy, and therefore imagination—understood as a cogni-tive independence from real-world limitations—is a formidable component as much of the ancient heroic epics as of even earlier oral traditions. This is not to say that autonomy has no developmental history of its own. It did not spring full blown from the mind of the first neolithic storyteller or Sumerian scribe. Literary autonomy grew and responded to changing contexts, literary and otherwise, just as it drew on its contemporary material and language use. What I am calling the autonomy of literature is the capacity of a text to resist reduction to an external reality, while aspiring to an internal formal coherence (no matter how flawed or elusive). And autonomy characterizes literature since its inception, because it derives from the symbolic character of language, which defines us as humans. We are human and therefore imaginative and literary. Literature is the tool with which humanity sharpens our power of imagination while adding to the eloquence of our language.

Literary autonomy implies two personae: the author and the reader. Across time, the ever sharper profiling of both these roles contributes to the modeling of autonomous individuality. The invention of authorship — Homer can stand as the emblematic model here — is fundamental to the historical development of notions of a free and dignified character. The manner in which an author completes a work stands as a norm of integrity for other forms of human practice. Similarly, the fact of written literature implies the presence of readers, and readership too models a subjectivity in a way that encourages the cultivation of an inner life of self-reflection. This subjectivity is not a literary fiction or an arbitrary invention by some nefarious ideology. On the contrary, it is grounded in the phenomenology of being human, the character of our bodies — our being in the world, as well as the physiological preconditions of language use. Subjectivity, the very nature of our self-consciousness, is unthinkable without language, which, however necessarily, also implies the creative use of language and therefore literature. Consequently, the functions of author and reader and the explicit thematization of subjectivity in literature — beginning with the epic heroes — allow for the articulation of Western notions of individuality: I insist on "Western" because of the characteristic combination of alphabetic literacy, which originated in Greece, and Judeo-Christian spirituality. This realization of individuality through literature anchors literature in the real developmental history that has generated those distinctively Western social institutions that are dependent on the vibrancy of individuals capable of choice: liberal democracy and the market economy. I therefore argue that the long history of autonomous literature is very much part of a specific Western teleology. Without imaginative literature, we would not be able to imagine the individuality to which we aspire and on which our institutions depend. The programmatic separation of literature from society — the autonomy of this form of imaginative language use — is precisely the path that allows literature to contribute to society through the elaboration of individuality.

To argue as I do that imagination is a function of language, and that literary autonomy is grounded in the cognitive function of the imagination, does not imply that autonomous literature, as it developed in the West, was a somehow necessary or inevitable outcome. Too much depended on the specific efforts of generations of authors, in their continuous expansion of the limits of human freedom. "A [literary] work is nothing more than a battle fought against conventions," wrote Zola.[1] More broadly, the contingency of the whole process is much too great to posit any deterministic necessity: Not all primates developed language, not all humans developed alphabetic script, not all literate cultures articulated transcendent religions with notions of holy scripture, which became fundamental to the Western understanding of the literary work of art — those are the evolutionary stages that this book will trace. There is clearly nothing necessary or preordained about our linguistic situation or, therefore, our literary tradition. The argument here is consequently not that autonomous literature is somehow inevitable or universally valid. On the contrary, it emerges through a set of very contingent choices, perhaps even accidents or freaks of nature (such as early humans' learning how to speak). Still, fully recognizing this contingency, we can nonetheless study the tradition that did indeed take shape and that remains ours to inherit and cultivate.

The introduction explores some basic points about the relationship between literature and history that are pertinent to the argument in this book and to contemporary criticism. The core claim is that imaginative literature contributes productively to the long-term civilizing process by fostering a capacity to project alternatives to any given context. The claim implies, however, the possibility of a big-picture account of civilization, a grand narrative, despite the predisposition in the academic humanities today to focus on narrower moments and ever smaller specializations. In contrast, I assert that literature is a dynamic force in social development; it plays a role within history, and it does so precisely through its autonomy, its distinctiveness from other, primarily referential, modes of language use. The interest is less in what distinguishes modern writers from the ancients than in how they participate in a shared project related to the character of literature, and how that character, the emphatic difference that is literature, informs the developmental history of society.

Yet literature does not only participate in a developmental history of civilization. That history is, also, internal to the literary work of art, shaping its very character. I explore the implications of this interrelationship in chapter 1. Despite its autonomy, its imaginative distinctiveness from real-world language, literature also conveys historical substance within itself. This history that is immanent within literature is, however, not only some positive knowledge about its own context but, more important, a particular relationship to its own temporality. Literature has the characteristic ability to survive its context, in space and time, and address readers in distant venues; it can move through time, separate itself from its initial surroundings, and therefore call into question narrowly periodic approaches to its history. These issues are pursued in the first chapter, which examines the problem of periodization. The historicity of literature is not one of context dependence but a capacity to overcome periodic or historicist time. The question, as Marx once put it, is not how Greek literature is rooted in an ancient context — this he assumes is obvious and trivial — but rather what it is about that literature from a very different time and place that makes it still a source of pleasure and admiration here and now. Walter Benjamin reformulated the same problem in a crucial way in his *Theses on the Philosophy of History*:[2] The transhistorical power of literature is greater than a historicism focused solely on periodization and contexts. For the argument in this book, the problem that ensues involves sketching a history of literature in relation to claims about social development without falling back into historicism. Literature participates in developmental history, not, however, because it can reflect its historical context but rather because it harbors a sense of time and a force of imagination that can call context into question in order to surpass it. A tension nonetheless remains between the autonomy of imaginative literature and the developmental frame, and this gap has important implications for the relationship between humanistic and social-scientific norms.

Chapter 2 examines recent discussions of human origins, particularly with regard to the emergence of language. While much contemporary literary study focuses narrowly on the present — grows presentist — this contrarian chapter stakes out a very distant starting point for a long history of literature. No literature without language: hence the decision to start the consideration of literary history with reflections on the origin of language. To be sure, this origins question is far from new in intellectual history. Yet rather than relying on older (merely) philosophical speculations on language history, we can now turn to contemporary human origins research with its social and natural scientific bases for insights into the consequences of early human language acquisition. When and why did *Homo sapiens* develop language? Can we correlate this inventiveness with other articulations of knowledge or cultural and technological change evidenced in the archeological record? How does speech acquisition distinguish humans from earlier hominids or, for that matter, other primates? In this chapter, three accounts of language origins, with very different disciplinary backgrounds, are discussed. I examine how Merlin Donald considers the archeological record in order to suggest a multistage cultural prehistory in *Origins of the Modern Mind: Three Stages in the Organization of Culture and Cognition*.[3] In contrast, Steven Mithen proceeds by way of cognitive psychology, in particular by posing questions on the modularity of the intelligence in his *Prehistory of the Mind: The Cognitive Origins of Art and Science*.[4] Finally, William Noble and Iain Davidson, in *Human Evolution, Language, and Mind: A Psychological and Archeological Inquiry*,[5] examine evidence that points to language acquisition, in particular a sudden leap associated with the facility to utilize symbolic knowledge. The chapter investigates these approaches and explores how each account leads to possible hypotheses on language, imagination, and literature.

The evidence of accelerated technological change among early humans, the emergence of the first art objects, and the archeological findings of the first gravesites (indicating a thematic awareness of death and therefore, presumably, a rudimentary religious culture) around fifty thousand years ago is linked hypothetically to a sudden transition to language use. As Noble and Davidson in particular underscore, language implies the use of symbols, the capacity to make reference: using a sign in order to invoke an object not present. This symbolism, which is the precondition for any genuine language, is integrally associated with imagination, that is, the capacity to envision absent contents. Literature is precisely that formalized skill that allows humanity to cultivate this imaginative capacity and, therefore, in an evolutionary feedback loop, literature refines language itself. The *Homo sapiens* capacity to shape tools faster than earlier hominids includes as well an ongoing effort to reshape the one species-defining technology, language. Moreover, Donald associates the capacity for linguistic creativity evidenced by seminal poets with the initial creativity of invention of language. It follows that the human-origins question is not just about the distant starting point of language and literature; it also sheds light on ongoing literary poetic practice. Literature's particular productivity for the refinement of language thus continues the original creativity that allowed for the initial species-defining entry into language.

Other questions follow: Once language was in place, but before the emergence of writing, what sort of literature (if that term is permissible) proliferated, what prehistoric stories and songs might have been conveyed through the symbolic expression of early language? Paleoanthropology and archeology have contributions to make in this area, which is crucial to literary history but which has been largely ignored in the humanities. For the historian of literature, of course, genuine evidence appears to be sparse: We have no direct records of the narrative culture of the prehistoric world. Instead of therefore avoiding the topic altogether, literary history will have to learn how to extrapolate from indirect evidence. For example, statues of creatures half human, half animal are among the oldest artifacts found in prehistoric sites. Yet written literature too has repeatedly, and throughout its history, reflected on this process of hominization through fictions of talking animals, echoing the conditions of its own origin. I consider Kafka's short stories "The Metamorphosis," in which the human becomes an animal and loses all but interior speech, and "Report to an Academy," in which the animal acquires elaborate speech on his way toward becoming human.[6] Both are taken as commentary on the relationship of literature to an original language acquisition. While Kafka makes the border between animal mutism and human communication thematic, an alternative example, a poetic stanza by Lamartine,[7] gets at the problem in a different way. Despite the lack of any similar direct thematization of language origins, the character of the verse itself is, one example standing for many, shown to indicate literature's ongoing concern with the status of language as such: literature as the perpetual refinement by the species of its linguistic technologies, and rhyme as a trace of a nonsemantic linguistic function. (Making reference to this literary material raises certain methodological questions, insofar as the argument moves between social-scientific and humanistic evidence and their different norms of truth. These issues are addressed at several points in the book in an ongoing methodological reflection on the questions of evidence and objectivity at this border between the humanities and the social sciences.)

Chapters 3, 4, and 5 discuss the transition in language use, which is surely foundational for our notion of literature: the development of written language. The question of the origins of writing has long been at the core of seminal scholarship, such as that of Walter J. Ong, Eric Havelock, Jack Goody, and Ian Watt. Key aspects of this scholarship are examined closely in order to explore the foundations of literature in the context of writing. Several basic conceptual issues emerge very quickly and are examined in chapter 3. Much existing scholarship is organized in terms of a binary historiography of (primary) orality and literacy. That developmental process is better understood, I assert, in terms of competing social or cultural sectors, such as literature, politics, and economics. This paradigm of sector competition is ultimately richer and more reasonable than a contrast between a once-upon-a-time of pure orality and a postlapsarian literacy. This approach is corroborated by the elusiveness of any clear borderline between the presumably separate phases. In particular, I show that many of the phenomenological aspects of the written word, on which Ong[9] insists, are not radical innovations in the context of newly acquired literacy but represent elaborations of aspects of earlier visual artifact production that dates from the period of original language acquisition. Thus, features such as material durability, portability, and the consequent separability from the producer, all of which characterize the written word and are absent in oral performance, nonetheless characterize certain visual arts, such as statue or vase production. Still another consideration highlights the inadequacy of the neat duality of orality and literacy, the overall problem of technological determinism. Media-historical foundations to a history of literature and culture surely depend on the acquisition of writing technology (just as the new electronic media of the late twentieth century may be ushering in a further techno-cultural paradigm shift). Yet it is hardly convincing to attempt to explain literary change solely through a reduction to this single technological factor, while excluding other components of social development.

The written work is the foundation of literary autonomy. Once written down, the text achieves a certain stability and a greater capacity for distribution. It thereby escapes the conformist pressures of the homeostatic adjustment processes from performer-audience interaction that burden oral performance. This transition is discussed closely in chapter 4, especially with reference to Donald's trajectory of cultural development but also Scribner and Cole's investigations of Vai literacy and its particular psychological consequences.[10] These approaches are then brought to bear, in chapter 5, on the standing of the heroic epics: the Homeric texts, *Das Nibelungenlied*, *La Chanson de Roland*, and, as an indication of generic continuity into the present, Derek Walcott's *Omeros*. Among the questions that ensue, Havelock's insistence on the distinctiveness of alphabetic writing is particularly salient.[11] Alphabetic literacy requires knowledge of a considerably reduced range of signs (as compared with ideographic or hieroglyphic literacy). Hence it implies a much greater potential for dissemination toward a generalized literacy, a greater access to information, and therefore also a greater prospect for democracy. But alphabetic literacy is, ultimately, a consequence of one singular world-historical process, the Greek adaptation of Semitic syllabary writing. (Korean represents a much later but nonetheless important exception). In other words, the discussion of the particular character of consistent alphabetization involves fundamentally distinctive processes of accelerated economic development, political democratization, and psychological individuation. The institutionalization of autonomous literature is an integral component of this transformation.

The significance of literature and its contribution to individuation are particularly noteworthy in the evidence provided by the heroic epics: the heroes ground Western individuality, and the epics are already, at their "early" stage, examples of aesthetic autonomization, thereby going well beyond what Havelock refers to as their function as "social encyclopedia."[12] The epics are crucial to any discussion of the relationship of orality to literacy while also providing a useful perspective on the profound and frequently competitive relationship between literature and political power. Without a doubt, preexisting tales were woven together to form these epics, but they very likely emerged in the context of beginning literacy. Intratextual evidence corroborates this claim. If that is the case, however, then an additional claim becomes more compelling: that the epic heroism, in its adversarial rejection of the given order, is nothing less than the objectification of the standing of the new medium, writing, in its challenge to traditional society.

Chapter 6 proceeds to a later historical stage. After the emergence of writing and its generic corollary, the elaborate heroic epic, the next transition involves the dissemination and consequences of the so-called axial religions, the great monotheisms. Judaism and Christianity, in particular, define religious cultures around the sacrality of central texts, a legacy later inherited by the literary work of art. The chapter traces several aspects, first of all the question of creativity as *creatio ex nihilo* and an orientation in literature toward the radically new, whereby the distinction between pagan and post-Christian accounts of transformation is particularly telling: that between Ovid and Kafka on metamorphosis. Second, canonicity as a sense of a relation to the past, the recognition of the importance of tradition as a transhistorical conversation, is discussed with regard to Brecht's "Hollywood Quatrain," leading, third, to an examination of the imagination as such and its relationship to religious sensibility. Fiction as the suspension of disbelief stands in a taut relation to belief; but faith and fiction both represent mental predispositions that stand at odds with a narrow empiricism. Literature, drawing on the cognitive structures of faith, allows for the cultivation of the imagination as the human facility to imagine change and transformation.

Why Literature Matters

This argument on religion and literature depends on a discussion of the linguistic turn in theology associated with the so-called radical orthodoxy in recent work, especially by the British theologians John Milbank and Catherine Pickstock. Milbank draws attention to older discussions of the distinctive rhetoric of biblical Hebrew poetry. The constitution of the Western work of literature depends, ultimately, both on Greek sources, rooted in the culture of alphabetization, and on biblical material, a consequence not of writing technology as such but the characteristic mentality of transcendence through faith. Our contemporary expectation that literature be more than entertaining, more than informative, that it instead promise a sort of redemption — as well as its strong tie to a promise of freedom — derive from these religious and historical roots. Understanding the origins of Western literature therefore requires recognition of the specificity of this sacred tradition. It also requires recognizing that constitutive difference: No matter how much works of literature imitate scripture, they are themselves not sacred, from which fact ensues an inevitable sense of incompleteness surrounding any given work.

Chapter 7 sorts through various approaches to the political character of literature, with the goal of distinguishing between those in which politics is, ultimately, merely a topic for literature and those that hypothesize fundamental political implications for the constitutive categories of autonomous literature and literary reception. That these implications have nothing necessarily to do with the allegiances or loyalties of the author is obvious. Of course, within contemporary literary studies there is much political or over-politicized questioning that instrumentalizes literary works for particular agendas. A genuine discussion of the politics of literature, however, must go beyond determining the party affiliations of the author or the idiosyncratic ideology of this or that text in order to focus, instead, on the inherent orientation of literature as such toward an implied reader, hence toward a public, and therefore toward the public life of the community. But if literature necessarily addresses a political community, it does so indirectly, through the reception by the reader as an individual. The very phenomenon of literary reception is therefore implicated in the duality of individual and community that is basic to the institutions of liberal democracy: the presence of the public — the community — is indisputable, but this community is always mediated through and restrained by the significance of the individuality of the reader. Indeed, one consequence of the dissemination of literary practices, the habits of reading poems and novels, is nothing other than the cultivation of the individualistic sensibility on which modern, Western political institutions depend.

In the final chapter, chapter 8, attention shifts to the question of economics and literature. My object here resembles the distinction made in chapter 7, literature instrumentalized by a partisan politics versus a democratic political substance inherent in literature as such. I try in chapter 8 to sort out various intersections of literary and economic concerns. One can easily enough identify literary works in which economic programs appear as thematic material, and one can of course similarly choose to study the industry of literature (or publishing) as an economic sector. Neither of these approaches, however, gets to the core question of how literature, understood as a formalized use of imaginative language within the framework of certain malleable conventions, might have cultural and evolutionary ramifications for the economic life of society. I argue that the cultivation of imagination as the capacity to posit alternatives to the historical conditions of material scarcity and the habits of judgment and taste, which are inextricably tied up with literature, disseminate value structures and mental habits that have important ramifications for the economy. Literature cultivates the imaginative prowess of entrepreneurial vision, and it nourishes the evaluation, judgment, and choice of consumers. Indispensable economic skills and practices are therefore deeply embedded in the literary enterprise. Just as the immanent political predisposition of literature is democratic (whatever the ideological allegiances of an author may be), so too does the individual character cultivated by literature contribute to the value structure and virtues of a capitalist economy. This holds despite the history of romantic and avant-garde anticapitalism in modern intellectual history.

Literature, this book demonstrates, has deep historical roots; it is linked to the behavioral adaptation of the species to speech, and it is decisively transformed by the ancient development of writing technologies. In the West, the cultural consequences of alphabetic literacy in Greece and the transcendent spirituality of the Bible are foundational for a specific cultural tradition, which supports interrelated institutions: liberal democracy, the market economy, and aesthetic, especially literary, autonomy. Indeed, all three components imply the autonomy of the individual, the free subject, who maintains a supple identity in an ongoing dynamic with the structures of the surrounding community. This outcome in freedom was not foreordained, but once the West began to take on its specific shape with its particular cultural and technical character, the autonomy of literature became a very likely outcome. Language meant imagination; written language meant a new relationship to the text, history, authorship, and readership. The distribution of the texts through printing and the market entwined with democratization, and the appeal to imagination and judgment defined the parameters of market mechanisms. Literature is therefore fundamentally associated with social development and democracy. Yet if writing implies individuation — which has been the case since the invention of writing and the beginning of the decline of oral performance — so too does reading, and it is therefore in the cultivation of imaginative literature, if not only there, that our freedom finds its sustenance. This is the emancipatory character of literature.

FICTION SETS YOU FREE

INTRODUCTION

AT ITS BEST, the study of the humanities amplifies our ability to understand fundamental aspects of our cultural, social, and existential conditions. Among the various humanistic disciplines, literature and history have figured prominently: the study of literature as a vehicle to explore the human capacity for imagination and its expression, and history as a reflection on our predicament as it changes through time. Yet in important and worrisome ways, scholarship on literature and on history both have declined, and the impact of this double diminishment is particularly clear at their intersection, in literary history, which is rapidly becoming neither literary nor historical. As today's academic criticism loses its grasp of the specificity of literature, opting instead for a broader and more diffuse notion of culture, it becomes unable — or unwilling — to distinguish the literary work of art from other modes of writing or, even, other sorts of objects altogether. Literary works become just so many cultural things among others, fundamentally undifferentiated from the array of objects that clutter our everyday lives. The work of literature therefore surrenders any claim to a special standing in our culture. At the same time, relations of continuity and change over long periods of time are lost from sight. Instead, scholars tend to dwell solely on the present; or they treat isolated moments in the past, as if each were just a snapshot of a present, with no pertinence to the larger flow of time. Time dissolves into a series of limited contexts. And such works become the studies of single moments of the past, historicist vignettes, as if one were always only in a present, without past, and without future.

As literature goes, so goes history, and both seem to be going away: Such is the state of the humanities. A premise of this book is that these two developments in the academic world, the withering away of literature and of history, are fundamentally connected to each other and that, together, they represent a significant impoverishment of our intellectual and cultural lives. Losing an appreciation for the distinctiveness of the literary work—I will call this distinctiveness "autonomy" in the course of the argument—we are robbed of the benefits of the aesthetic imagination, the capacity to articulate and envision possibilities of life and happiness that we might strive to attain. It is a sorry irony of critical history that the attack on this promise of happiness, the hostility to art's capacity to project other ways of being, is largely carried out in the name of an explicitly progressive political agenda. By attacking the distinctiveness of literature (and the other arts as well, but the arguments are not necessarily the same), radical critics lay claim to the honor of attacking distinctiveness in general, and hence privilege and inequality. High literature is imagined, strangely, to stand in some necessary relationship to upper classes, and this shared altitude is evidently enough to confuse critics into thinking that a programmatic antiaesthetic suffices to qualify them as good democrats. Such is the sad logic of leveling that has long haunted radical thinking: from Heinrich Heine's worries facing early communist activism in Paris of the 1830s to George Orwell's dissection of Stalinist totalitarianism in the 1940s or the refuge that an engaged critic, if there ever was one, Edward Said, found in the aestheticism of Theodor W. Adorno. Art may have a radical potential, but radicals are usually hostile to art.

Yet it is not only today's radical critics, the consistent "cultural materialists" reviving some of the more dogmatic aspects of Marxism, who call into question the literariness of literature.[1] A much broader change of sensibility is afoot in the academy, where the traditional aesthetic understanding of the term *culture*—literature and the arts, above all—has gradually been displaced by an ethnographic definition: the values and practices of a community. Through the influence of cultural anthropology on literary studies, the work of art has become redefined as one artifact among others. Suggesting a link between aesthetic objects and surrounding society is of course in and of itself neither novel nor destructive. It is certainly the case that the traditional aesthetic usage of the term *culture*, which insisted on the distinctiveness of the cultural object as a work of art, nonetheless allowed for diverse claims linking that work to its extra-aesthetic context, while simultaneously insisting on the difference between the work and its context.[2] A specifically aesthetic criticism need not hesitate to talk about context and society, but only by maintaining a recognition of the distinct standing of the aesthetic object.

Yet precisely this appreciation of the difference between art and its context disappears in the ethnographic recasting of culture. Without this separation, we lose the critical potential of literature, its capacity, due to its distinctiveness, to suggest, however implicitly, an alternative to the current state of affairs. The study of literature becomes instead the study of existing communities or identities — the empirical collection of all the objects and practices that just happen to be — devoid of any basis for distinguishing the specific nature of the literary text, and devoid of the critical tension that prevails between autonomous literature and its social surrounding. Yet in order to study these communities, it is not the case that literature, characterized by its fictionality, the programmatic deployment of counterfactual statements, offers a particularly auspicious access. An intellectual orientation toward empirical facticity would in fact have little reason to pay much attention to the unreal claims that make up literature. A historian, for example, may perhaps make reference to novels in order to illustrate or bolster certain points, but the same historian is unlikely to base claims about historical change primarily on their novelistic representation. As I will argue in the course of this book, fiction is in fact of central importance in human history, but the particular statements made within literary fiction do not provide very compelling evidence about empirical historical conditions. To appeal to literary works for evidence about culture implies a basic disregard of their fictional or imaginative character.

Within the university, the transition to a cultural approach to literature implies the loss of the logical basis for a separate disciplinary grounding for literary studies. The *raison d'être* of literary studies, trapped between the expansive fields of cultural anthropology and history (itself increasingly pointed toward culture), disappears once the literary work is denied any differential standing. The primary concern here, however, is not the academic question of a disciplinary legitimation for literary studies (as important as that question remains, given the present crisis of the humanities in the university); nor am I concerned here with the character and causes of this shift, the loss of an understanding of the distinctiveness of literature (be it due to cross-disciplinary influences, or intra-academic dynamics, or even a wider shift in public sensibility). The point, rather, is that this salient feature of literary scholarship today is fundamentally antithetical to the specifically aesthetic character of the literary work as art. Hence the claim that literary history, as it is currently practiced, is, unfortunately, ceasing to be *literary,* as it widens its field of study to other sorts of material, renouncing any claim for the distinctiveness of literature. The resulting scholarship may be of interest to anthropologists or cultural historians or perhaps even some philosophers, but it is handicapped, as literary history, by a blindness to the defining features of literature as art, as imaginative, and as autonomous. This is a scholarship devoted to the study of a material, the defining characteristics of which it refuses to recognize. Literature is marvelously different, fundamentally separate from the nonaesthetic concerns of everyday life, and this difference is inseparably linked to deep historical elements within literature: its relationship to language as such, the dynamics of writing as a technology, and an overlap with foundational religious traditions. (These three points are discussed in detail in chapters 2, 4, and 6 respectively.)

The decline of interest in the specifically aesthetic character of literature in the context of a certain cultural studies is, significantly, accompanied by a declining historical sensibility in general and, in particular, a diminished regard for the historical character of literature. While considerable attention is frequently paid to the context of the production of literature — and much more will be said later about the category of context — a more complex historical sensibility is in decline. Bigger questions about the relationship of literature to long-term historical processes are excluded by an overriding emphasis on context, the single instant in time when a work is written: as if the identity claims of the present generation necessarily outweighed the legacy of past generations or the obligations to the descendants in the future. Indeed, the historical character of literature ought to be conceptualized in terms of two interrelated aspects. On the one hand, literary autonomy — the distinctiveness of imaginative literature, its fundamental difference from other modes of language, such as informational, communicative, devotional texts — is by no means a recent invention, but rather rooted deeply in the long-term developmental process of civilization. One theme of this book is the role this literary autonomy has played in that civilizational process: how literature, through its distinctiveness, contributes to the developmental character of society. On the other hand, individual literary works are themselves resonant with their own temporality, their unique relationship to the past as part of a literary tradition as well as their characteristic capacity to imagine possible futures. It is this dual character of literature that defines its historicity: It remembers and it projects. As much as we can think of literature within the process of history, we can also recognize history, the past and future, within each work. Ever since Homer and Hesiod literature has been understood as a repository of "things that were, things that are, and things that will be."[3]

I argue in this book that literature, being autonomous, plays a role in a long civilizational history, and that successful works of literature are themselves, individually, resplendent with a complex historicity. Literature is in history, and history is inside literary works; or, phrased differently, history that surrounds literature is external to it, but history is also internal to each work in the forms of memory and anticipation. For the moment, however, I note that the failing of contemporary criticism is double: Hand in hand with the suppression of aesthetic autonomy, one finds also a growing reluctance to recognize the complex and dynamic temporality of literature. By dynamic temporality I mean that immanent sense of time within the literary work, its ability to reach backward, as part of a tradition, and forward, as a vehicle of innovation and anticipation. This sort of temporality is quite different from a single-minded and frequently reductionist focus on historical context. As much as a work of literature may give expression to features of its momentary context, the fundamental literary project involves overcoming that narrow context through an imaginative capacity that calls the limits of the respective empirical conditions into question. By calling the present and its claims into question, the literary work attempts to give the past and the future their due.

The late twentieth century saw the blossoming of a new historicism, a reaction against the neoformalism of the deconstructive literary criticism of the 1970s. One might take that new historicism as evidence of a renewed interest in history, and as a corrective to deconstruction it certainly was that. Nonetheless, the concept of history at the core of the new historicism remained deficient; its mission involved locating the work of art, as text, in a particular historical context, the present of its writing, outside any larger developmental frame and with scant attention to the aesthetic substance of reception in the present. The double temporality just mentioned consequently disappears from sight, as does the dynamism of the historical process, which could imply a particular relationship between the past of the work and the present of the modern reader or critic. If, for example, a contemporary critic understands a Shakespearean play only or primarily as a complex set of references to particular circumstances in Elizabethan England, it is then not at all clear what the grounds would be for a contemporary interest in the text, except perhaps for professional scholars of the Elizabethan world.[4] The more rigorously criticism historicizes a work of art, in the sense of lodging it in the context of the moment of its production, the less likely it becomes for criticism to be able to explain either its own subsequent interest in the work or the possibility of lay—that is, nonacademic—interest in reading it. One can, however, hardly be satisfied with the assertion that literature ought to be of interest primarily in order to justify the existence of academic criticism. On the contrary, the problem for academic criticism ought to be: What is it about literature that explains its ongoing interest to generations of readers? How does this special usage of language maintain its grip on a public? Why can the work of imaginative literature animate the imagination of its recipients, in particular those of a different place and time, that is, a different context? Therefore, the programmatic contextualization of the new historicism tends to miss both the specifically autonomous character of literature and the dynamic of the long-term historical process. This is not a surprising result of the ethnographic influences;[5] indeed, new historicism can be thought of as cultural studies of the past. The work of literature, even the Shakespearean play, is reduced to a documentary artifact of its cultural context. Thus the impact of the new historicism was precisely to wedge the literary work into its moment of production; however, the urgent question for criticism is not the significance of the context but the possibility of reception, how a work remains viable outside its initial context, how it can still speak to us.

Why has historical thinking so declined, at least in the study of literature? Increasingly, the temporal categories underlying contemporary literary criticism are narrowly presentist. Presentism implies not only a shift toward contemporary material (older material is denounced polemically as tied to dead authors), but an implicit structuring of time as always only a present, without a recollection of its past, without an aspiration to a future. This flattened, one-dimensional structure of time derives in part from anthropology, which, particularly in its structuralist variant, has long been recognized as inimical to historical accounts, preferring instead to locate artifacts in an ethnographic present.[6] More broadly, this dehistoricization draws on a postmodern sensibility, with its suspicion of master narratives and accounts of teleological development. Against the narratives of consciousness (German idealism) and against narratives of emancipation (Marxism, but more broadly all notions of social progress, indeed of economic development in general), Jean-François Lyotard, in his seminal account *The Postmodern Condition* (1979), articulated a deep suspicion of any broad historical vision and treated it as hostile to the fragmented reality of contemporary experience and legitimation needs.[7] Hence his exhortations to promulgate *petits récits*, rather than master narratives. Part of the compelling force of Lyotard's argument derived from the erstwhile viability of his primary target: the orthodox Marxist insistence on the historical-materialist narrative of progress through economic stages to a revolutionary future. A key component of the communist ideology of the twentieth century, and very much a piece of the intellectual landscape at the time of Lyotard's writing, that notion of progress did indeed have a mythological status, and it was appropriately debunked by postmodern skepticism. There is no reason to be nostalgic for a narrative of progress that culminated in the primacy of the Communist Party of the Soviet Union.

Much more than historical materialism, however, was under attack in the polemics of postmodernism. The critique of historical teleology that emerged from classical postmodernism has been transformed by subsequent criticism and expanded into an attack on targets well beyond the ideological historiography of Soviet-style Marxism. Indeed, Lyotard's dismissal of narratives of progress has turned into an authoritative prohibition of any account of developmental progress, individual or social. This means, in particular, that along with the defunct Marxist mythology of progress, humanistic scholarship now tends to avoid any long-term descriptions of civilizational development or progress altogether. For to suggest even the possibility of progress and advancement implies a value judgment, the insinuation that later stages of the process — social, cultural, or economic — are somehow superior to the former ones, and this insinuated superiority is taken to represent a hierarchical denigration of what postmodern relativists would prefer to regard as merely different ways of life. In order to avoid this hierarchy and value schema, the temporal structure of progress has to be jettisoned. Without any explicit value orientation, postmodernism can describe a multiplicity of presents but no coherent, and certainly no developmental, linkage among them.

With its denunciations of narratives of progress, postmodern historicity maps quite neatly onto the still standard anti-imperialist opposition to development, that is, economic development, even though that same antidevelopmentalist opposition frequently articulates its economic position in precisely those Marxist categories that postmodernism rejects. Moreover, the same sort of antidevelopmental opposition underpins contemporary "green" resistance to globalization, whether it derives from postmodern, Marxist, or other intellectual legacies. I point this out in order to suggest the scope of the resistance to those temporal structures that imply social development. Postmodern theory provides this antihistorical predisposition with its most elaborate articulation, but whether postmodernism is the intellectual source or not, it is evident that a vocal resistance to development and to developmental narratives is afoot, with considerable influence in academic life, at least in the humanities. The crisis of historical thinking is a direct corollary to this resistance to development.

The widespread antidevelopmental stance contributes to the erosion of a dynamic sense of history because models of history as frozen context replace narratives of history as progress and change over time. For the purposes of this book, it is important to note that this diminishment of history is closely linked to the seemingly separate problem of the loss of a sense of the specificity of literature. The simultaneous transformation of historical and literary sensibilities suggests that the two processes might plausibly have much to do with each other. Why do these transformations take place in tandem? Do they derive from features of a larger social condition, an end of ideology, of history, and of art, or are they indicative of a peculiar shift restricted to academic culture, explicable in terms of an imaginable sociology of intellectuals? These are questions that ought to be treated in the context of a critical analysis of contemporary intellectual life. My central concern here, rather, is somewhat different: the character of literature in history. The simultaneity of the disappearance of literature (as aesthetic) and history (as development), which we can observe around us in the academy, points to a fundamental commonality; unraveling one implies unraveling the other, since both are grounded in the same goal-oriented structures that postmodern sensibility opposes. Both civilizational history and autonomous literature are constitutively teleological, dependent on notions of progress toward goals, and they both therefore face resistance from the antidevelopmentalism of contemporary intellectual life.

Critics of development can attempt to evade the challenge of historical progress by exaggerating the idea *ad absurdum* in order to reject it by ridiculing it. Progress is, one would have to concede, in fact not necessary in some ultimate ontological sense. One can still agree to this point quite easily and nonetheless insist on the progressive, developmental character of history and literature. Nor need one claim that progress is inscribed in the human condition, for there are surely multiple examples of ways of being human that do not participate in consistent aspirations of development. Yet it is also the case that a civilizational trajectory can be described, one that demonstrates a progress, despite reversals, a cumulative process of knowledge and the development of institutions that define a Western tradition in a

Introduction

broad sense. It is a tradition that includes, among its characteristic features, a nonparochial inclusiveness that helps explain the attraction Western culture has consistently held — and continues to hold — for other traditions and that lends it an increasingly universal appearance. The specificity of this tradition, its contingency — that is, the fact that humans may well live otherwise, despite the universalist opening of this tradition — does not undermine the internal logic of the tradition. The Western tradition with its developmental trajectory is, in other words, not an obligatory option for all humans; one can live a human life outside it. Yet the tradition is driven by its own internal project, a universalist teleology nonetheless deeply rooted in specifically and uniquely Western institutions and values.

Progress and modernization are not humanity's fate. There are other ways to be human: paleoanthropology describes long swaths of the prehistory of the species without noticeable progress, and one can point as well to aboriginal societies to find other modalities of social life.[8] But progress is surely humanity's destiny, in the sense that the tradition — I choose this term to underscore its contingency and particularity — that has come to define the predominant aspiration of human society involves a set of overlapping terms embedded in the Western historical teleology: rational explanations of the world, an increase in the production of wealth in a market economy, an improved standard of living, political equality, literacy, and universalism. These choices entail certain consequences. A cultural relativism is certainly possible that refuses to adjudicate between Western notions of progress and aboriginal society; but, once one enters the logic of Western development, there is also no doubt that liberal democracy is superior to, say, apartheid, or that the market economy is more effective than Soviet communism, or that with the spread of literacy, democracy and the market are more likely outcomes than dictatorship and central planning. These matters are not legitimately adjudicated by cultural relativism as equally viable cultural options or merely diverse ways of life.

The foregoing argues for the possibility of positing a civilizational history with a teleology: not one that is necessary for all humans, not one that is ineluctable, but one that has indeed transpired and continues to proceed and that, moreover, points toward values and institutions that are worthwhile. This is a history that stretches from hominization and the acquisition of language, the transition to agriculture, state-building, and the development of writing, particularly alphabetic writing; and the emergence and elaboration of the social institutions and categories of thought that became characteristic of modern societies: universalistic religio-ethical systems, scientific knowledge, conceptual thought, and autonomous art and literature. It is the last item in that list that is the concern of this book: within the frame of a long-term developmental history, what is the standing of literature; in particular, autonomous literature?

This book argues that autonomy — the constitutive distinctiveness of imaginative literature that implies a complex and multidimensional temporality — is central to a long history of civilization. The tendency of imaginative literature to become autonomous, to become distinct from other types of writing, while also setting itself up in opposition to the empirical conditions of existence, arises at the latest in the literate ancient world: No matter how the Homeric epics may have also conveyed nonaesthetic, historical knowledge or practical information, they were above all imaginative literature. The Greeks could clearly distinguish conceptually between the epics as poetry and Herodotus's writing as historiography. The institutionalization of the imagination in the form of literary autonomy introduces an emancipatory dynamism into cultural history. It is this long history of autonomy, a constitutive component of literary art for millennia and not simply a late product of modernity, that allows us to raise the question of its role and function in the developmental process of civilization.

1

Periodization and the Canon

ESTABLISHED LITERARY judgments are typically anchored in arrays of corollary claims, not the least of which pertain to the contours of the specific history in which literature is presumed to play itself out. For scholars and critics, and even for the lay reader, the path to the work or the author passes through a landscape of periods, which indirectly structures the possibilities of reception. The importance ascribed to the period, or the historical context, of a work is frequently so great that it shapes the reading altogether. Indeed, a constitutive element of contemporary reading practices is the need to integrate into our "horizon of expectations"[1] the expectations of the earlier period when the work in question was produced. Asserting the need to consider historical context is truistic only because it is an unquestioned habit that Shakespeare is read as Elizabethan, and hardly a performance of Brecht goes by without reflections on the Hitler era: two examples of explicitly political periodizations that set boundaries for sanctioned receptions. Other periodizations may not stamp the face of a sovereign on the coin of literary judgment, but they nonetheless order and regulate reading in ways that are equally influential: Hugo in the romantic period, or Woolf and modernism.

Still something is certainly missing if we think of Shakespeare as solely Elizabethan. The enduring interest in his plays indicates the insufficiency of explanatory models that posit the priority of period over literature. While literature is surely in history, it is not only a matter of the single moment of its writing. What is then the status of the relationship of the work of literature to its presumed period, how significant is the period attribution for an understanding of the work? What, moreover, motivates the scholarly interest in attaching considerable significance to period assignments? With regard to the larger argument in this book, the problem of periodization is of interest because it reveals assumptions about the temporal character of the literary work. To the extent that scholarship chooses to attribute major significance to the period identification of a work, it implies that the work's location within its period, or, to repeat the term used above, its context, is somehow of defining significance. What precisely is the significant definition implied by a periodizing approach to literature? How does an insistence on the priority of period modify the standing of the autonomy of a literary work?

The assertion of a periodic frame around multiple phenomena implies that their contemporaneity is itself of determinative importance to their understanding. Periodization of literature is comparable to the periodic groupings of other historical phenomena and is in itself not a specifically literary-historical method. One might collect eighteenth-century German literary works, just as one might describe sets of eighteenth-century legal judgments, or paintings, furniture, clocks, or medical reports, and then decide what they have in common: whether they should be labeled Friederician or absolutist or prerevolutionary — a choice that would be based on the evaluation of the presumed common denominator. Ultimately, a claim is made that some contemporary condition is of defining importance for the diverse items grouped together under the periodic rubric. Things that are of the same time — the same historical period — are likely to share some features in common, to the extent that one assumes that the "same time" imbues its inhabitants with a common identity. It is nevertheless presumably not the time, not a *Zeitgeist*, itself that projects this commonality, but a particular component of the social order that the scholar assumes exercises a defining influence on the other components.

The fundamental argument is put forward by Marx in the *Introduction to the Critique of Political Economy* of 1857: The character of Greek art depended on Greek mythology, which was in turn a result, according to Marx, specifically of the low level of technological mastery of nature. The period is a significant category because one of the features of the historical moment has the capacity to shape other contemporary phenomena: for Marx, this one feature is the conditions of production. Marx's position leads to the famous rhetorical questions that underscore the priority of periodization by insinuating the absurdity of temporal displacements: "Is Achilles possible with powder and lead? Or the Iliad with the printing press, not to mention the printing machine?"[2] The modern technology of warfare, powder and lead, render the ancient warrior obsolete; modern print technology precludes the viability of ancient literary forms. For our purposes, the key issue is not whether the specifically Marxist focus on economic conditions, represented here by forms of technology, is the appropriate vehicle to generate a category for a period (literary or not), but rather, much more fundamentally, the historicist gesture itself, the hermeneutic practice of establishing a period frame altogether, resting on an argument about a defining logic of an age. It is the assertion that the literary work participates in a larger contemporary terrain, and that this terrain is determined, ultimately, by a single feature.

It is hardly surprising to find Marx claiming that cultural phenomena stand in some secondary relationship to material conditions. If it were not for his emphatic insistence on economic matters, the interpretive move would be indistinguishable from other modes of literary historical contextualization, new historicist or otherwise. Periodization always involves lodging a work in its context, on the basis of the assumption that it is the context that imbues the work with meaning. It is, however, precisely at this point that Marx's argument takes an unexpected turn that separates him from standard contextualizing critics, as well as from commonplace associations with Marxism. Despite his prior recognition of the period character of a work, he suddenly ascribes to literary objects a distinctive character — precisely that specificity to which I have been referring as the autonomy of literature, a difference that sets them off from other sorts of objects — which runs counter to the significance attributed to contemporaneity, thereby considerably loosening the grip of the periodic attribution. The literary work, as literature, does not belong neatly to its moment of production, an observation that implies that the context is not the crucial source of the work's meaning. For Marx, the contextualizing argument is the simple, perhaps even trivial part of an interpretation. "But the difficulty lies not in understanding that the Greek arts and epic are bound up with certain forms of social development. The difficulty is that they still afford us artistic pleasure and that in a certain respect they count as a norm and as an unattainable model."[3]

Evidently Marx reserves for literary works a very distinct status, a specific temporality that allows them to retain a pertinence despite considerable remove from the context of their production. This is a unique feature of aesthetic material, which is thereby set apart from the other artifacts of social life. While one might, for example, cultivate an antiquarian or scholarly interest in the Greek economy as a component of historical knowledge, the relationship to ancient literature is fundamentally different from any possible engagement with ancient market forces. For the modern reading of ancient literature involves a mode of reception that is not merely scholarly or antiquarian. Instead, aesthetic experience allows for a direct relationship between reader and work, despite the historical distance. Today's consumer cannot participate in the ancient economy by trying to use an Athenian coin as legal tender; but today's reader can participate in the ancient literary imagination through an authentic engagement with the Homeric text (no matter how much contemporary circumstances necessarily also enter into that encounter with the ancient text). Thus the historicist imperative of periodization evidently stands at odds with the potential for immediacy associated with literary reception and aesthetic experience.

Having conceded the embeddedness of the literary work in its historical context (defined characteristically if not necessarily in economic terms), Marx promptly surpasses this contextualizing historicism as he recognizes the specific nature of literature bypassing the boundaries implied by periodic distinctions. The imagination allows for more complex temporal arrangements, memory and anticipation, bringing past and future into play, in ways that stand at odds with the necessarily presentist logic of any periodizing scheme that foregrounds all that is contemporary. The point is not that contemporaneity is insignificant, for surely Marx can hardly stand accused of ignoring a decisive role of social conditions in relation to works of culture. It is rather that there is something more important at stake in the temporal character of literature: its relation to history, understood as change and development, rather than as context and frame. Marx's reflection, strikingly antideterminist and stunningly at odds with the dogmatic historical materialism that Marxism would become, suggests a definition of the temporality of the literary work in terms of the large frame of civilizational development, a capacity to escape the sequestration in a single moment by recovering an emphatic relationship between past and present. In contrast, periodization appears to be little more than a strategy to restrict temporal experience by limiting the imagination to the respective historical present. Literature must be *zeitgemäß* or timely, to use Nietzsche's ironic term: The contextualizers reduce the significance of the literary work to its moment of production and rob it of any larger, diachronic resonance. As it becomes more an artifact of a single moment, it loses a capacity to serve as a cultural legacy, speaking to different recipients across generations and in quite disparate contexts. Meanwhile, as it is reduced to an example of its contemporaneity in which all objects of the same moment conform to an underlying logic, it surrenders any strong claim to individuality and distinction.

The Marxian tension between a deterministic moment of periodization and an activist dimension of aesthetic subjectivity echoes deep-seated conflicts both in Marx's own biographical development as a thinker and in the classical social democracy of the nineteenth century: between evolution and revolution, and between socialist models of linear progress and anarchistic radicalism. Marx's recognition that the very act of reading ancient literature upsets any neat order of historical periods that he himself had labored to construct anticipates the seminal theorization of political time in Walter Benjamin's "Theses on the Philosophy of History" of 1941.[4] The tensions within these reflections on history are revealing, not only for the antinomies within Marxist thought, and not only for the often gravely problematic character of Benjamin's own political judgments, but, more important, as a framework for considering the standing of history within any literary historical project. Marx's own ambivalence between a deterministic materialism and aesthetic autonomy recurs in Benjamin in a complex form directly relevant to the project of literary history.

Benjamin wrote at a moment of historical despair: Weimar democracy had collapsed seven years earlier, Hitler was fully in power in Germany, the Western democracies appeared unable to mount much resistance, the Soviet Union had compromised itself desperately with the Hitler-Stalin pact. What had become of the history of progress, the optimism of the nineteenth century and Marxism, as its ideology, par excellence? Benjamin attempts to provide an answer by characterizing two opponents. He designates the first as historicism, a term he uses in a specific and distinctive manner. It suggests, of course, Ranke's mandate to study the past "as how, essentially, things happened,"[5] but Benjamin underscores another feature, the corollary injunction to ignore the consequences of the past moment under study, as well as the scholar's present. Historicism becomes the examination of an isolated moment of time, with no aftermath (which might color one's judgment on a period) and no implication for the present (which might undermine one's objectivity). The historicist holds the past at an infinite distance; it exists in no relation of continuity with the present and certainly in no framework of a shared history of progress. The approach is emphatically anti-Hegelian in its rejection of a dynamic temporality.[6] Historicism therefore necessarily prohibits the possibility of empathy with the past, and hence also the motivation, so important to Benjamin, to redeem it. Indeed, he asserts precisely such a redemptive mission, the obligation to seize the moments of the past in an emphatic loyalty across generations.

In Benajmin's account, historicism suppresses that loyalty by insisting on an objectified separation from the historical period. It represents the isolation of the historical moment as a unique context, and it therefore, if unexpectedly (since it is, after all, a historical contemplation) participates in this amnesia, insofar as it lodges the past in what is describable as an empty space, fully apart from the rest of historical experience. Historicism therefore functions like literary-historical periodization. It can provide detailed elaborations of context, but it ignores those longer developments that sustain cross-generational links. Thus, one can also see historicism functioning for Benjamin in a way that a determinist contextualization functioned, implicitly, for Marx in the 1857 passage just discussed: recognitions of moments in the past without any diachronic signification. Neither does past meaning acquire contemporary relevance, nor is contemporary affect obligated to past experience. Historicism might account for the emergence of the Homeric epics, but it would never ask the question why those epics might remain relevant for subsequent readers.

Benjamin confronts a second opponent as well. Whereas the conservative historiography of Rankean historicism separates the past from the present, social-democratic historiography, in its perpetual celebration of progress, in effect also separates the present from the past: Today is always the latest moment of triumph over the backwardness of yesterday. Empty space is Benjamin's master image. It pertains not only to conservative historicism, which scatters past moments in a random array, with no logical coherence, but also to the social-democratic progressivism of linear time. Unlike the historicist, the socialist assumes that progress unfolds in history, but it is progress through the same empty space, and its sole focus on a perpetual amelioration of the human condition severs the affective relationship to the past. Historicists study past moments in detail but deny a continuity with the present; socialists insist on a continuity of progress, but their celebration of improvement, in a panglossian disregard of the world catastrophe of 1941, overshadows any memory of the past and therefore prohibits any substantive link with it. While Benjamin commences with the attack on conservative historicism, the fundamental thrust of the "Theses" is the assault on the optimism of socialist or, by extension, any naïvely progressive, whiggish historiography, including the core Marxist paradigm. Although its political agenda is quite distinct from that of historicism, the basic understanding of time and change in both models is the same.

By this point in the recapitulation, it has become evident that Benjamin's argument displays much of the political irresponsibility that contributed to the end of Weimar democracy. Accepting his codings of the specific positions, to wit, historicism as conservative and the narrative of progress as socialist, he comes close to equating the Social Democrats with the antidemocratic right, which was the stereotypical stance of the Weimar Communists. Their theory of social fascism insisted that the Social Democrats were no better than the Nazis, an argument that debilitated the left and cleared the way for the National Socialist ascendancy. Yet no one has ever considered Benjamin a particularly astute observer of the real world of politics, and in any case, he wrote the "Theses on the Philosophy of History" well after the demise of Weimar. Against the Right and the (socialist) Left, Benjamin nonetheless tries to sketch out a third philosophical position. In contrast to both, he proposes a notion of redemption that implies an emphatic relationship to the past, a version of a traditionalist obligation, linking subjects across time. Remembering the past becomes a mandate, a resistance against all the cultural forces of amnesia that would sever our substantive ties to the past. In the end, and against both his foils, Benjamin draws close to a sort of radical traditionalism: politically radical in its ethical predispositions, but backward looking, rather than fixated on some utopian socialist future. By strangely choosing to label this third way as historical materialism, however, he would seem to identify it with Marxist or communist discourse, a move quite consonant with the demonstrated parallel to the theory of social fascism. Nonetheless, Benjamin's usage is extremely idiosyncratic, and the content of the third term, neither historicist nor linear progressive, turns out to be deeply aesthetic: closer to Kant's Third Critique than to Lenin's Third International.

Strictly speaking, the term *historical materialism* refers to Marxism after 1845, the turn away from Hegelian idealism, and the insistence on the periodization scheme of succeeding regimes of production. This doctrine becomes a lynchpin of orthodox Marxism. It represents, for example, the insistence on the priority of the economic context in the 1857 introduction that, as we have seen, even Marx himself regarded as insufficient. In the "Theses," however, Benjamin nearly inverts the significance of the term, deploying it in order to gesture toward a decidedly antiperiodic capacity to bridge the gap between the present and the past. Benjamin's historical materialism therefore becomes unexpectedly comparable to Marx's speculation on a modern reading of ancient material. Yet where Marx, sentimentally, framed that reading in terms of irredeemable loss and unattainable norms, Benjamin describes the revolutionary moment when the past suddenly bursts into the present, as if rising from the grave to rectify the wrongs it suffered at the hands of a banally triumphal progress. Thus Benjamin's historical materialism implies a capacity to link otherwise separate and distant moments in time through a profound empathy. This empathy takes on a revolutionary character by disrupting the regularity of quotidian temporality. Without this sort of tie to the past, no critical stance in the present is possible. Finally, Benjamin's phrasing suggests that the link to the past typically has an aesthetic character; hence his references to the image of the past. His peculiar usage of the term *historical materialism* is inseperable from an aesthetic sensibility.

Periodization sequesters human experience. The historicist separation of the past from the present prohibits empathy with the past and therefore precludes criticism in the present. It leaves unanswered the question of why we can read and appreciate the literature of other times and places. Progressive history may recognize a developmental continuity, but its presentist triumphalism leads to the same enervating result. From that follows Benjamin's account of the socialists' failure, and the communists' as well, after the Soviet Union's alliance with Hitler in the face of the rise of fascism. Their determinist optimism canceled their capacity to act. He therefore pursues the third option of aesthetic temporality. Drawing on mystical and theological imagery, Benjamin describes an emphatic present, a *Jetztzeit*, in which the extent of past suffering becomes evident and its present redemption therefore becomes realizable. Instead of a collection of neatly defined periods, isolated from one another for the conservative historicist or concatenated in a grand narrative of progress for the socialist, Benjamin sketches a perspective that surveys all of time in a single instant. That perspective informs the famous gloss in the ninth thesis on Klee's Angelus Novus painting, read as the angel of history: looking backward toward paradise, transfixed by the continuity of postlapsarian destruction, with his wings caught in a storm that blows him ever further away: "Where we perceive a chain of events, he sees one single catastrophe which keeps piling wreckage upon wreckage and hurls it in front of his feet. The angel would like to stay, awaken the dead, and make whole what has been smashed. But a storm is blowing from Paradise; it has got caught in his wings with such violence that the angel can no longer close them. This storm irresistibly propels him into the future to which his back is turned, while the pile of debris before him grows skyward. This storm is what we call progress."[7] The "we" who are trapped in the discourse of progress are the carriers of a whiggish socialist historiography, blindly trusting the movement of history—which, however, the angel can recognize as a single catastrophe. In this crucial text, Benjamin's dismissal of Rankean historicism is ultimately less germane than his disappointment with the historical consciousness of the Left, which shares the same assumption of empty time, having long ago abandoned more radical forms of temporality.[8] Progressivism severs the tie to the past, which is rendered forever distant. It is disciplined, controlled, and objectified, and it is therefore no longer accessible to the sort of immediate aesthetic encounter that could overturn a moribund status quo. Against strategies of periodization, designed to separate the readers of the present from the claimants of the past, with consequently conformist political implications, Benjamin appeals to the aesthetic ability to overcome the separations of time, allow for critical empathy, and escape restrictive determinism.

Overcoming the determinism of context suggests the possibility of strong relations between texts across time: This makes canonicity a key problem for literary history. Canonicity, to which we will return in later chapters, plays a crucial role in the discussion of the historicity of literature. Here, however, the relevance of canonicity has nothing to do with the notion of codified establishments of hierarchical judgment (for which it typically attracts revisionist hostility). Instead, canonicity is important as the capacity to permit vibrant reading relationships to works from the past. Marx's suggestion that Homeric epics invite contemporary readers entailed recognizing their canonic power. Whatever else the canon may do, its primary function has been the preservation of the reception of literature across periodic borders, thereby calling into question the significance of those borders or the fetishism of contexts. The canon tunnels under the Berlin Wall that periodizers erect between literary regimes. At a fundamental level, therefore, periodization stands at odds with canonicity. Canonicity maintains, cultivates, and develops community over time and across generations; periodization breaks up that identity and suppresses the historical continuities through a strategy of temporal separation. Canonicity is backward looking, like Klee's angel; it insists on the presence of the past and resists its suppression. Periodization is presentist, establishing contemporaneity as the defining principle of the social condition. Canonicity corrects the present through a constant recollection of the past in order to envision a future. In contrast, periodization asserts the hegemony of any given present and therefore to value conformity.

This assertion of the priority of contemporaneity, the celebration of the present, defines the politics of periodization. It is either a matter of our present, defined as the vanguard of historical progress, or it is the historical present of the objects of study, presumed to be fully grounded in that single, isolated moment of time. In either case, the classificatory impulse inherent in periodization tends to proscribe the more complex temporalities of tradition and anticipation. If the shared present becomes the organizing principle of meaning, then past and future wither, a dialectic that describes the inherent political program and sheds light on our contemporary loss of historical sensibility. The suppression of traditions, particularly in the guise of the dismantling of the canon, puts an end to any future that goes beyond the present. Periodization is the disciplinary strategy with which the present establishes its rule over all time and encourages conformism, to the detriment of autonomy, individual and aesthetic. The argument pertains to periodization as such, not only revisionist periodizations, to the extent that any such organization of historical time underscores the separation of past and present. The reified focus on the moment of literary production, in a distanced context — the typical topic of periodization — suppresses the experience of reception, the actualization of the past in the reader's present.

It is not the case that historical contexts or literary periods are without relevance. Periodic categories certainly have a didactic value, just as they may be helpful in characterizing particular attributes of specific works, such as style, genre, institutional setting. But the fundamental issue involves gauging the importance of such period attribution in relation to the full substance of aesthetic reception. A literary critical culture that primarily values historical frames rather than the artistic pleasure of which Marx wrote tends to dismiss the diachronic moment in any reading, and with it the potential of tradition, the capacity precisely to transcend the constraints of the isolated historical moment. Literature transformed into historiography, however, would be as impoverished as a religion reduced to the scholarly study of its texts without an experience of their holiness. Historicism runs counter to the specific capacity of the literary work to escape the limits of historical time, to allow for the cross-generational flourishing of tradition, and open the present to a multidimensional temporality.

Moreover, to approach literary works primarily as period pieces necessarily entails several further problematic assumptions. It asserts, above all, the priority of the age over the work. This criticism sets as its goal the organization of literary material in terms of the overarching temporal category. It tries to fit the texts in or, in the case of revisionism, to redefine the categories so that the fit works better. In either case, the autonomy of the literary work dwindles in relation to the scholarly rubric: The art becomes proof for a historical claim. It is a dubious strategy in any case, since it necessarily bypasses the logic of the individual work itself, but it is particularly problematic where the period is defined in nonliterary, typically political, terms. The politics of a politically defined periodization scheme is the assertion of the priority of the state over the poets, Elizabeth over Shakespeare, a choice worthy of Platonic republicans.

Contemporaneity, the principle on which periodization schemes are based, is of course pertinent to nonliterary material: legal history, economic history, and so on. Moreover, there is no doubt that literary works, like laws or economic practices, have some period character and participate in the features of their age, the point in time when they were written. But literature goes further; it maintains a distinct relationship to time, in its ability to remember — a phenomenon that occurs in every act of reading — and its imaginative capacity to project, equally inherent in all reception. Recollection and prophecy are the defining potentials of literature, no matter how much any individual work may display the stylistic signs of its age. Periodization is therefore not inappropriate to the study of literature, but by definition it addresses only the most dated aspect of the material. It is antiquarian, at best. At worst, it is implicated in the programmatic suppression of tradition.

This criticism of historicist periodization coupled with appeals to the constant presence of the canon is likely to elicit attacks as conservative from scholars more concerned with the allegedly deleterious consequences of the hierarchical implications of canon. It is therefore worthwhile to recall the emancipatory substance associated with autonomy and the democratic ideal inherent in the reception of literature unrestricted by artificial restrictions, insisting on reducing the significance of periodization altogether. W. E. B. Du Bois presented an alternative strategy in a memorable passage from *The Souls of Black Folk*, which stands as a testimony to the entwinement of emancipation and canonicity, undisciplined by linear-historical markers: "I sit with Shakespeare and he winces not. I move arm in arm with Balzac and Dumas, where smiling men and welcoming women glide in gilded halls. From out the caves of evening that swing between the strong-limbed earth and the tracery of stars, I summon Aristotle and Aurelius and what soul I will, and they come all graciously with no scorn nor condescension. So, wed with Truth, I dwell above the Veil. Is this the life you grudge us, O knightly America?"[9] Du Bois's immediate concern was racial segregation, but the passage simultaneously subverts the temporal separations of his present with reference to the inclusiveness of literature unhampered by the restrictions of time. This is precisely the aesthetic experience that Marx invokes as a correction to the logic of social conditions and that reappears in the mysticism of Benjamin's *Jetztzeit*, and it is the sort of wild time that every historicism seeks to constrain. As scholars we are predisposed to seek recognition from professional colleagues, our contemporaries, in forums of peer review; and academic historicism transforms that principle of contemporaneity into a strategy of scholarship: judging material in terms of its age. Periodization may therefore be a characteristic undertaking for literary scholars, reflecting a guild psychology, but the narrow focus on the single moment in time is incompatible with the specific capacity of literature to reach beyond the limits of its age. This discrepancy points to the deep gap between the presentist predisposition of scholarship as profession and the complex temporality inherent in the successful work of art.

A final comment on Benjamin's historiography is in order. The aesthetic temporality that links the past and the present represents his alternative to the competing strategies that hold the past at bay. The suggestion that successful literary works can transcend the limits of their original context and therefore speak to each other as much as they can be appreciated by readers from other times and places is at the core of the notion of canonicity, suggested above. Canonicity is therefore also at odds with historicism and progressive historiography. For the purposes of the argument here, however, it is worth noting the tension between the aesthetic temporality strangely labeled historical materialism by Benjamin and the prospect of a developmental historiography that I have set as one of the goals of this book. The character of developmental narratives and their dismissal by postmodern critics were examined in the introductory chapter, where socialist progressivism figured as one variant of accounts of development. Furthermore, the insistence on the possibility of a developmental history, an account of a civilizational process that entails progress, is a core premise of this book. It might appear that this assertion of long-term historical development could be susceptible to Benjamin's injunction against linear history.

The problem is genuine. It is not resolved but is at least mitigated by keeping in mind the distinction between the two core poles of my argument: the *external* temporality of literature, its participation in the process of civilizational development, and its *internal* temporality, the temporal construction of the individual work of art. The first, the external aspect, involves a historical claim but borders on the social sciences: the history of imaginative literature participates integrally in a long social history, starting with the process of human origins, the character of language acquisition, and continuing through the emergence of writing technologies and the differentiation of value spheres in a long-term developmental and modernizing process. The second claim, much more a specific matter for humanists, concerns the unique logic of literature. A notion of developmental temporality is appropriate for the discussion of certain social processes; an aesthetic temporality is appropriate for the examination of the singular work of art. The following problem ensues for this book: within the process of social development, how and why does literary autonomy arise, recognizing that social development and literary autonomy imply alternative structures of time. Underneath this distinction, one can perceive deeper differences between the two modes of scholarship. The social sciences, ultimately, are about patterns, rules, and phenomena available to certain objective forms of explanation; the humanities, especially the study of literature, are about exceptional cases, singular works, and individuals that require subjective understanding. Rules and exceptions: With this in mind, one can formulate an interlinear project of this book as an inquiry into the very rules that allow for exceptionality, and how exceptionality responds to the elaboration of rules. This exceptionality takes on historical shape as individuality. The history of literature is, in other words, deeply involved in the emergence of concepts of individuality — the heroic individuals of epics, the incommensurable individuality of works of art, the private individuation of the reader — and this individuation is, simultaneously, constitutive of key social institutions: the individuality of liberal democracy and the individualism of the capitalist market. Literature became that field of society dedicated to the cultivation of the imagination, and therefore also imaginative individuals, that form of subjectivity that has always allowed humanity to aspire for other, and better, ways of life.

Human Origins and Literary Beginnings

THE STUDY OF human origins concerns the biological and behavioral adaptations that led to the evolutionary emergence of modern humans. Scientific inquiry into this process of hominization is necessarily an interdisciplinary undertaking because of the range of evidence available: comparative anatomy for the study of physiological transformations, archeology and physical anthropology for the examination of artifacts and remains, but also linguistics and psychology for the emergence of language — typically taken as the defining feature of the human condition — and its impact on consciousness. Do the discussions of human origins have ramifications for the humanities as well? As profound as the developments in human origins research have been in recent decades, very little of it has affected the cultural fields (linguistics is perhaps the sole humanities field that is significantly involved in the discussion), and none of it has reached into the field of literature. Yet, as I will argue in this chapter, the human origins discussion is pertinent, indeed indispensable to the formulation of a project of literary history. The origins of language and literature are intertwined. As Vico wrote in *The New Science*, "In the world's childhood, men were by nature sublime poets."[1]

Typically, literary histories, conceived in national terms (or imperial terms, e.g., histories of Spanish literature that include the literature of the former colonies in South America) commenced with the establishment of the respective state. Alternatively, literary beginnings have sometimes been identified with the earliest documents of the particular language. State and language: It is the case that the condition of literature throughout much of its history betrays a strong, if often tension-ridden, connection to the political formation in which it is harbored, and there is no doubt that literary works are typically embedded within a particular linguistic tradition and the literature of a particular language or language group. Yet prior to these questions of literature and state, literature and national tradition, literature and language specificity, is a more fundamental matter that has been ignored: the origin of literature as such and its relationship to initial language acquisition in the process of hominization. French literature begins with the first literary use of French, and this may overlap with the beginnings of the French state. When, however, does literature begin altogether, the initial use of language for imaginative and fictional purposes? Precisely the recent developments in the study of human origins can shed light on the likely origins of literature, the prehistorical starting point of literary history, and therefore the standing of literature within the evolution of the human condition.

To suggest a link between literary history and human origins pushes the hypothetical beginnings of literature far back in time: further back than the histories that shadow state formations, which, for the modern European languages, typically start in the Middle Ages. Indeed, I am proposing a move even further back than the other origins discussion, which studies the transition from orality to written language, the origins of literature as written text. This latter (and chronologically much later) topic will be addressed in later chapters. Now, however, before wondering about the relationship between the Homeric epics and the development of alphabetic script around 700 B.C., or about the writing technology of cuneiform and the *Epic of Gilgamesh*, the matter at hand here is the origin of language and the standing of an imaginative use of language within it during preliterate, prehistoric times. For the biologically modern human who emerged anatomically some hundred thousand years ago, how and when did language and literature — literature understood as a specifically imaginative language usage — develop, and what role did they play in the defining transition of the cultural explosion between thirty and seventy thousand years ago?

At first glance, the suggestion that human origins have anything to do with literary history could seem both obvious and hopeless. It is obvious because of course there could be no literature without humans and their distinctive behavioral adaptation, language use; and it is hopeless, from the point of view of scholarly research, because we surely have no direct evidence of the initial narratives and songs of early humans. There is by definition no written record of that oral past. Yet the implications of the suggestion are in fact by no means obvious, nor do they present a reason for scholarly despair.

They are not obvious because a close look at hypotheses about the hominization process discovers complex and distinct characterizations of language origins, which in turn have considerable significance for the possibility of literature and its hypothetical operations. If there could clearly be no literature without language, the nonobvious and nontrivial corollary hypothesis might well be that there could no language without literature, that is, the imaginative use of linguistic symbols, their utilization for aesthetic representational rather than solely informational processes, may define the very possibility of language. If language originates as symbol usage and therefore as metaphor, then literariness is a defining potential of the human condition (literariness not taken, however, in the specific sense of letters and therefore written, an aspect treated in later chapters).

To argue along these lines is not impossible because of the lack of direct evidence, the sort of accumulation of texts or works that are the grist for the mills of standard literary history. On the contrary, existing human origins scholarship typically extrapolates from the sometimes sparse evidence available, and much the same would apply for a potential paleohistoriography of imaginative language use. Prehistoric artifacts that shed indirect light on symbolic and therefore imaginative, even literary, possibilities would be pertinent — neolithic cave painting or stone figures, for example — as would anthropological studies of existing preliterate cultures. Thanks to recent developments in several sciences, we are beginning to get a much better picture of human prehistory, and it is here that a potential history of literature ought to begin. Much remains speculation, but it is speculation that extrapolates from genuine evidence. It is therefore different from the long-standing literary and literary-critical tropes of literary beginnings: the language of Adam, for example, or romantic projections of poetry backward in time, such as Rousseau's speculations on the origins of language, German romantic images of poetry as the original language of humanity, or extensive accounts of an original bardic song, including Vico's claim cited at the outset of this chapter.[2] Language may well indeed have been poetic from the start — in the sense of a profound creativity and a metaphoric capacity to make reference to absent contents — but these claims can now be examined in the objective light of the evidence of human origins research.

PROGRESS IN VARIOUS scientific disciplines has enabled recent scholarship on human origins to generate several accounts of the transition from advanced primates and early hominids to modern humans, *Homo sapi-*

ens. Supporting evidence includes behavioral studies of primates, artifacts documenting changing tool-making techniques, migration patterns, and comparative anatomy: the transition to bipedalism, the development of the modern vocal apparatus, and encephalization. In order to construct a comprehensive account, multiple elements have to be pieced together; this is a scholarship based, on the one hand, on very hard evidence, but on the other, on considerable conjecture and surmise. The questions addressed are crucial for our inquiry into the possibility of literature: What sort of consciousness had to develop in order to allow for imagination or for that concatenation of fictive events that defines narrative? How can we think about the relationship between the emergence of a consciousness capable of imaginary narrative and the acquisition of linguistic facility? And how do these developments fit into a plausible account of evolutionary adaptation — in other words, in what way did the changes that contributed to the development of a literary facility constitute effective adaptations to the environmental challenges that early humans faced? The point is not to suggest some sort of triumphal evolutionary history — the caricature of evolutionism that postmodern critics of teleology present in order to denounce it — but rather, on the contrary, to recognize the deeply contingent character of this development. Language acquisition and its consequences — an increase in the size of social units, accelerated technological change, and, above all, the dynamic use of symbols — should not be thought of as necessary, an unfolding of some idealist truth, but rather as the specific and very curious adaptation that this one peculiar species pursued.

Several accounts of this adaptation process, the transition from the common ancestor of humans and chimpanzees to the emergence of the modern human, are available and posit discrete points of particular relevance to our concern with the origins of a facility for literature. Humans are the literary animal; other animals do not tell stories (although humans certainly imagine stories about talking animals, and this fundamental fiction is one of the defining characteristics of literature's embedded knowledge of its own species-historical standing). In order to make the human origins discussion as productive for a potential literary history as possible, it is useful now to proceed to a review of several of the key treatments of hominization, particularly on the question of the emergence of modern consciousness and language use.

In his *Origins of the Modern Mind,* Merlin Donald proposes an evolutionary schema of hominization, the passage from the common ancestor to modern human, with particular reference to cognitive capacities, including the sense of self-consciousness, the capacity to know the world in a way that permits innovation, and language use. Not only is the overall schema productive for the arguments pursued here on the origins of literature; at several points Donald himself teases out specific links between the evolutionary account of consciousness and modern human cultural, especially aesthetic, facilities. Yet the argument itself proceeds through extrapolations from the physical record and, above all, the varying rates of cultural and technological changes among hominid species. *Australopithecus* dates from four million years ago; *Homo erectus* emerges some two million years ago, and although the Acheulian culture of *erectus* displays a greater sophistication than the Olduwan culture that preceded it, during more than a million years it changes only very slowly. "The main impression *erectus* leaves is one of a systematic, organized creature who was able to hunt and manufacture tools cooperatively, cook food, transmit skills across generations, and grow culturally, albeit at a snail's pace compared with modern humans."[3] The last remark points to the touchstone of Donald's account, the criterion of a capacity for innovation. *Homo sapiens* emerges between one and two hundred thousand years ago, with a 20 percent increase in brain size; not only does a more advanced culture develop, but the rate of cultural change stands in marked contrast to the stability of Acheulian culture, despite the fact that no further growth in brain size took place. The transitions from Mousterian to Mesolithic and Neolithic cultures, for which the physical records demonstrate greater technological and social capacities, cannot be mapped onto encephalization data alone. On the contrary, something takes place in the evolutionary adaptation of *Homo sapiens* that specifically allows for dynamic change. "Ritual, art, myth, and social organization developed and flourished in rapid succession. A new cognitive factor had obviously been introduced into the equation. The human capacity for continuous innovation and cultural change became our most prominent characteristic."[4] That new cognitive factor was — and this is the crux of the hypothesis — linked directly to the development of language, a relatively late feature in the hominization process. It is unclear whether archaic hominids, especially Neanderthals, utilized some primitive speechlike behavior, perhaps with regard to tool manufacture. In any case, they certainly lacked the dynamic use of symbols characteristic of high-speed modern human speech, which defined *Homo sapiens* and marked a profound rupture in evolutionary development.

Yet this rupture has a long prehistory, which Donald traces through a series of stages in the hominization process. In general he argues (following Darwin) that the adaptations achieved in the course of evolution remain present, no matter how dormant, in later stages. In other words, the forms of archaic consciousness that may have preceded language acquisition still inform modern consciousness, carried on underneath subsequent and more advanced developments. He therefore turns to an examination of the question of cognitive capacities in primates, in particular experiments with language facilities in apes. With regard to experiments in training an ape in American Sign Language, Donald concedes that apes may have an ability to learn language. Nonetheless, it is clear that apes do not develop language independently in nature; and, moreover, to the extent that some rudimentary language training can be carried out in experimental contexts, the apes never show the ability to develop new symbols with the creative rapidity shown by young humans. In other words, even if the linguistic difference between apes and humans is not absolutely watertight, the difference in quality is enormous and unmistakable. It is the human capacity for innovation in language that is distinctive (rather than the ability to use linguistic symbols at all), leading to a human semantics with "an infinitely expandable symbolic set."[5]

Donald designates the consciousness attributable to apes as "episodic," a minimal understanding of one's presence in a specific contextual moment. Behavior is instinctive, without reflection or communication, although it can be strategic, in the sense of responding to a danger. The first significant transition in consciousness that he describes corresponds to the Acheulian culture of *Homo erectus*, with significant advances over *Australopithecus*, but nonetheless clearly very much a prelinguistic environment. Language, which Donald comes to describe as a "revolutionary system,"[6] is still absent, which accounts for the very slow rate of change for more than one million years. Yet a change has indeed taken place, a transition from "episodic culture" to "mimetic culture." Without language, without a capacity for symbolic representation, *erectus* nonetheless is presumed to have a facility for mimesis, for a sort of imitation that is linked to a set of functions that are surely preconditions for language: "intentionality, generativity, communicativity, reference, autocueing, and the ability to model an unlimited set of objects."[7] It involves a sort of communication, but one prior to anything readily describable as words, hence a nonverbal communication. It is interesting that these nonverbal mimetic gestures, for example, how adults speak with babies, remain largely constant across modern culture, indicating their

Human Origins and Literary Beginnings

origins in "an ancient root culture that is distinctly human" although not at all modern human.[8]

Furthermore, we should note how Donald draws a strong connection between this archaic mimetic capacity and the centrality of mimesis in the arts, with references to Arnheim, Auerbach, and Frye. At stake is nonverbal — or preverbal — elements in aesthetic production; his choice example is the depiction of Socrates in Aristophanes' *Clouds* and the comic effect generated by the conflict between the verbal discourse of the philosopher and nonverbal action on stage, the motion of the actor's body.[9] The insight supports the recognition that the arts, as such, are not fully dependent on language: drama, dance, painting all have modes of existence independent of linguistic components, and rudimentary forms may well have preexisted the later development of language. If, for the purposes of a prospective literary history and the determination of the standing of literature within society, the acquisition of language is no doubt the defining moment of origin — no literature without language — language in general builds on the prelinguistic skills associated with mimetic culture. Moreover, that form of language that becomes literature retains an emphatic tie to the prelinguistic mimetic phase of cultural development. Other forms of language usage, especially theoretic or scientific language use, pursue the refinement of concepts or the communication of information. In contrast, literary language use retains both a sensibility for the nonlinguistic aspects of language, for example, the possible musicality of words and an anchoring in the mimetic project to become like that which is different. The tension inherent in that formula — the imperative to become similar, while also recognizing difference — anticipates in a rudimentary way the aesthetic condition of autonomy. As little as one can imagine a literature before language, it is also the case, following Donald, that language itself, and in particular literary language, builds on and integrates the legacy of prelinguistic behavioral patterns.

Donald's account continues with a second transition, from mimetic to what he designates "mythic culture." This new formation is specifically dependent on the invention of language and is associated with the emergence of modern humans, one hundred to fifty thousand years ago. Neanderthals were present between 150,000 and 35,000 years ago; modern Cro-Magnon dates from 50,000. While Neanderthals may have had some rudimentary languagelike behavior, evidence suggests that they lacked the dense, high-speed speech of modern humans. Language may have emerged as a result of interspecies competition; or it may have represented an evolutionary response to the challenges posed by the environmental adversity associated with the last period of glaciation. In either case, Donald's argument is that the primary evolutionary advantage of language was precisely not in the transmission of technological skills, such as modes of tool manufacture, which are typically much more dependant on imitation than on articulation. Rather, language development allowed for the development of integrative models of the universe and the human condition, which, in narrative form, become myth. Therefore, in contemporary "stone-age peoples," hunter-gatherer cultures, technology can remain relatively stable, but there is typically an extensive interpretation of the world that allows for causal explanations as well as group identity.

Characterizing mythic culture by the comprehensiveness of narrative explanation, while pointing toward a link to a specifically literary problem, Donald's remarks nonetheless suggest a closed and nondynamic consciousness. To the extent that one assumes that the cosmic explanation provided by mythic narrative bolstered existing group cultural identities, the constraining character of mythic knowledge comes to the fore. Yet myth is more complex: An explanatory model of the world, and, hence, in a sense an archaic forerunner of science, it can also enable a practical progress in the mastery of nature. In this sense, Eric Havelock proposes the "Homeric encyclopedia" thesis, discussed in later chapters, the claim that the oral epic provided a vehicle for transmitting extensive knowledge of the world in order to allow for ongoing pursuit of practical activities.[10] Moreover Donald's description does not only underscore the cognitive standing of myth, but also the particular inventiveness associated with the acquisition of language. Chomsky's "linguistic competence," the child's inventiveness in acquiring linguistic facility, itself implies an innovative capacity associated with language.[11] For Donald, however, the original invention of language betrays an extraordinary ability for innovation and one that continues through the history of language. In other words, the innovation at stake is not merely the invention of language as an evolutionary adaptation by early modern humans, but rather the invention of rapid innovation, dependent and nearly coextensive with that specific invention of symbols associated with the revolutionary system that is language. Literature is a particularly productive site of linguistic invention, with consequences that define cultural traditions: "Some individuals have had a determining effect upon an entire culture; their efforts at linguistic invention created new words and phrases — and, perhaps more importantly, new grammatical conventions — that endured across centuries: Spencer in the English language and Dante in Italian, for example. They and other great innovators were probably close to the kind of linguistic invention that led to the initial creation of language."[12]

It should be noted with interest that Donald's reference to relatively "late" literature — late, if measured on the time scale of human evolution — suggests that this literary material sheds light on the original process of human language acquisition. The creative originality of Spencer and Dante are cut from the same cloth as the creative originality at the beginning of language; this is a striking approach from the social sciences toward an otherwise humanistic notion of the creative artist. Ultimately, the connection suggests a rapprochement between artistic innovation and the civilizational innovation at the core of progressive development. The methodological ramification is that recent literature can be understood as a specific linguistic activity that stands in a strong relationship to the defining linguistic character of human society.

Theoretical culture, Donald's third stage, is characterized by written language with profound consequences for the objectification, refinement, and transmission of ideas. At the outset, however, it should be noted how rare and particular this development was. According to Roy Harris, of the many thousands of languages that humans have developed, only one in ten has generated a writing system, and of those perhaps one hundred produced a significant body of literature.[13] Indeed, one can add that if, as the next chapter reviews, the utilization of a specifically phonetic, that is, alphabetic language is deemed crucial, it is only a matter of ancient Greece, and the cultures that adopted and modified that alphabet. To insist on the importance of alphabetic script therefore gives classical Greek a unique standing in cultural history. As chapter 3 explores, it is precisely on this point that a discussion of an explicitly Western cultural teleology could be grounded.

It is similarly useful to reflect on the prehistory of writing and consider the production of relatively permanent visual artifacts and symbols that preceded the elaboration of coherent writing systems. Advanced cave paintings have been dated at twenty-five thousand years ago, and clay sculptures and figurines at fifteen thousand years. They are pertinent here not so much as art (and therefore antecedent to imaginative literature), but potentially as examples of an objectified, artifactual, and therefore also visual record of subjective intentions. Painting and sculpture can consequently be seen as forerunners of writing; surely both can lay claim to a capacity to record and convey narrative, even if the dynamics of representation operate differently from those in literature, oral or written.

The cognitive skills associated with prehistoric visual-symbolic representation predated and then underpinned the emergence of early writing systems: pictorial, ideographic, hieroglyphic. The growth of agricultural surplus and economies in the ancient Near East required the maintenance of lists and types of records, hence the emergence of cuneiform writing, with its specific advantage of portability. Cuneiform developed into a syllabic script around 2800 B.C.; by 1800 B.C. in Akkadia the usage had spread from commercial lists to legal historical texts. A gradual transition takes place from various Semitic scripts, via Phoenician, to the adoption of the Phoenician letters by the Greeks, who, however, adapted and utilized them in a newly phonetic and, strictly speaking, alphabetic manner. New capacities for the dissemination of literacy ensued, insofar as alphabetic writing, compared with ideographic or hieroglyphic systems, massively reduces the number of symbols to be learned by a potential reader.

Writing has multiple consequences: literacy, objectification of thought, dissemination of ideas. For Donald, however, one issue stands out that is particularly significant for our explorations. Writing initiates an ongoing process of "demythologization."[14] Precisely the core achievement of mythic cultures, the capacity to generate comprehensive explanatory models of the world, is called into question by theoretic culture. Texts, of course, gain a sort of material permanence, thanks to writing, which can encourage, or at least support, a text-critical stance. In oral cultures, we know, literary performance is typically associated with phenomena of homeostatic adjustment, that is, the oral narrator may adjust the tale in order to curry favor with the public, whose reactions may be quite visible. That connection breaks down with writing, which is to say that the writer is freed from the immediate (physical or even threatening) pressures of an audience. In Greece, in particular, the consequences of writing, as the visual symbolization of ideas, were explored most deeply. Hence, Socrates' readiness to call official ideas into question in a process of demythologization and to present instead dialectics, the competition of ideas rather than a new orthodoxy.[15] More generally, writing changes the cognitive psychological environment for humanity (and this argument applies of course to all scripts, not only alphabetic ones) by providing an "external memory": allowing for greater accuracy in the cultural memory, while also freeing up the brain for other sorts of activities beyond the memorization that predominated in the primary orality of mythic cultures.

For Donald, language acquisition is a unique species adaptation, and writing emerges in response to particular social needs; both are behavioral developments pursuant to prior anatomical evolutionary change. Steven Mithen comes to a compatible conclusion, but with a different disciplinary approach, in his *Prehistory of the Mind*. While Donald writes as a psychologist drawing on archaeological data, Mithen is an archeologist seeking support from cognitive psychology. Both Donald and Mithen ultimately reflect on the same evolutionary process and the data available for the transition from *Australopithecus,* through *habilis* and *erectus,* to *Homo sapiens.* Yet while Donald attempts to underpin his model of several cognitive stages of culture with archeological data, Mithen pursues an alternative strategy. Guided by a fundamental debate within cognitive psychology over the structure of the mind, he attempts to speculate on the cognitive transformations that might account for the varied archeological record in the history of hominization.[16]

At the core of his argument is the debate over the so-called modularity of the mind. Is the mind best conceived of as a single and relatively undifferentiated processor of information, or is it more reasonably described as subdivided into separate units or modules, each dedicated to a particular intelligence? The arguments for the latter include the possibility of refined distinctions, accelerated learning possibilities, and more efficient decision-making. Yet this "Swiss army knife" model of the mind suggests a greater complexity than the single processor model and requires further elaboration. It implies the development of content-rich mental modules, dedicated to some fundamental areas of knowledge and hard-wired into human intelligence: for example, a language learning facility (consonant with Chomsky's work), an intuitive biology (an ability to recognize animals and their groupings), an intuitive physics (an ability to understand basic physical principles, for example, expectations that things fall or that walls are solid), and an intuitive psychology (an ability to attempt to predict the likely behavior of others). Recent research demonstrates how much of this basic intelligence appears to be innate in the early child's mind. "Are children really born with content-rich mental modules that reflect the structure of the real (Pleistocene) world . . . ? The answer from developmental psychology is overwhelmingly [affirmative]. Young children seem to have intuitive knowledge about the world in at least four domains of behavior: about language, psychology, physics and biology."[17]

Yet even if one were to argue that this fundamental knowledge represents a survival advantage for early humans, and even if one claims that the division of labor among the multiple intelligences entails an important efficiency, the modular model of the mind is hardly self-evident. Indeed, it is not difficult to consider common situations in which behavior reflects extensive transgressions of the borders among the various intelligence domains. Thus Mithen: "Recall for a moment the way in which a child will play with an inert doll, investing it with the attributes of a living being. A critical feature of that child's mind is not simply that she is able to apply the evolutionarily inappropriate rules of psychology, biology, and language to play with her inert physical object, but she is utterly compelled to do so."[18] He then proceeds to elaborate on the phenomenon of cross-modular knowledge, the specific cognitive psychological phenomenon of the ability to link different domain-specific knowledge contents to each other. Indeed, this demodularization appears to be a defining feature of modern human intelligence and a source of creativity. Mithen cites Susan Carey and Elizabeth Spelke's comment: "Although infants the world over share a set of initial systems of knowledge, these systems are spontaneously overturned over the course of development and learning, as children and adults construct, explore and adopt mappings across knowledge systems."[19] The accumulation of specialized knowledge allowed for particular efficiencies; but the dedifferentiation among the specified domains is crucial for their innovative deployment. In the words of Annette Karmiloff-Smith, "knowledge becomes applicable beyond the special purpose goals for which it is normally used."[20] This distribution of knowledge outside the content-rich modules and its reorganization in creative situations leads Dan Sperber to propose the notion of a "module of metarepresentation," precisely in order to explain this ability to escape the narrow modular perspectives.[21]

Mithen's strategy involves mapping the cognitive psychological discussion onto the archeological record of hominization: from an undifferentiated general intelligence, through the gradual emergence of domain-specific intelligences — which, however, remain sequestered from each other — to a flow of knowledge between the specialized intelligence regions. Thus he speculates that in the common ancestor of the *Homo* lineage and chimpanzees a minimal general intelligence existed as well as some specialized knowledge: physical intelligence pertinent to foraging and social intelligence in the sense of predicting another's behavior through an awareness of self; but that self-awareness is restricted to the social knowledge and does not lead, for example, to a reflexive knowledge in the physical, let alone technological, area. In the Olduwan culture of *Homo habilis* one finds evidence of a greater technological facility than with chimpanzees. Although chimps may use sticks, as tools, to probe anthills, early humans not only manufactured tools, but also were also able to manufacture the so-called flakes, tools used in the manufacture of other tools. Nonetheless, specialized intelligence in *habilis*, Mithen concludes, was probably quite limited, and it was general intelligence, not modularized knowledge, that remained predominant. It is rather with *Homo erectus*, 1.8 million years ago, that separate and specialized domains of knowledge begin to appear clearly. An example is the sophistication of the hand ax, sometimes characterized by a multidimensional symmetry, indicating considerable planning and attention. As dramatic as this advance over Olduvan culture was, its limitations are equally apparent. Tools were made only from stone, rather than from ivory and antlers; nor were they made for specialized tasks. For example, the hand ax was used for all functions. In addition, tools were simple, never entailing multiple parts. Finally, there was little variation in technology over time. This early human culture was marked by little innovation during more than one million years. Mithen concludes that a specialized realm of technological intelligence had indeed developed, but it remained fully separate from other modules, such as a natural history intelligence, which facilitated the colonization of much of the world outside Africa.

Donald emphasized the transition from mimetic to mythic culture, associated with the transition to language. Mithen's narrative is in effect congruent: *Homo sapiens* appears about one hundred thousand years ago, but a "big bang" does not take place until sixty to thirty thousand years ago, a cultural explosion marked by the simultaneity of new technologies and the origin of art. It is in this period that the final colonization processes take place, especially Australia (to which, as Noble and Davidson underscore, no land bridge ever existed, and nautical skills and associated social cooperation were therefore required); and it is in this period that religion and a confrontation with death — evidenced by ritual burial sites — apparently emerged.[22] Neanderthal culture displays no comparable evidence, while *Homo sapiens* leaves cave paintings dating from thirty to thirty-five thousand years ago. Some of this art involves nonrepresentational symbols, as in the cave paintings in the Dordogne. Elsewhere it is representational, albeit imaginatively so, as with the statuette of a man with lion's head, found in Hohenstein-Stadel in southern Germany. As enduring artifacts, designed for the visual transmission of symbolic knowledge, they stand in an anticipatory relationship to the development of writing, as noted above.

Mithen, however, underscores the innovative character of this art and its cognitive preconditions. Production of these objects entailed at least three components: the ability to execute a mental template, the willingness to associate a meaning with a visual image, and an intention to communicate that meaning to another party.[23] Taken independently, none of these functions was new. The technical ability to plan and execute had long been associated with toolmaking ability; the natural-historical modular intelligence had similarly permitted the association of a particular meaning with, for instance, an animal track. Mithen has also assumed that some primitive early language existed as part of the social intelligence, and therefore the intent to communicate through the art object was not new. The novelty, rather, was the sudden coincidence of these otherwise segregated knowledge domains. Language, which for Donald clearly stands at the center of the cultural and cognitive advance of early humans, is somewhat displaced by Mithen, who treats it, instead, as one among the several modular specializations. The lynchpin is not the transition to language as such but to the demodularization of knowledge, the ability to link the specialized knowledge domains, including linguistic knowledge, to one another in complex ways.

It is therefore in this period, around thirty to fifty thousand years ago, that natural historic and technological intelligences become linked, leading for example to the first needles made of bone. Similarly, social knowledge and natural history merged in anthropomorphic representations, such as the lion man of Hohenstein-Stadel. Mithen suggests that anthropomorphic thinking may have represented a competitive advantage to the extent that it linked an effort to predict others' behaviors, heretofore restricted to the social realm of other humans, to natural history knowledge associated with hunting. Artistic exploration of the border between humans and animals, therefore, is treated as a source of potential knowledge of value in the hunter-gatherer economy.[24] At the same time, Mithen's frame implicitly suggests more. The proliferation of symbolic expression indicates a capacity to recognize an emphatic but ultimately arbitrary relationship between a sign and its referent: to maintain the distinction between the sign and the referent as well as their resonance with each other. In other words, the capacity to move between intelligence modules implies a capacity for symbolic thought, in particular the ability to utilize a present symbol in order to invoke a distant referent. This play of presence and absence is also at the heart of the simultaneous innovation of burial, indicating a transformed understanding of mortality. Early humans discover art and death just at the point that they discover language: All three are implicated in the semiotic dynamic of meaning, reference, and absent referent.

This question of symbolic capacity is central to the third treatment of human origins under consideration here, William Noble and Iain Davidson, *Human Evolution, Language, and Mind*. While they cite various criticisms of Donald's work, particularly claims that the archeological record does not support his narrative as neatly as he suggests,[25] they shift attention away from his three-stage process and focus instead on his characterization of human consciousness: "The useful feature to appreciate about Donald's point is the recognition that consciousness entails intentionality (aboutness). Just as speaking is speaking *about* something, consciousness is consciousness *of* something. The position we develop in discussing 'mindedness' . . . is that human consciousness *of* things is another way of describing human speech *about* things," and they continue with the emphatic proposition "We identify absence of language as the feature that limits the consciousness of non-human animals to that of sensory sensitivity (conscious sensitivity). Human mindedness is essentially marked by the conscious attentiveness and articulateness that language enables."[26] Mindedness and language are not identical, but they are in effect mutually dependent; rather than imagining that ideas exist in the mind first and that early man invents language to express them, Noble and Davidson argue that the very contents of our minds, our ability to have ideas, imagination, concepts, and so on are a function of our unique social behavior, the use of language.

To demonstrate this, they insist that while there are of course physiological and anatomical preconditions of language, it is not the case that the anatomical changes, especially an increase in brain size, leads necessarily to language. Anatomically modern humans appear some one hundred to one hundred and fifty thousand years ago, but language emerges, for Noble and Davidson, around seventy to fifty thousand years ago. In other words, the anatomical changes may have been preconditions but were not sufficient explanations for the emergence of language. The key to the development of language, and therefore human consciousness, within a context of evolution-theoretical argument, is therefore to posit a series of primate and hominid adaptations, in particular social adaptations, that would produce human language acquisition.

Insisting on the importance of evidence to sustain claims of language use, Noble and Davidson reject claims of early language usage, of one or two million years ago, because the Olduwan tool manufacture could well have proceeded without language, and there is no evidence of the specific characteristic of language usage, the ability to use signs symbolically.[27] In other words, the question involves the manner in which to trace the transition between, say, primate gesture calls and human speech; in the former, while vocalizations occur in response to particular conditions, such as danger, no semanticity, in the sense of a meaning recognized by a consciousness, is present. Moreover, it is only in human speech, and the attendant consciousness, that reflection on meaning takes place. The use of the symbol entails suppleness absent in the gesture call, which is typically linked to an immediate situation (or *episode* in Donald's sense of "episodic culture"). "The detachability and objectifying force of linguistic signs enables reference to what is not immediately present."[28]

Noble and Davidson proceed on multiple levels, examining what might be considered as constitutive of language and exploring the evidence of hominid behavior in order to identify the earliest indications that might point to language use. Their primary conclusion involves the insistence on the late emergence of language, that is, *Homo sapiens* acquires language use around sixty thousand years ago. The key dating involves the colonization of Australia: While it may well have been discovered accidentally by seafaring early humans, the navigational technology and organization required for the sea voyage itself is unthinkable without the conscious planning that presumes speech. In contrast, the much earlier human migrations beyond Africa are explicable in terms of the movement patterns of a carnivorous species (carnivore population densities are typically lower and therefore engage in migration). The colonization of the Americas takes place later. Crossing the land bridge to Alaska does not allow for the same sort of argument, as does a marine approach to Australia. Nonetheless, the hardships of Arctic conditions during a period of glaciation (the prerequisite for the land bridge) presented challenges of a magnitude that could have been mastered only through planning operations of complexity comparable to the Australian colonization. Similarly, after a passage over a land bridge into Alaska, the access to the rest of the Western Hemisphere, blocked by glaciers, very likely required considerable coastal navigation. Such navigation presumably required the same technology and social organization, premised on language use, that must have characterized the colonization of Australia.

In addition to migration, Noble and Davidson cite other evidence. On the one hand, they argue that earlier artifacts do not support insinuations of a modern consciousness and language usage; on the other, they point to the proliferation of symbol usage around thirty thousand years ago, especially art, in the context of other innovations in technology and living conditions, such as regular control of fire and the first shelters. This is the same late dating presented by Donald and by Mithen. Noble and Davidson in addition suggest an admittedly speculative evolutionary adaptation thesis on language utilization — speculative, but nonetheless supported by existing evidence and addressing key points that any comprehensive hypothesis would necessarily face. One aspect of the argument involves the particular social conditions that would allow for the maintenance or transmission of language skills, a "social context of learning" that could support the "reinvention of language skills."[29] As frequently with evolutionary processes, the path appears indirect. Some early hominids adapted to bipedalism, which may have allowed for a more effective mobility in the African savannahs in search of nourishment, since bipeds were able to cover territory more quickly. Bipedalism and the savannah environment had thermoregulatory consequences, advantaging increased blood flow to the brain, for a cooling effect, and also selecting for a disappearance of body hair to allow for greater cooling through sweating. With the disappearance of body hair and the upright posture, infants could no longer cling to the back of adults and would henceforth be carried in front, permitting an ongoing interaction between adult and child. To the extent that such interaction involved symbolic activity, the social context for language transmission and reinvention was established.

A second process hypothetically underpinned the first process. An increase in encephalization is often cited as the cause of cultural and linguistic change. Noble and Davidson explicitly reject such biologically deterministic claims. Indeed, an increase in brain size plays a very different role in their story: As an energy-intensive organ, it contributed to the need for an increase in caloric intake and probably encouraged carnivorousness, and hence hunting and bipedalism. In addition, the greater adult brain size affected birth and childbearing. The postnatal growth of the brain, and therefore head size, is much greater among humans than among other primates. This contributes to a longer period of altriciality, that is, infant dependence on the adult caregiver, and therefore a longer period for the potential of learning.

Finally, and most speculatively, Noble and Davidson suggest a specific origin of a particular semiotic capacity within their evolutionary narrative. For the frame elaborated thus far, setting up a possible learning context between infant and caregiver, does not yet have anything to do with language per se. They argue rather from the behavior of stone throwing among chimpanzees and assume a natural selection for greater accuracy among early hominids. Evolutionary development of the motor skills implied not only greater hand-eye coordination but also anatomical adjustments in the arm and thorax that arguably contributed eventually to the modern vocal system, and the extensive control it permits. Yet before the vocal system could develop as a vehicle for language, a more profound notion of semanticity had to develop, the link between a sign and a referent, precisely that capacity that other primates (at least in nonenculturated states) do not display. Noble and Davidson suggest "that if throwing at a target is selected for, an inevitable posture, as a feature of the end-phase of the throw, is orientation of the arm to the target. . . . For an observer, this posture directly indicates the whereabouts of a target. The posture achieves the communication of information. Were it imitated as a posture in appropriate circumstances, it would come to signal the presence and whereabouts of potential predators, prey or antagonists without revealing the presence and whereabouts of the signalers to that predators, prey or antagonist."[30] This is their hypothetical origin of pointing, that distinctive behavior that involves an implied communication of a meaning, and one specifically not found in nonhuman primates. The increase in altriciality and the potential for adult-infant interaction could bring pointing, and imitative pointing, into play in the process of ontogenetic development. This sense of semanticity hypothetically spread from its origins in the anatomy of throwing to other physical marks made by early humans but gradually recognized as carriers of meaning: marks on bones, for instance.[31]

Noble and Davidson present an evolutionarily plausible sequence of adaptations that could support their argument for the late, explosive emergence of language. The prerequisites included the social context (adult-child interaction), the anatomical transformations (muscle control and vocal tract), but above all the semantic capacity, the transition to pointing. In the context of the last ice age and, perhaps, out of interspecies competition with *Neanderthal,* the modern human suddenly develops the symbolic capacity that is language and with it the concomitant form of consciousness, intentionality, that defines human mindedness. These adaptations, however, built on several other pieces that had emerged much earlier in evolutionary history.

The three accounts summarized here agree on the late development of language. Whether one dates it from the evidence of art in Europe — for example, the paintings at Chauvet of 30,000 years ago — or from the colonization of Australia at 55,000, or, more controversially, the recently discovered South African artifacts from Blombos of 77,000, for our purposes the result is the same: the sudden emergence of a capacity to deploy symbols, evidenced by artistic objects and accelerated technology, both of which are unthinkable without linguistic facility.[32] Moreover, that language use is linked, via art, to a specifically imaginative capacity, grounded in the very nature of symbolic communication. The consequences for a history of literature, that is, a history from the beginning of language, are complex and multidimensional, because of the various implications of the three human origins stories. Literature is unthinkable without language, and language involves fundamentally, and presumably initially, a symbolic capacity that implies a detachment from the merely present context, hence an imagination of that which is absent. The standing of that imaginative capacity and the pressures acting upon it, however, differ somewhat in the three accounts.

Despite different orientations, both Mithen and Donald in fact underscore an innovative capacity in language that bears on literary creativity. In Mithen's cognitive-psychological account of the emergence of content-rich intelligence modules followed by a demodularization allowing for a deployment of knowledge outside its initial context, language appears to involve a systematic usage of symbols defined by its mobility or interdisciplinarity. In other words, Mithen's account suggests that literature might be conceived as the peculiar language use that is not specific to a narrow specialization and is precisely therefore the potential source for a cultural creativity. Imaginative language use, or literature, would consequently play a central role in a dynamic culture, as a source of innovation (as Donald suggests as well) rather than being a marginal phenomenon (marginal for its lack of precise referentiality) or historical and atavistic (again, the other side of Donald's argument). In the end, Donald's three-stage schema tends to locate literature in historical strata that fall short of theoretical modernity, while Mithen suggests treating it as the metadiscourse, beyond any specific module, which therefore can drive the motor of cultural innovation.

All three human-origins accounts, but especially Noble and Davidson's, insist on the complex cognitive psychology of symbol usage. Language and therefore literature presume the ability to manipulate arbitrary signs and to indicate absent contents. The capacity for an imaginative use of language is implied by the very nature of language itself: "imagination is among language's several fruits."[33] If this is the crux of the argument, two further elements are particularly germane for a potential literary history. One is the insistence on altriciality, the extended infant dependency and its consequences in human prehistory, or more broadly the recognition of the social context of learning that language use requires. Language acquisition requires cross-generational relationships, in which knowledge and language skills (and the cognitive capacities those skills presume) are transmitted. While one thinks initially of parent-child relations, the extension to schooling follows quickly. Language learning and literature, as a specialized language use, maintain a fundamental tie to questions of education: both as a topic of literature, for example, in novels of education, and as a venue in which knowledge of and access to literature are provided systematically.

The second element of the Noble and Davidson argument that is vital to a potential literary history is a broader version of the consequences of altriciality. Literature is not only, as just discussed, rooted solely in educational processes; it is, as language, a more broadly social phenomenon. Language use is not an individual matter, no matter how it is a precondition for individuation, but rather part of a social network of language speakers. It is the vehicle for strategic planning, projective action, and technological undertakings in the face of natural adversities. The relationship of a specifically literary language use to this social character is complex: literature is social, presuming a reception process, but it may also be defined by a creativity that puts it at odds with an established social order (an opposition that is moreover heightened once primary orality gives way to literate culture, as explored in the next chapter). Indeed, the communicative character of symbol utilization, that is, the social function of the symbol as a carrier of meaning between an originator and a recipient, stands in some tension with the semiotic arbitrariness of any symbol, as well as with the absence of the referent, two distinct components of its imaginative nature. Does literature maintain group identity or does it transform it? Is it a force of social cohesion, the expression of a particular culture, which its adherents intend to maintain, or is it a source of innovative change? Is the appropriate criterion of literary success the quantitative distribution to a mass audience of readers comfortable only with received opinion or is it an incommensurable quality even if that means an inaccessible hermeticism? The problematic itself, a constant in literary history and a site of perpetual critical irritation, is rooted in the very nature of the social and semiotic arguments about the origins of language.

Thus, the three accounts point in several rich directions for literary history. For now, however, we should hold on to the very fact that human origins research can provide a starting point for a history of literature, with ramifications that extend through subsequent forms of literary expression. By shedding light on the origins and defining conditions of language, which implies symbol usage, prehistory becomes relevant to the humanistic study of art (for which artifacts themselves exist) and literature (about the oral-history past of which we are forced to speculate, although we can do so by extrapolating from other evidence: the art, burial practices, accelerated technology, and migration patterns). At this point, three general conclusions are allowable:

1. Language use, understood as the precondition for literature, as the specifically imaginative use of language, represents a unique and highly contingent social behavioral adaptation. While we may assume that modern human life is unthinkable without, and therefore dependant on, language, it is clear that all other species survive without language in the human sense. (No matter how many gesture calls one can cite, no matter how many chimpanzees can be trained to manipulate cards, none of this approaches the quality of human language.) Indeed, other hominids very likely had no language in the modern sense, and the language originators were a very small group of *Homo sapiens*. In other words, even *Homo sapiens* presumably existed without language for tens of thousands of years. Far from some necessary or teleologically foreordained outcome, language use is close to an evolutionary accident, and literature, consequently, is not an ontological necessity. These comments do not detract from literature, but they call upon us to recognize its specificity and distinctiveness within our human condition. Language use is a curious behavior, but once the transition to language is made, literature is a likely consequence, since it is linked to the dynamic of the linguistic symbol through the functioning of the imagination.

2. Language use is a particular behavior that entails the utilization of symbols, which in turn implies a specific set of cognitive abilities. These include, aside from communicative intention, a facility with arbitrary signs and a capacity to make reference to an absent referent. Hence the coincidence with the recognition of death as evidenced by burial practices, that is, the deceased can be absent and present within a presumed prehistoric religious sensibility. Hence also artworks, as symbol deployment, and the cooperative efforts in technological innovation and social organization that require complex planning and the capacity to project into the uncertainty of the future. Inherent in language is evidently an ability to allow for projective thoughts, to conceptualize that which is not real, and to imagine: hence literature. The capacity to imagine counterfactual and qualitatively new contents (new in the sense of different from that which is already and merely present) suggests the pos-

sibility of attempting to realize them, and therefore also purposive action. Imagination and teleology are intertwined in their common embeddedness in the linguistic condition.

3. The culture of oral literature, which presumably emerges among early humans coincidental with or soon after the acquisition of language — fifty thousand years ago — lasts until the establishment of writing (and of course continues albeit in the transformed context of literacy). Alphabetic writing appears around 700 B.C., but it is preceded by various other modalities: pictographs, hieroglyphs, cuneiform, and so on. Yet these too are relatively late, much closer to the end of the preliterate cultures than to their beginnings. Nonetheless, it is crucial to remember that preliterate cultures do display early evidence of art, including painting and sculpture, which is to say visual symbols. Writing too is a form of visual symbolization, although it involves a different systematicity than do the visual representations of drawings or abstract design. During the period of oral cultures, it was not the case that oral transmission was the only vehicle for shared memory transmission: visual art may well have served that purpose as well. Works of visual art, relatively permanent, and clearly detached from their producers, anticipate some of the phenomenological characteristics of written literature. Oral literature coexisted with these other modes of memory and expression.

While we cannot know the character of the oral literature that existed in prehistory, we may be able to extrapolate from existing oral literature. Considerable caution is due. The appropriate comparison to the hypothetical oral literature of early humans is precisely not the literature of oral performance in contexts of existing literacy; even oral performances by nonliterates in such contexts are not pertinent. In any context where literacy, no matter how restricted, has been established, the cultural standing of oral performance has been radically altered, since it has ceased to represent the sole mode of verbal memory. For example, in settings where a priestly literature has been established or where missionary Christianity has become present, the orality of a nonliterate population has been irreversibly relativized. As Jack Goody notes, "Since religious practices and beliefs are largely based on scriptures and in the hands of literate priests, what is left in the oral tradition tends to be magic rather than religion, the peripheral rather than the core. In other words, the content of the oral tradition tends to be marginalized."[34] Thus, for example, the classic studies of Yugoslav oral epics by A. B. Lord and Milman Parry, from which the thesis of the orality of the Homeric texts was extrapolated, are flawed to the extent that they draw on oral performance in the context of a restricted literacy, not a genuine preliteracy.[35] More broadly, we should be careful not to reproduce the eighteenth and nineteenth century romantic fascination with presumed oral bardic origins, Ossian being the best-known example. To be sure, that concern with origins and historical development, embedded in European romanticism, is hardly unrelated to the intellectual context of Darwin, whose work is foundational for the human origins discussion and therefore for the arguments in this book as well.[36] The point here is that all literature, or all serious literature, no matter how advanced and modern, carries with it the marks of the past, the entry into language and orality, as well as the later transition to writing.

The border between written and oral cultures, the main concern of the next chapter, is indeed blurry; it is of significance here to the extent that it is relevant to determining which oral material might be productive for modeling early human literature. On the one hand, oral performance—and of course nonliteracy—can continue within cultures where some forms of writing and literacy had been established. As already argued, the cultural transformations pursuant to the introduction of writing transform the status of oral performance and therefore make less useful this comparison set, which Walter Ong designates as "secondary orality." [37] On the other hand, we have also seen that long before the development of writing, forms of visual art are present, indeed presumably since the beginning of language use. Before the development of written language, oral performance, the utilization of imaginative language, therefore coexisted with the relatively permanent material artifacts of painting and sculpture, which carried distinct forms of cultural knowledge, and this in turn demonstrates that a nonoral mode of cultural transmission predates the development of writing.

We are approaching the disciplinary border invoked in the introduction. The human-origins discussion, though frequently speculative, is grounded in constant references to relatively hard data, sometimes natural-scientific (comparative anatomical or, increasingly, genomic), sometimes archeological and social-scientific, but still subject to frequently quantitative analysis. The material of oral literature has a mixed character, available both to anthropological and to humanistic inquiry. Yet for this current project, it is of vital importance to insist on the possibility of citing relatively recent literature (and to clarify the terms on the basis of which such literature might be cited) as evidence for the standing of literature within a civilizational process, in particular a process that commences with human origins. The first chapter presented an argument against a narrow periodization of literary history or a primarily contextualizing approach. It is the specific character of literature to be able to appeal to readers from contexts quite distinct from the point of production of the specific work. This implies that the current reader can find nonspecialist interest in the literature of an older period. In fact, we saw Marx insisting that Homer's epics retain interest for the nineteenth-century reader. The claim should now be expanded to the suggestion that the twenty-first-century reader might engage with even more archaic material. This distinctive temporality of literature, its ability to appeal across time, is amplified by a second diachronic feature, the manner in which any work is linked, via inheritance or competition, to earlier writing. Writing is always subsequent to prior literature, the past echoes through the present work, and the present work carries within it a deep memory of the past of literary life. Every work responds to its predecessor, in a chain of backward infinite regress. Hence the possibility of examining recent literature as a particular sort of evidence for inquiring into literary origins. If literature is not (or not only) contextually determined, if each work is resonant with evidence of the condition of literature as such, and if each is inescapably lodged within diachronic or cross-generational concatenations, then an inquiry into present (or relatively recent) objects ought to be able to shed light on the distant past of literature.

IF, AS CONTEXTUALIZING critics would have it, a work of literature is defined primarily by the social, cultural, and intellectual frames in which it is written, said work is then ultimately only about its point of production, its first time and place. In this sense, Kafka's writings would only be about early twentieth-century Prague, and they should consequently interest only aficionados of that early twentieth century and that locale. No doubt, there may be ways to read Kafka as a regional author, and local patriots in the Czech Republic may claim him for their own. One can observe that similar restricted localization of authors in other settings where local authors who reach international acclaim are turned into tourist attractions: the many Dante sites in Florence or the Neruda homes in Chile. Such celebration of local heroes is merely the popular version of contextual reading: new historicism for the masses.

This sort of restricted definition of an author, in temporal or spatial terms, shares the weakness of all contextualization, an inability to account for the specifically literary capacity to transcend time and space, evidenced by the appeal to distant recipients. One can read Dante in Chile and Neruda in Florence, as well as Kafka in locales far away from Prague. This is an important point to reiterate now in order to understand the significance about to be attributed to several literary examples. They are not being read, primarily, as expressions of their time and place, but as intratextual reflections on the condition of literature per se. Contextualizing readers of Kafka might regard his story of the talking ape in "Report to an Academy" as a literary manifestation of various early twentieth-century intellectual currents: Darwinism and, perhaps, Nietzsche's related imagery of the transition from ape to man and to superman.[38] The possible constellation of influences is not at all uninteresting, but to the extent that it lodges Kafka in the debates of his age, it does little to explain his interest to today's readers—a point intended not to lead to a discussion of relevance, that is, the reduction of a historical work of literature to emphatically current, present meanings. Rather, consistent contextualization evades the question of the specificity of the author of literature, Kafka, by suggesting that the fiction writer is little more than a channeling of other great contemporaries.

It is no doubt true that works of literature may invoke their context (or the author's), but what defines their literariness is precisely their ability to transcend these contexts, because of their autonomy, and to reflect immanently on their own preconditions and on the specificity of the standing of the literary work in general. Therefore, Kafka's fictions of animals and language may tell us, ultimately, less about Kafka's reading of Darwin and Nietzsche (as intriguing as that may be as part of the intellectual history of modernism) than about an internally literary knowledge of the relationship between human speech and animals, the standing of human language, and the substance of human creativity. Rather than imputing some ultimately arbitrary allegorical message to his stories, the suggestion is to take their subject matter very seriously as reflections on language as a defining feature of the human condition, a feature that is, moreover, the indispensable precondition of literature and also the dividing line with the animal world. The argument, in other words, is to take Kafka's allegories of language acquisition and loss literally. The literature of talking animals concerns a fictional trope that points to the very foundation of the possibility of literature itself. Human specificity therefore emerges through the irony of presenting animals imbued with speech, and these stagings of the human-animal problematic stand in a tradition that stretches from the early human anthropomorphism of the lion-man of Hohenstein-Stadel through Kafka's fictions, and beyond.

In fact, the literary tradition of talking animals is ancient and extensive: Aesop, Cervantes, La Fontaine, E. T. A. Hoffmann, and George Orwell come to mind as canonic examples.[39] The talking animal proliferates in cartoons, in a range of registers from the comic entertainment of Mickey Mouse to the Holocaust narrative of Art Spiegelman's *Maus*. Frequently associated with children's pedagogy, fables, and cartoons, all low genre, other forms of anthropomorphism and totemism point to a minatory potential for individual psychological regression: Freud's Wolfman, the Circe episode in the *Odyssey*, or the horror of dehominization implicit in the tales of vampires and werewolves. The very scope of this tradition should be viewed as evidence of a sort of objectivity of a cultural fact: A constant feature of literature (although not in all works, of course) is the interrogation of the border between animals and humans and therefore a referencing of the problem of hominization and language. The point is not animistic ignorance, some erroneous belief that animals really discourse like humans. That sort of imputation is as inaccurate for readers of *Animal Farm* or Aesop's *Fables* as it is for the sculptors of prehistory or ancient Egypt. Rather, these representations testify to the sophisticated capacity of culture — by definition, culture with language — to reflect on the relationship to and the transition from nonlinguistic animals, or rather, the transition from animals to humans, which is the passage into language.

A possible social-scientific objection to the extrapolation from literary examples to social developmental claims is that the literary texts may appear to have been chosen arbitrarily. While humanists explore individual cases, social scientists prefer large data sets in order to support generalizing assertions. In this case, at least, the examples, two stories by Kafka, have been selected as unique but nonetheless representative examples of a set of literary objects of considerable scope. A major body of literature involves animals and speech. The claim here is that this thematically defined text set reflects implicitly on the origins and preconditions of literature and autonomy: Hominization takes place through language acquisition, and this transition allows for literature. Literature, which is systemically predisposed to inquire into its own specificity, consequently interrogates the standing of language at the border between humans and animals. Kafka explores precisely this problem in these two narratives, which have become emblematic for twentieth-century writing, "A Report to an Academy" and "The Metamorphosis." The former treats the fiction of an ape's hominization process through language, the latter describes the reverse, a human's transformation into an animal and its consequences.

"A Report" is an uninterrupted first-person narration, directed to the silent addressees of the "Academy," and this illusion of direct speech lends a bizarre authenticity to the conceit of the fiction: It is an ape who is speaking, and speaking moreover on the topic of his hominization. The silence of the addressees puts the ape's speech in greater relief, as does of course the uncanny congruence of the reader with the addressee. The structure of the text locates the reader in the position of the fictional addressee. The tension between authenticity and fiction is underscored by the language act, which the speech itself entails and, indeed, names. It is a *Bericht*, a report, and a generic designation that appears in the title and both at the beginning and the end of the text, seemingly emphasizing the veracity of the narration. The insistence on the truth claim only heightens the irritation of the fiction for the reader. Of interest for us, however, is not primarily this cognitive dissonance that contributes to the characteristic strangeness of Kafka's vision, staging an irresolvable logical problem about the objective character of fictional assertions. Rather, our concern involves the thematic material itself, the presentation of the hominized ape precisely as a speaker, as a language user.

Thus, it is the first-person narration that magnifies the point, the absurd fact of the animal endowed with speech. Through language acquisition, he has taken on the defining characteristic of humans, even though he remains an ape. In fact, he even refers to his "apeness" as lying far behind him, as distant from his present state as the primate ancestors of the members of the academy. Indeed, his evolutionary acceleration is referred to in the text, amplified by the fiction of his address precisely to an academy and his highly conventionalized and formal syntax. Nonetheless, we also know that he remains ape. He refers to his fur, for example, as well as to his apelike pleasures in his private life. Yet here too we face a structural conundrum characteristic of Kafka. While the narrator references his own body as that of an ape, the direct evidence that we have before us is his speech, which demonstrates his humanity. His standing as ape or as human therefore remains ambiguous. The narrative is located precisely in the border zone of hominization through language.

The content of the ape's evolution, from his capture in the African jungle to his acquisition of language and to his success in the circuses of Europe, is complex and involves several intertwined themes. These include a critique of civilization, a consideration on repression and freedom, the function of imitation or mimesis (which resonates obviously with standard associations with monkeys and apes), the existential search for an exit from his condition, and his own circus performances. This material makes up the content of the report, which it is not our task to unravel here. It suffices to note that in this short story of hominization, Kafka has chosen to foreground the fact of language itself through the choice of narrator. The ape's definitive entry into humanity involved his sudden leap into language; hence his eligibility for participation in society. This is the case, however, even though the fact of language acquisition is set in parallel to another imitation of human behavior, drinking alcohol. A sardonic evaluation of human identity ensues, and this pejorative judgment is consonant with the thematic material of the narrative, the ape's indications that his evolutionary progress comes at the high price of degradation. While he does not regret his hominization, he clearly indicates an understanding of his condition as one defined by force, to which his strategic response of imitation — imitative drinking and imitative speech — amounts to an effort to find an escape. Yet even that notional escape is presented with resignation, considerably less than an emphatic notion of freedom, and at best an accommodation with the ultimate constraints of the condition of civilization.

That cultural pessimism and criticism of civilization arguably correspond to what might be considered Kafka's intention or message; the stance is, ultimately, not at all atypical for the intellectuals of the early twentieth century. In this context, however, the concern is different: the attraction to the problematic of hominization through language as a fundamental predisposition of literature. Kafka addresses the problem in reverse in "The Metamorphosis," where the central figure, Gregor Samsa, seems to fall out of the human community, precisely as he becomes an animal and loses language. Here too the narratological structure amplifies the thematic topic: The hominized ape in "The Report" is the vehicle of the first-person narration because he can talk, while Gregor, losing his humanity, becomes the object of a third-person discourse. This reduction through language loss is staged as an allegory in the second paragraph of the story, the brief description of an image that Gregor had hung on the wall of his room, "a lady, with a fur cap on and a fur stole, sitting upright and holding out to the spectator a huge fur muff into which the whole of her forearm had vanished!"[40] The woman in fur is taking on animallike features by disappearing into the muff. This dehumanization takes place in the context of an illustration, indeed, its visual character is underscored: It was a picture in a magazine, which Gregor had cut out and then framed, marking again its standing as image. Yet precisely as image it is without language. The passage allegorizes the association of dehominization and language loss, which is the substance of the main narrative and which, moreover, is at the core of widespread tales of regression: the evil spells that turn humans into animals and rob them of speech.

What of Gregor's speech? As already noted, "The Metamorphosis" is a third-person narrative, unlike "The Report," which highlighted the ape's ability to use language. Gregor's exclusion from the human community, which the ape had joined, is marked by his reduction to a topic of the narrator's discourse. Moreover, the loss of speech, as topic, contributes to the macabre humor of the first part of the story, while Gregor, as insect, is locked in his room, with his family and employer standing outside the door. His attempts to answer their questions highlight the transformation of Gregor's voice, at one point described as an animal voice. The irritation is magnified by the interior monologue, that is, Gregor's thoughts continue in human language, although his ability to articulate them audibly disappears. Indeed, Kafka plays with a variation between Gregor "thinking" to himself and "saying" to himself. But no matter what Gregor has to say, he cannot change his situation. Whatever fragmentary language ability he has retained, it is ineffective: "No entreaty of Gregor's availed, indeed no entreaty was even understood." That the underlying issue in the passage has to do with voice, however, becomes amply evident, when we learn of the other metamorphosis, the change in the father, who is beating his transformed son back into his room: "Maybe he was now making more noise than ever to urge Gregor forward, as if no obstacle impeded him; to Gregor, anyhow, the noise in his rear sounded no longer like the voice of one single father."[41] Language has turned into noise, and the single father has lost his individuality, as much as the son has turned into an animal. The confrontation between father and son, and the story as a whole, bear witness to Kafka's pessimistic account of family relations and modern society in general. For our purposes, however, the key is the entwinement of language and hominization or, rather, the loss of language, degradation, and an erosion of particularity. Read side by side, these two Kafka texts highlight a concern with the standing of language in the human condition and, moreover, the correlation of linguistic facility and individuation.

ONE MIGHT OBJECT that the discussion of Kafka stacks the deck through the choice of examples of direct topical relevance. The two texts have as their central topic linguistic borders at major points of developmental transition between humans and animals. As interesting as these illustrations may be as comments on the topics of language acquisition and literature, they do not provide conclusive proof of a general claim about literature. Are the choices therefore arbitrary? Hardly, since language acquisition recurs frequently as a topic in wide swaths of literary history. As a favored topic, it evidently points to early stages in the history of literature; its continued presence in modern writing follows from the internal clock of literary works.

Still, the general argument would be strengthened by a literary example with a linkage to the problem of language acquisition that is not primarily topical. It would be advantageous to identify formal and nontopical characteristics of a literary work of art that arguably point to the derivation of literature from the prehistorical fact of language acquisition. How does this origin, the specific species adaptation of a transition into talking hominids, constitute literature and — this the precise crux of the matter — how does that origin somehow remain germane to the nature of literature? This is the case that has to be made in order to insist on the fundamentally anamnestic character of literature, its capacity to remember its beginnings at the origin of language. Can one demonstrate a language bias in literature, a specific orientation to its own standing within language and, moreover, to the originality or historical standing of that linguistic definition?

Consider a stanza from Alphonse de Lamartine's "Pensées des Morts":

> C'est la saison où tout tombe
> Au coups redoublés des vents;
> Un vent qui vient de la tombe
> Moissonne aussi les vivants:
> Ils tombent alors par mille,
> Comme la plume inutile
> Que l'aigle abandonne aux airs,
> Lorsque les plumes nouvelles
> Viennent rechauffer ses ailes
> A l'approche des hivers.
> [This is the season when everything falls
> To the redoubled blows of the wind;
> A wind that comes from the tomb
> Mows down the living too.
> They fall by the thousands
> Like the useless feather
> That the eagle abandons in the air,

Human Origins and Literary Beginnings

When the new feathers
Come to warm his wings
At the approach of winter.][42]

In contrast to the previous examples from Kafka, this verse includes no thematic link to processes of hominization. Perhaps, one might read the association of the eagle with the *plume*, the feather but also the pen, as approaching the problematic of animals and language, but the following argument does not depend on that link. On the contrary, it is a nontopical aspect of the poem, the regular rhyme scheme that is worth considering. Lamartine maintains it through the full, lengthy poem. There is in addition some considerable internal rhyme: *tombent* pursuant to the punned rhyme of *tombe* (falls) and *tombe* (tomb), or the alliteration between *rechauffer* and *approche*. Note also the complexity of the last four verses: while *airs* rhymes with *hivers,* the *v* in *hivers* echoes *nouvelles,* just as — more graphically than acoustically — *airs* and *ailes* are linked by their initial letters. Yet it is the very fact of the rhyme that is of interest. As we will see in the next chapters, Havelock (following Parry and Lord) argues that the literatures of primary oral cultures were rhymed in order to assist in memory. Oral literature was — so goes the argument — the sole repository of cultural memory, and cultural transmission required memorization. That hypothesis is designed to account for the preponderance of a literature characterized by mnemonic devices, especially rhyme. But even if one concedes that rhyme supported memorization practices, and even if one overlooks nonrhymed forms of oral literature (stories, sayings, and proverbs), one faces the irksome fact that rhyme persists throughout the history of literature long after the appearance of writing, and even after the wide distribution of writing beyond the restricted literacy that surely characterized it in premodern settings. How does one account for the persistence of rhyme, even after it had become obsolete as a vehicle of memory?

There are two possible types of answers, in principle not mutually exclusive, and both of which support the claim that the very character of the literary work includes a long-term literary-historical memory. The first involves accepting the assertion of an oral literature as rhymed, perhaps for mnemonic purposes. The persistence of rhyme, after the development of writing and the emancipation of literature from its erstwhile function as primary cultural memory, should be taken as evidence of the backward-looking character of literature: Literature has a predisposition to orient itself toward prior literature (be it for reasons of traditionalism or competition, within the complex dynamic of canonicity). Rhyme is a kind of vestigial organ, a fact of literary form that has lost its original functionality but is maintained in the anatomical conservatism of cultural evolution. This hypothesis of course ought to proceed into a consideration of the extensive abandonment of rhyme in much twentieth-century poetry, a phenomenon that would require examination within the frame of long-term literary historical developmental trends.

There is, however, a second, stronger argument. Instead of regarding rhyme in modernity as an atavistic persistence of the "really existing" history of literature — a claim that links Lamartine's rhyme to the mnemonic character of the oral — one can point to the persistence of rhyme as evidence of a continued functionality. Rhyme becomes elaborate and complex as literature's concern increasingly become the words themselves, and language, rather than their referents. Rhyme is a play with signifiers themselves, whose relationship to the referents has been loosened if not severed. Sonority drowns out signification. Rhyme is the celebration of the sound of language, heuristically separated from semantics by the elegance of the echoing. It in effect recalls the evolutionary heterogeneity of vocal tract development and eye-hand coordination, the calling and the pointing. The anachronism of rhyme is therefore an indication of memory, but not (as in the first argument) memory of oral literature's form; it is rather a memory of the origin of orality altogether, the origins of voice as speech.

Beyond the question of rhyme and its relationship to orality, the Lamartine stanza exemplifies another issue through the complexity of the rhyme, but also in the pattern of verse, the pun, and the arrangement of images: Poetry is a language act, the very point of which is the forming of language. There is to be sure a content or a topic in the stanza — human mortality — but the lyric character makes that content secondary to the labor of language formation itself. This tension between the content and the language is a historical process, reflective of the nature of autonomy, and leading, in the extreme, to an expulsion of content. The work of literature gradually becomes open to any content, since it is not primarily content that matters. Against modes of academic taste or generic distinctions reflecting social hierarchy, Bourdieu reports how Flaubert suggested that for a literature that is consistent in pursuit of its own internal logic, its autonomy, there is no preferred subject (just as no subject is impossible).[43] This democratization of contents is not driven by an external agenda of engagement; it derives instead from the recognition that literature, existing in language and therefore carrying with it semanticity and, hence, referentiality, is nonetheless not primarily about its referents. It is not the encyclopedia of the community. Literature is, instead, specifically about language, its refinement and, arguably in some contexts, its perpetual revitalization. This explains the emancipation of literature from referentiality in the hermeticism of symbolist poetry.[44] Another example is the eruptive crudeness of language in Louis-Ferdinand Céline's novels, a Nietzschean rebarbarization, regaining for language an endangered expressivity. If Stefan George's abstraction and elitism and Céline's populist vocabulary — taken not only as antinomic positions within modernism but as paradigmatic alternatives for literature as such — both represent possible labors on language, then the rhetorical positions of the dual corollaries, high and low literature, are themselves consequences of the language bias of literature. Literature is the specialized language use that steers and repairs the culturally available language: Literature maps onto a range from high to low not primarily somehow as a reflection of class differences (which in any case are only ideologically associated neatly with high and low tastes). Rather, the alternative modes of literariness reflect contrasting operations on language, such as refinement and revitalization. Some authors may teach us how to speak with greater subtlety and others with greater force, but in either case more effectively.

In the end, literature is less about its ostensible topic (here: Lamartine's views on death) than about how to form, in particular, how to form language. That the Lamartine stanza enacts an elegant forming of language, independent of the topic, points out the crucial connection between successful literature and any notion of conscious labor or praxis. We learn from the human-origins discussion that there is a profound and complex entwinement of language with the forming of tools. Not that tool usage is the defining criterion in hominization (it is not, as Jane Goodall has shown), and not that prelinguistic hominids did not have tools (of course they did, but technological progress was painfully slow). Rather, with language an epistemic orientation toward symbolic behavior takes place that implies a capacity to impose form on the environment, on tools, and on language itself.[45] Language acquisition entails a sophisticated system of symbolic invention that loops back onto language: *Homo sapiens*, one might say, starts — thanks to language — to shape tools in more elaborate ways than had been previously done, to shape art works, and to shape language — the tool par excellence — as well. Such formed language is literature, and the obligation of literature, through its history and including recent literature, to the necessity of form testifies to the original condition of literature and language.

The attention to poetic structure in Lamartine's stanza points to this formal imperative in literature as such. The emancipation from the restrictiveness of any particular content is grounded in the autonomy of literature, which, pointing back to its origins, reenacts forming and at the same time models of innovation. The antinomy of form, however, is decomposition, and death as well, which is, after all, Lamartine's topic. The stanza announces the coming of winter, nature's disregard for the poet — the useless feather, the plume, the pen — and perhaps the uselessness of literature altogether. Death is the fate that the poet faces, about to be pushed aside by nameless others, and the response to this imminence of death is verse, an attempt for immortality. In a situation of ultimate adversity, poetry is a strategy of survival through the imagination.

Yet that gloss is, arguably, Lamartine's content, while the point in these pages has been to proceed in a way less arbitrary than through a reiteration of the arbitrarily chosen single poet's single choice of thematic material. Lamartine's views on death obviously do not prove the case for a human-origins starting point for literary history. More compelling is the fact that the topicality of death in poetry, while surely a preferred theme for Lamartine and romanticism, is at least just as much, if not more, fundamentally a parameter of literature in general than even talking animals or exotic civilizations. Moreover, archeology can show us that language emerges simultaneously with art, hence literature, and with a knowledge of death as indicated by burial practices. That particular pairing of literature and death is therefore much more than nineteenth-century romanticism. At the roots of literature altogether is an affinity with death, a result of the nature of the symbolic capacity that is language. The semanticity of language involves the ability to invoke the absent; the absent, and the deceased, are therefore never fully gone, always available to poetic conjuring. Literature can grant the author immortality; or it is Orphic and retrieves the dead. This knowledge of death is, as we will see in the next chapters in different ways, foundational in literature: the epic hero who does battle with death, the authors' aspirations to overcome death through the act of writing, and the religious promise of eternal life in holy scripture. For the moment, however, it suffices to note that the problematic of human origins, which are in effect the origins of language, and hence the capacity to engage in literature, recurs insistently in literature as topic and as form. Literature conveys an archetypical memory of these beginnings. We can speculate on the beginnings of literary history, the oral performances of preliterate humanity, by extrapolating from the human-origins discussion or through comparison with contemporary nonliterate cultures. But for the humanist as literary historian, it is through the examination of literature—Kafka and Lamartine have provided trenchant examples—that the complexities of the origins of language and the condition of literature take shape most vibrantly.

3

Writing and Heroism

ELABORATING A TEXTURED sociological description of literary autonomy, Pierre Bourdieu cites extensively from a range of nineteenth-century French authors, notably Flaubert, in order to demonstrate the complexity of the simultaneous engagement with and revulsion from contemporary society. Thus Flaubert to Maxime du Camp on September 28, 1871: "Everything was false: a false army, false politics, false literature, false credit, and even false courtesans."[1] How can the author make these adversarial judgments? Why does the public lend any credence to a novelist's judgment on the nonfictional context? What brings the author to adopt such a forcefully adversarial stance? Flaubert poses as the outsider with insider information who excoriates a reality as degraded and mendacious. It is as if the literary standing of the author in the world of imagination and fiction paradoxically grants him a greater access to the truth than would be available in the falseness of empirical existence. Flaubert had been even more emphatic earlier the same year, writing to George Sand on April 29: "All was false! False realism, false army, false credit, and even false harlots. . . . And this falseness . . . was applied especially in the manner of judging. They asked art to be moral, philosophy to be clear, vice to be decent, and science to be within the range of the people."[2]

The notion of literary autonomy depends on a strong relationship between the author and creativity, which confers on the author a capacity to turn a critical eye toward aspects of the social condition inimical to creativity. The process of literary creation is not merely a matter of producing works of literature, comparable to other goods and services; rather, it concerns the very act of producing creativity. The author's work allows him, as Bourdieu puts it, to "to produce himself as a creator, that is, as the *subject* of his own creation."[3] Hence the trenchant overlap of literature, subjectivity, and creativity within the terrain of autonomy, which, as a result of its capacity to criticize the limits of the social condition, enables society to engage in dynamic self-transformation. By insisting on its difference from the empirical social world, literature becomes all the more profoundly, if counterintuitively, a motor of the world's development. Literature is most social when it is least social. In this sense Bourdieu recapitulates Baudelaire's apotropaic account of the lyric: "An autonomous reality, with no referent other than itself, the poem is a creation independent of creation, and nevertheless united with it by profound ties that no positivist science perceives, and which are as mysterious as the correspondences uniting between themselves beings and things."[4]

The positions associated here with Flaubert and Baudelaire point to two sides of the same coin of autonomy: Where Flaubert emphasizes the adversarial character of art against social reality, Baudelaire traces the particular sort of engagement in reality associated with the distinctiveness of art. This is the love-hate relationship of the autonomous work for surrounding society and the source of the dynamic force of literature in the social process. The author enacts a heroism of authenticity directed against the falseness of the world, while also modeling individuality in a world of conformism. The author represents the possibility of creativity against a constant human temptation to lethargy and stultification. There is no social progress without the integrity of individuals, for whom the creative author serves as the model. Where does the strength for this heroism arise? What are the social sources for this antisocial but nonetheless social-transformative capacity of the author?

This chapter explores the ancient origins of literary autonomy as well as its subsequent and continued entwinement with the condition of individual autonomy in general. Literary autonomy and autonomous individuality, it turns out, are constitutive components of Western culture, rooted importantly, if not solely, in the emergence of habits of literacy. The previous chapter was concerned with the transition to language, some fifty thousand years ago; this chapter addresses the transition to writing several thousand years ago (if one dates writing from the earliest precursors of cuneiform; alphabetic writing is a still much later phenomenon). As writing and, therefore, literacy develop, deep transitions take place in society and culture, despite the fact that literacy skills frequently remained restricted to narrow segments of the population. Among these several transitions, however, it is the vicissitudes of literature that concern me: No longer oral but henceforth inscribed on surfaces — stone, bark, parchment, paper — the very nature of the text is changed. Imagination, a function of language as such, always presumed some autonomous separation from the given real, but it is with writing, for reasons discussed below, that autonomy takes on material form.

Does the history of literature begin with the invention of writing? The obvious objection is to point to the phenomenon sometimes designated as oral literature. It is important to address the objection raised by Walter J. Ong on this point. Scholarship, because it is itself written, tends to project categories of writing onto other material, including oral presentations; moreover, the very analytic character of scholarship derives, for Ong, from writing, further biasing scholarship toward conceptual structures implicated in writing. For this reason there is need for caution in the selection of categorical designations. As Ong points out, the term *oral literature* may be attractive precisely because it misrepresents the oral performance as a text to be read, which is implicit, etymologically, in the very term *literature*. "Thinking of oral tradition or a heritage of oral performance, genres and styles as 'oral literature' is rather like thinking of horses as automobiles without wheels. . . . No matter how accurate and thorough such apophatic description, automobile-driving readers who have never seen a horse and who hear only of 'wheelless automobiles' would be sure to come away with a strange concept of a horse. The same is true of those who deal in terms of 'oral literature,' that is 'oral writing.'"[5]

Since terms such as *oral literature* or even *preliterate* are seen as privileging the categories of writing in contexts where they are inappropriate, Ong opts for *oral performance* to indicate the mode of presentation in cultures without writing. At times, he has recourse to the notion of verbal art, a designation capacious enough to include both oral performance and written literature. In any case, both oral performance and verbal art avoid the term *literature*, which is taken to mean conveyed by letters, and therefore writing. At the very least this argument should give us pause before subsuming aspects of oral cultures willy-nilly into the prehistory of literature. Writing, as Ong persuasively argues, transforms culture and consciousness profoundly. In the light of his arguments, it is not easy to treat oral performance in preliterate or, more neutrally, nonliterate settings as merely a prehistory to writing. The relationships to the preliterate past are more complex. While the material of an oral performance may seem to be like a prehistory to literature since both are imaginative, the distinction between them is so great that more attention has to be paid to the character of the transition and its deep implications for the development of culture.

According to Ong, oral performance is not appropriately characterized as the first chapter in a history of literature because it is not part of literacy, from which we derive our expectations about the character of texts. It would then follow that literature should be dated from the origins of writing. While compelling in some ways, this single focus on the medium of writing brackets those aspects of literature that derive from its standing in language in general, including the imaginative character, which is grounded in the dynamic of the symbol. If, following Ong, one excludes oral performance from the category of literature because it does not depend on the technology of writing, then one would reduce literature to a function of its particular material apparatus, that is, writing technologies. This reductionism, however, is problematic. The written literary work inherits other aspects of the culture of the world before writing, aspects that are associated specifically not with oral performance but rather with the character of the visual works of art that began to emerge simultaneously with the invention of language.

Whether the material of oral recitation is understood as the first stage in literary history or as an alternative to literature (defined in Ong's narrow sense of written texts), it is important to follow how scholarship has been able to characterize the phenomenon. Oral performance in preliterate cultures is typically short, a matter of sayings, songs, or brief tales. Extensive narratives are not common, and great epics are rare. For Jack Goody, in fact, the lengthy epic is not associated with primary orality at all, but is rather a form symptomatic of a society with incipient literacy. Indeed, composing an extended epic depends on writing for the planning and execution of the large texts, no matter how they may still have been destined for oral performance.[6] This writing establishes the formal integrity of the text, independent ultimately of the oral performance. Literature dates from the origins of writing not because of the etymology, as Ong would have it by claiming that *literature* means letters. Rather, the materialized realization of language in writing is the condition that allows for the autonomization of literature (even if such autonomy was inherent as a potential in the use of imaginative language in general, before writing).

Writing transforms human society and culture. Alphabetic writing transforms society and culture in distinctive ways, leading to a particularly dynamic process of civilization. There are, to be sure, critics of the thesis that writing elicits a great divide in human culture, and in some ways the absolute insistence on that divide has been modified even by its defenders: The transition to writing is no longer seen as a gap between savages and civilization.[7] While that large civilizational transition is the context for the material discussed in this chapter, of greater interest is the specific impact of writing on literature, the impact of writing on that imaginative use of language, which is at the foundation of all literature, as well as the implications of that transformation of literature for social development. It is with writing that the autonomous work of literary art appears, and it is through the literary work that authorship and readership emerge as models of an emphatic subjectivity. Thus it is with the autonomous work, as a consequence of writing, that these paradigms of autonomous individuality are born. The sort of strength of individual character evidenced in Flaubert's comments, based on the cultivation of art as a vehicle of a higher truth against a mendacious society, derives from the character of writing itself. This chapter explores how.

LET US CONSIDER the historiographic frame within which the binary opposition of orality and literacy is typically discussed, that is, the foundational vision shared by many scholars of an epochal distinction between oral and literate phases in human history. On one level, of course, this distinction is undeniable. The shape of human history is such that a long period stretches between the invention of language and the invention of writing, tens of thousands of years in which language is only oral or, to be more precise, oral and gestural (body movements), but in any case not objectified in written symbols. The invention of writing systems — cuneiform in Mesopotamia is the first, but also Chinese ideographs and Egyptian hieroglyphs — takes different forms and has different consequences, but with the transformation of cuneiform into the Semitic syllabaries and then into the Greek alphabet a world-historical change takes place. That one alphabet, the phonetic representation of spoken words, becomes the basis of most alphabetic writing in the world (Korean, an independent alphabetic invention, is an exception) and is associated with irreversible cultural and social changes. Nonetheless, the neat division into oral and literate historical phases should be treated with some caution. It is vital to distinguish between claims pertaining to large epochal frames, defined in terms of their linguistic modalities, and claims specifically about the mode of transmission of imaginative language acts (literature in the sense used above). Thus we might consider, as does Ong, the hypothetical character of society and culture in general in a context in which writing does not exist. Alternatively, we may ask specifically about the limited and differentiated social sphere of oral performance or oral literature. These two projects are, at least heuristically, distinct from one another. The same holds on the other side of the watershed. We may pursue an inquiry into the general character of societies that have developed the specific technology that allows for a (relatively) permanent record of language in writing. Alternatively, we may focus on the specific vicissitudes of imaginative literature, once writing technology becomes available. (And as it develops: The spread of paper, movable type, the rotation press, and electronic media represent key moments in that technological history of literature.)

To pursue the larger change of society in general, one would depend on the claim that the single technological factor defined each epoch. A mode of language — oral or written — would then be cast in the role of the mode of production for an erstwhile Marxist historiography. If instead one were to focus solely on the development of the single sector, literature, in the relationship to the technology of writing, then one moves closer to a consideration of a multiplicity of distinct factors in civilizational development, the relationships among which can be thought of as dynamic and unstable, allowing for different processes over time as well as multiple trajectories leading to differing outcomes and traditions. Such a differentiated account of sectoral development invites a greater precision in the observation of literature, not to be reduced to the single dimension of writing technology. It would moreover be able to draw on the cognitive psychological model of multiple intelligences presented by Mithen, as reviewed previously. In addition, a model of differentiated sectoral development is a reasonable and more likely response to the heterogeneous character of the physical environment and the social condition, both of which elicit complex, not monovocal, responses. In other words, the technology of writing is one way society responds to challenges, but it is surely not necessarily the sole variable, and those other elements are likely to affect literature, no longer reduced to its technological underpinning.

Sectoral development — rather than a historiography that prioritizes the single global shift from orality to literacy — is all the more likely because writing itself represented a particular response to other civilizational changes.

While it is possible to argue that original language acquisition amounted to a behavioral adaptation driven by exogenous factors — the adversity of the environment in the period of glaciation or interspecies competition with other hominids — the much later acquisition of writing responded to endogenous civilizational challenges. With economic growth, such as the achievement of a surplus of goods from an agricultural economy and the political process of state building, the need developed for records to support the organization of wealth and the administration of power.[8] Yet this account indicates that significant civilizational development predates writing, which, evidently, then responded to that prior development. The developmental acceleration attributed to writing and literacy, especially by Goody and Watt, may still have taken place, but it is not the case that writing is the sole source of development. At the very least one would have to conclude that economic capacities, political complexity, and language technologies (writing) proceed in an intertwined development with both relative autonomy and reciprocal influences. The single factor theorem of a mode of language, like a mode of production, becomes untenable. After the end of Marxism, there is no reason to salvage its heritage of technological reductionism. (Indeed, we have seen that even Marx, in the gloss on reading Homer, underscored how the important questions are all located beyond simplistic, contextual determinism.) The option of reducing human history or, more narrowly, the history of literature, to a technology history of language is hardly attractive.

The thesis of separate sectoral development is of particular importance to the shape of the history of literature. As writing, literature always stood in a relationship of dynamic exteriority to the politics of state building and the economics of wealth accumulation, precisely as it also preserves its distinction, its autonomy. Literature therefore enters into a competitive relationship with the multiple spheres of social activity, and this competition defines central concerns of literature from the start. Because writing responds to political and economic development, literature, as a distinctive mode of writing, appropriates those relationships between writing and power, and between writing and wealth, and integrates them as points of reference or topical material into the literary works. At the outset of the first tablet of *The Epic of Gilgamesh*, the eponymous hero of this point of literary origin arrives as the carrier of a fundamentally political wisdom: "he who saw the Deep, the country's foundation," the defining terms of the community. His first acts are, however, literary — oral and written:

He saw what was secret, discovered what was hidden,
He brought back a tale of before the Deluge.

He came a far road, was weary, found peace,
And set all his labors on a tablet of stone.
He built the rampart of Uruk-the-Sheepfold,
Of holy Eanna, the sacred storehouse.[9]

The unknown author of the first written epic, in the context of the relatively advanced state-building of the Mesopotamian city-states, casts the demigod political leader as, first of all, a teller of tales and a writer. No matter how much the great epics may draw on elements of preliterate oral lore,[10] the defining feature is their written status, and it is from this point, four thousand years ago, that the competition between writing and politics, literature and power, can be traced. Is the world of writing a passive, reflective option in contrast to the world of political deed, or does writing try to claim for itself the same heroic status as authentic action? Meanwhile, the author of the epic casts the writer-hero-politician as also the manager of wealth. The competition between literature and wealth production — art and commerce — begins to take shape. Autonomous literature comes to stand for both an alternative to the worldly accumulation of goods and itself an object of luxury, dependent on the production of an economic surplus and distributed unequally within society. (Literature and economy are the topics of the final chapter of this book.)

By treating language-technological change (the acquisition of writing) as one of several relatively independent, if reciprocally interrelated, axes of civilizational development, one can distinguish among different cases, instead of attempting in vain to impute a single developmental schema, despite different cultural traditions, social institutions, and natural resources. The consequences of literacy in Greece and the societies that build on its cultural legacy were different from the consequences of literacy in India and China.[11] A lack of writing could coexist with relatively high levels of scientific (calendars, astronomy) and technological (building) skills in ancient American civilizations. Reducing the distinctiveness of a Western tradition to the specific consistency of the alphabet (Havelock) or the dissemination of literacy subsequent to the alphabet (Goody and Watt) overburdens a single factor and, precisely therefore, avoids the textured and complex character of history. In fact, however, the Western tradition includes a multiplicity of factors in a multidimensional constellation of interrelationships, which distinguishes it from other cultural constellations but also allows for a heterogeneous range of positions within the tradition. Autonomous literature is one of them, and this autonomy is related to (but distinct from) the parallel categories that emerge in other spheres of social activity — the autonomous individuality at the base of notions of citizenship and the private property of the acquisitive individual. The strength of character exhibited by Flaubert against political power and against commercialism is, as we saw in the material cited at the outset of this chapter, informed by the structures of individuality that are foundational for the political and economic spheres. It is the particular configuration of these multiple axes of civilizational development that define the specific character of the cultural and institutional frame within which literature — imaginative, autonomous, and written — takes shape.

FROM THE ABOVE, it should be evident that too stark a distinction between oral and literate social formations is untenable. Other social sectors — the state and the economy — maintain a significant degree of independence, despite complex interrelationships. The emergence of state building and the accumulation of an economic surplus as causes for the invention of writing systems indicate that they commence prior to the writing systems, no matter how writing may accelerate their development. From this we conclude that the mode of language, oral or literate, should be thought of as a relatively independent axis of social development and not as its single driving motor, as is frequently implied in orality and literacy studies.

Yet even with this cautionary remark, the standing of the phases — oral cultures and literate cultures — requires further scrutiny, particularly with regard to the ramifications for the autonomous literary work. Let us consider first the paradigm of an oral culture understood as the presumed alternative to a later phase marked by writing technology. This oral world is therefore defined by a lack: the lack of the permanent records and expanded memory that writing provides, the material and durable inscription of certain accounts that are preserved outside the consciousness of either individuals or the cultural group. The oral world lacks this "external memory storage," so crucial for Donald's account of civilizational development.[12] It relies instead on what Ong describes as the "evanescence" of the spoken word, rather than the permanence of the written trace.[13] Hence the claims by Havelock and others that oral performance — such as, hypothetically, the heroic epics — is structured around the mnemonic devices that support memory in the absence of writing: strong figures, memorable action, regular meter and rhyme.[14] Evanescence appears as a deficiency of orality, which the generic conventions of the allegedly oral-performative epic correct for.

While by definition oral cultures lack writing, and it is precisely this "lack" that underlies the predominant characterizations of orality, it is not clear that the oral world is fully devoid of relatively permanent external memory banks. Indeed, scholarship that assumes that memory can be stored only in the repositories of writing, and therefore defines orality as the lack of writing, is at fault for not searching for the durability, permanence, and externalization — otherwise associated with writing — in other objects. In contrast to the relative late phenomenon of written language, visual works of art, painting, and sculpture are present considerably earlier and presumably emerge nearly simultaneously with language itself. Both cave paintings and sculpted objects are characterized by durability, providing a temporal longevity in contrast to Ong's evanescence of the word, and both are objectifications and hence separable from their originator, the painter or sculptor, in a manner that anticipates the separation of the author from the written work. Sculpture (as figurines) is furthermore portable, unlike cave painting, although, at later dates, paintings on portable objects, such as vases, could well be disseminated and therefore anticipate an additional aspect of writing. The concern here is not the distinctions among the various visual arts, or their development between their early emergence in the history of human origins and their transformations in the context of writing. Rather the point is that against the theoreticians of orality who define it above all as the absence of writing and the specific memory capacity associated solely with writing, one can locate aspects of that durability, objectivity, and portability precisely in the visual arts that long antedate writing.

Objects of visual art of course are themselves not writing in a full-fledged sense. They lack the detail and suppleness of language, and they cannot accurately reproduce anything like the full semantic substance of an originator's message. Nonetheless, they can record meanings and serve at the very least as a memory prompt in the context of oral performance. In more sophisticated versions, nonlinguistic visual records can reach the considerable detail implicit in calendars, maps, and charts. It is therefore evident that the absence of writing systems is not an adequate basis for the argument that cultural memory depended solely on the spoken word. Of course, the introduction of writing transformed the social capacity to operate with language, magnifying memory and its accuracy; it is with writing that a genuinely text-critical perspective on cultural material can begin to develop.

Writing and Heroism

Nevertheless, the baseline for memory in oral cultures is misunderstood, if the record of the visual artifact is ignored. The visual record can in fact convey considerable knowledge: One picture, for example, a cave painting, can be worth more than a thousand words of informational content.

This point is all the more pertinent in light of the visual character of developed writing systems themselves. Writing is nothing if not the visual representation of language; this fact underlies Ong's insistence on the phenomenological shift from ear (spoken word) to eye (literacy). The case is most obvious for semipictorial writing systems — pictograms or hieroglyphs — but the difficult case of alphabetic writing is more interesting. The letters of the alphabet are the visual representations of phonological actions, themselves acoustic representations of semantic contents: the alphabetic word is therefore a sign of a sign, more precisely, a visual sign of a phonetic sign. At this fundamental level, therefore, writing retains a link to visual representation and therefore to the features of the visual artifacts that predate writing itself. Moreover, even in the context of alphabetic writing, the phonetic principle is frequently overridden by iconographic elements. For example, the space between words is not typically a pronunciation but rather a visual indication of a nonphonetic meaning. Similarly, readers typically do not sound out the words on the page before them but have internalized a capacity to recognize the visual icons: While they may have been learned phonetically, they are subsequently recognized as ideographs. This feature is all the more the case when one encounters new words composed of recognizable components.

Thus the continuum between the visual arts and writing is twofold: It is historical in the sense that the visual artifacts in oral societies anticipate aspects of the memory capacity inherent in language, and it is phenomenological in the sense that writing systems, including advanced alphabetic writing, remain visual and therefore share aspects of the visual arts. One short-circuits the history of language use if one reduces it to a binary of orality and literacy or a simple two-phase narrative, a before and an after the invention of writing. Moreover, and more relevant to our concern here, a simplistic binary of orality and literacy also misrepresents the history of literature. For precisely this complex relationship to visuality turns out to be a constitutive component of a literary phenomenon. Literature does not have an existence separate from the visuality inherent in manuscripts or typescripts. The specifically literary, or autonomous literary, aspects of the work stand in a complex relationship of dependence and competition with the work's own visual presence, be it a matter of the illuminated manuscript, the engravings in early novels, the illustration in the children's book, or the cover of a modern bestseller. The competition between the visuality of language and literary autonomy is the terrain in which theatrical production takes place, the tension between spectacularity and speech. As Donald points out, precisely this tension repeats a much older evolutionary transition, the interplay of mimetic and mythic cognitive capacities.[15] It is furthermore precisely this terrain where literature, since the end of the nineteenth century, has encountered its strongest rival: cinema, and then later television and video production. The history of literature involves a constant, and constitutive, competition with the visual image.[16]

Evidently the neat distinction between oral and literate phases of language and literature is blurred by the continuum of visual representation, with its own implications for memory and the relationship to the visuality of script. The permanence of memory attributed to writing has a significant antecedent in prehistoric visual art. Yet the hypothetical binary of oral and literate formations is difficult to maintain for a second reason as well. The invention of writing and the spread of literacy do not do away with orality. The point is an obvious one, and the theoreticians of orality versus literacy studies go out of their way to concede it;[17] yet the fundamental premise of their paradigm is the defining character of writing for postoral society. Rather than thinking of a mode of postorality, however, it is more appropriate to consider the continuity of the oral, the ongoing competition between the oral and the written, and, particularly with regard to the conceptualization of literature and its history, the standing of orality with regard to literary works. As far as the blurring of the two phases of orality and literacy goes, we can see how visual recording predates writing, just as orality continues to thrive after the invention of writing. The binary historiography is therefore undermined by two overarching factors.

Despite the magnitude of the technological change associated with writing, social institutions and cultural values continue in many ways to be defined in terms of orality. "The letter kills; the spirit gives life." Ong quotes 2 *Corinthians* 3:6 in order to demonstrate how, even in the context of holy scripture, and particularly in the passages defined in genre terms as epistolary, a bias continues toward the priority of spoken language coupled with a mistrust of the written letter and law.[18] That suspicion of the written text and the preference for oral assertions continues for centuries, as M. T. Clanchy has demonstrated for medieval England.[19] In the context of greater specialization, writing does undeniably move toward an ascendancy. Modernity is characterized by spheres of professional specialization, in which written evidence is accorded priority. This is particularly the case in scholarship, where the published article has greater significance than the oral discourse (including the orality of the classroom setting, since the academy values the written text over the spoken presentation, the published book over oral teaching). Legal documents are a similar case. Yet popular adages warning of dangers of the fine print in contracts testify to an ongoing suspicion of the written word. It therefore becomes clear that the second phase of the presumed chronology should not be characterized as literacy but as the era of the competition between orality and literacy.

Autonomous literature, as written, evidently exists in a competition both with visuality and with orality; it is the thin line between sight and sound. Even conceiving literature in its most written character, it is consistently positioned toward the spoken word as much as we have seen it competing with the image. The orientation toward vocalization is most obviously the case in drama, written works of art understood as a collection of speeches and typically, if not necessarily, intended for oral performance. Lyric verse is stereotypically associated with song, and it retains an institutional relationship to speech in the convention of the poetry reading. For much of its history, the novel too (let alone shorter prose fiction) was experienced in the form of reading aloud, and the very texture of written fiction is, arguably, very much still a function of its presumed aural resonance.[20] Even more obviously, though, the autonomous work of literature since its inception — the heroic epic — as well as in its modern derivative, the novel, retains the relationship to orality in the form of spoken dialogue. Aristotle's *Poetics* testifies to the Greek recognition of the distinctiveness of fictional writing over against history — ergo, aesthetic autonomy has a long history, even if Aristotle would not have used the term *aesthetic* in the modern sense — when he praises Homer for the dramatic character of his epics, that is, the preponderance of speaking characters and the relative reticence of the narrator to intrude on their dialogues. The epic is therefore the written record of speaking people and as such reenacts the competition between writing and speech. The history of literature, particularly of the novel, invites interrogation on this particular feature: the scope and transformation of fictional speech. Such written representation of speech ranges between the preponderance of dialogue in popular or low literary forms and the emergence of the foregrounded, vocalized narrator in sophisticated forms of fiction, such as the modern novel. In both cases, however, the written fiction becomes the vehicle to generate speech, and an illusion of orality.[21]

THE INITIAL ACQUISITION of language by early humans was a unique behavioral adaptation of a particular hominid species. The possibility of language was predicated on a host of earlier physiological and cognitive transformations, but there is no evidence that language itself was an independent piece of a biological evolution. As a result of the extensive transformations, especially in the vocal tract, linked in complicated manners to other anatomical components, language use had become possible. Language furthermore represented an adaptive response to particular environmental pressures. The invention of writing was similarly a behavioral change, but in the sense of the establishment and refinement of a new technology (and therefore it could long be restricted to particularly defined subsets of the population, rather than, as with language itself, be available to all members of the population: Only some people may be able to read and write but everyone can speak, a distinction that implicates language in a dialectic of equality and differentiation). The specifically technological aspect of writing remains evident; indeed, we continue to speak of *writing tools,* while university writing instructors talk of *toolkits,* and this dimension of writing is especially salient in the development of new writing vehicles that are obviously technologies, such as computer hardware and software.

Ong is emphatic on the technological character of writing. "Because we have by today so deeply interiorized writing, . . . we find it difficult to consider writing to be a technology, as we commonly assume printing and the computer to be. Yet writing (and especially alphabetic writing) is a technology, calling for the use of tools and other equipment: styli or brushes or pens, carefully prepared surfaces such as paper, animal skins, strips of wood, as well as inks or paints, and much more. . . . Writing is in a way the most drastic of the three technologies. It initiated what print and computers only continue, the reduction of dynamic sound to quiescent space, the separation of the word from the living present, where alone spoken words can exist."[22] Hence the centrality of technology to Ong's account, which explains the subtitle of his seminal book: *The Technologizing of the Word.* Although he takes pains to avoid a solely pejorative account of the transition from orality to literacy, he repeatedly describes the oral word as somehow living and natural in contrast to the artificiality and mechanically isolating character of written language. The introduction of technology into language changes the character of language use, restructures consciousness, and alters the substance of culture. There can be no doubt that the difference between the two modes of sociability depends, in a clearly deterministic manner, on technology. The great divide in human cultural history is, it would seem, a function of a single technological change. It is, however, important to interrogate this determinism.

While the shift to a technologized language had enormous ramifications, other independent variables played a role in the emergence of the new cognitive structures. At stake here is therefore not the incontrovertible assertion that the shift to writing had an effect on social and cultural history — including the character of literature — but the suspicion that technology should not be singled out as the indisputably overarching factor. Consider an analogy from the political sphere. It is one thing to say that alphabetic writing had an innate tendency toward a greater distribution of literacy than did prealphabetic scripts because of the more expeditious learning strategies appropriate to a consistently phonetic writing system; it would be quite another to derive Athenian democracy solely from this technological change and therefore to disregard all other social or cultural resources on which ancient democracy drew. The following pages examine the implications of treating technology as a causal factor in literary history.

The previous chapter discussed the origin of language and its possible relationship to literature: no literature without language, although the specific potential within language that enables it to generate autonomous literature still requires further specification. The fact that literature exists within language (it exists nowhere else) does not imply that language necessarily produces literature — for there are plenty of other modes of language use that are not reasonably described as literary. Not all language is imaginative, which is the defining feature of literary language, even though, precisely as language, it is always symbolic. The symbolic character of language implies the cognitive capacity to refer to counterfactual conditions, and this in turn implies the imaginative facility that, objectified in formalized language, becomes literature. Yet how and why precisely does the imaginative potential inherent in the symbolic usage of all language become amplified and transformed into that specific language use that is literature? Writing plays the key role in this metamorphosis, transforming the general imaginative capacity of language into the autonomous works of literature. But exactly what are the significance and the limits of the significance of the new technology, writing, in the history of literature? How is it that writing turns oral performance into literature? How does the performance turn into the "work"?

Recall the fact that Ong insists on separating oral performance from any literary history precisely because, as oral, it does not appear within the domain of the defining technology of literature and literacy. In his account, writing is the source of the very essence of literature; literature is, in other words, an effect of writing. Alternatively, literature can be derived, not from the fact that it is in *letters* (the etymology that Ong underscores), but that it is imaginative and hence implicit in the very symbolic logic of language. The two approaches have different ramifications: Is literature primarily grammatological, a function of its status as written, or is it primarily symbolic, deriving from the character of language as such? To be sure, the choice relies to some extent on a false distinction: The written letters themselves imply symbols, just as much as spoken words do. (In fact, the written word implies symbolism doubly so, especially in the alphabetic context, with the overlay of phonetic and semantic functions: The written symbols stand for a phonetic sign.) This objection does not disqualify the question, and instead only refocuses the attention: Is literature grammatological, a direct effect of a technology called writing? Or is literature—a more restricted claim—one particular use (among many possible ones) of that technology? In that latter case, one would be called upon to explain that selection and its particular character. If writing generates literature, why is literature different from other modes of writing, particularly that writing that is not imaginative, or not as distinctively and consistently imaginative as autonomous literature, in the standard understanding of the term?

A strict technological determinism cannot provide grounds for an emphatic distinction between literature and other modes of writing, but this dedifferentiation of genres stands at considerable odds with the historical record. The introduction of writing in ancient Greece leads, more than anything else, to an amplification of the distinctions among genres. That is, because literature loses the encyclopedic function ascribed by Havelock to preliterate oral performance—maintaining the collective memory in the absence of any permanent (written) record (an argument that requires modification in light of the comments on visual artifacts made above)—some of the specifically nonimaginative functions migrate to newly emergent genres. Written literature is no longer burdened, for example, with maintaining a historical record, since that task is taken up by the henceforth differentiated rhetoric of the historians. Poets and historians may both deploy rhetori-

Writing and Heroism

cal strategies, but that does not mean that Homer (taken as an exemplar of imaginative literature, not as an oral bard conveying a cultural encyclopedia) and Herodotus are indistinguishable from each other.

Both novels and historiographic texts are written, and they may even share certain rhetorical features. They nonetheless have distinct social functions, we have little difficulty distinguishing between them, and we certainly apply different criteria in judging them. Similarly, it is only with writing that a certain concept-critical and text-critical mentality emerges and hence philosophical writing (that the first philosophical author chooses a genre, the dialogue, that feigns orality is itself testimony to the technological transition underway). Plato and even more so Aristotle proceed with discussions that suggest a rapid differentiation of knowledge: poetics is different from ethics is different from metaphysics and so on. Thus one can conclude that the introduction of writing as a new technology contributes to an amplification of tendencies toward specialization in the variants of language use: literature, historiography, and philosophy and its subfields.

We are left with two quite distinct explanatory paradigms. A technological deterministic account that insists on the priority of the introduction of writing points toward a dedifferentiation of genres: In a world described as one of the "technologized word," what is at stake is the proliferation of writing, not the distinctiveness of any particular mode of writing, and, in turn, the obviation of the question of literary autonomy. The postmodern leveling of all writing to the status of texts ensues. Alternatively, one can describe a model of generic division of labor: Autonomous literature becomes one among several distinctive usages of writing. It is language, in writing, but different from other modes of writing.[23] Because literature is written, it is delimited by precisely those conditions that we have already mentioned in passing as associated with writing. For example, the written text is separable from the author in a way that the oral statement is not separable from the speaker. Recall, however, that we have seen how this objectifying separability of the written sign is not unique to the act of writing. On the contrary, it was anticipated by the prehistoric visual arts, as were other features of the visual semiotics of written language. The nature of the written work of literature, in other words, is defined by certain characteristics of writing in general. These include the separation from author, in clear contrast to the situation that prevails in oral performance. This objectifying separation of the written sign is not unique to writing and therefore not dependent solely on the new technology of writing.

The question can now be reconsidered: Shall we think of literature as primarily grammatological, an effect of writing, or as symbolic, and a use of language in an imaginative manner? If the answer were only the first, then a technological determinism would be warranted, but the situation is evidently more complicated. Both tendencies are present in the sense that autonomous literature remains a matter of writing, but it stands in a competitive relation to other kinds of writing. It shares their grammatological character, but it is simultaneously distinct from them in its emphatically imaginative agenda. On this complex terrain the position of literature is doubly contested: by other arts (visual but also musical, oral), with which it shares certain phenomenological characteristics related to the counterfactuality of imaginative contents, and by other writing, with which it shares the fact of writing but from which it is distinguished by its lack of significant informational content. Literature therefore takes part in two competitions: with the other arts and with other (nonartistic) writing. Facing these other modes of cultural expression, literature takes shape as an agonistic assertion of its own identity. This is its autonomy, the embattled assertion of its place in the universe of human expression. The foundational literature — heroic epics and sacred texts — draw on some oral legacies, but they begin to exist as literature in writing, and at the same moment necessarily enter into competition with other cultural forms. This struggle itself becomes the substance of literature, which is to say that the agonistic establishment of aesthetic autonomy, against literature's rivals, is one with the plot of the heroic narrative. This assertive establishment of autonomy is objectified as the substance of heroic narrative. Indeed, the insistence on the autonomy of the epic as work and its fictional hero lay the foundation of the cultivation of autonomous individuality, arguably the most dynamic component of civilizational development. The freedom of literature and the freedom of the individual share this ancient origin in the heroic model.

This revision of the technologically deterministic approach is particularly fruitful for literary scholarship. Instead of the mechanical claim that the new technology, writing, produces a mentality that translates, rather murkily, to new literature, we can now identify the multiple components within the civilizational process that frame the emergence of autonomous literature and that also leave their marks within the texts: Literature is that particular sort of artifact (a result of human practices) that includes a reflection on the conditions of its own emergence (a vehicle for human reflection on human practices). Three parameters have been identified. First, literature is in writing, but writing emerged in response to other sectoral development; written literature typically concerns itself with those developing sectors as its topics (politics, economics, religion). Second, literature is not only writing, but also a symbolic formation, sharing features with other non-written symbols and competing with them, especially visual, gestural, and oral modes of expression. Third, as writing, literature — far from being subsumed under a general grammatological category — insists on the cultural division of labor and attempts to distinguish itself from nonliterary writing, especially historiography and philosophy. Hence, in the context of this multiply contested terrain, autonomous literature emerges, perhaps a meta-intelligence (as Mithen suggests, against specialized intelligence modules), but in any case embattled. No wonder that literature begins with the heroic epic, the real substance of which is the heroic assertion of literary autonomy against the resistance of the cultural world.

These parametric conditions of the emergence of literature describe the origins of the genre of the heroic epic not only in general terms but also in the particular texturing of the works, as three examples can demonstrate. I have already touched in passing on how the competition with other societal sectors, especially politics, emerges at the very outset of *Gilgamesh*. The eponymous hero is political leader and writer at the same time. Literature is about politics from the start. To think literature is to think politics, even when literature apparently turns its back on politics. Literary writing is predominantly about the powerful of society: The tradition, through the eighteenth century, was to restrict the high genre of tragedy to royalty. The modern shift to accounts of bourgeois or popular strata, especially in the novel, takes places only as a political move, and only in a context where the democratic notion that sovereignty derives from the people became current. Needless to say, there are exceptions, as in the comic tradition of treating slaves or lower classes, but that is ultimately a secondary effect of the positioning of literature toward the polarities of power, an internalized compass from which it cannot escape.

The second parameter, the competition with alternative modes of symbolic expression, is evidenced in the Homeric epics. Despite the tradition since Milman Parry, asserting that the *Iliad* and the *Odyssey* are products of a preliterate society, Goody insists that extensive epics are effectively absent in genuine oral cultures and that the grand epic is more characteristic of cultures with emerging literacy. The claim that Homeric Greece was an oral culture is, as even Rousseau knew, countered by the very text of the *Iliad*, where, in the Bellerophon episode, one reads of a written message being carried, with fatal consequences. The incident has to be read as evidence of a restricted literacy, belying claims of a primary orality. In this light, the poems treat the emerging literary culture, and the difficulties it faces as it develops in the context of older cultural formations. Indeed, the multiple encounters with the alternative civilizational stages that define Odysseus's itinerary could well be mapped onto a conflict between the rationality of writing and preliterate cultural formations.[24]

After the competition with other societal sectors in the process of an ongoing division of labor; after, second, the competition with other modes of symbolic expression, a third feature of autonomous written literature also defines the emergence of the epic: competition with other writing. Literature, as written, is "grammatological," it is in a field with multiple other written texts, with their durability, in contrast with the evanescence of the oral performance. Written texts malinger, defining a context in which any new text intrudes; in order to assert its identity and its autonomy, it has to define itself against them. The problem emerges in a paradigmatic national epic: *La Chanson de Roland* marked, internally, by efforts to define itself over and against alternative textual modalities. The next two chapters provide a more elaborate discussion of the epic as genre and its relationship to the historical process of individuation. For the moment, however, it is important to attend to a narrow point: intratextual evidence within the epic for its competition with other writing. In *Roland*, this takes place through the reference to the "book of Mahomet" as a foil to the Christian literacy of the *Chanson* itself, but this is at one with the substance of the plot, the military competition of an emerging Christian Europe with the Islamic world.[25] Similarly the *Chanson* repeatedly points to historiographic texts in order to establish a generic contrast. Not only does the epic exist in a world of writing; that world is also characterized by a generic division of labor. In the midst of battle and after a record of the massive slaughter that the Franks have accomplished, the archbishop announces:

> Il est escrit en la Geste Francor
> Que vassals est li nostre empereür (*laisse* 111)
>
> [*Gesta Francorum* says of our emperor
> That he was served by heroes one and all.][26]

The record of killing takes place in the "Geste" or history; which stands in contrast to an alternative genre of "Chanson" (*laisse* 115). Similarly, in *laisse* 127:

Cels qu'il unt mort, ben les poet hom preiser;
Il est escrit es cartres e es brefs,
Ço dit la Geste, plus de .IIII. milliers

[We know what happened according to the *Geste*,
Chronicles, records bear witness to the fact:
Four thousand pagans by those few Franks were slain.][27]

The reference to the historiographic source both confers a certain accuracy onto the current account, comparable to the effect of a footnoted reference, and also distinguishes the present text from the other account. Indeed, at key instances throughout the *Chanson* we find evidence of a sense of weakness, fallibility, and betrayal, the defining concerns of the epic, as opposed to the facticity and certainty that it projects externally onto another genre (the distinction echoes the antinomy of authenticity and fiction identified in Kafka's "Report to an Academy"). In other words, the disparate references to the certainty of historiography not only define the *Chanson* negatively, as precisely that which is not a factual record. The contrast also implies that the *Chanson* represents the genre that is devoted to the dimensions of language and therefore those social conditions that are not circumscribed by factuality: betrayal and faith (moreover, with regard to that one faith, Christianity, which is centrally concerned with betrayal).

This section has demonstrated how too simplistic a sequencing of orality and literacy obscures important aspects of the substance and history of literature. It is not merely the fact of writing that is determinative, but rather precisely the emergence of writing in relationship to other, relatively independent, sectoral developments. For these reasons, no literary history can ignore those other sectors and remain convincing. Furthermore, it is evident that phenomenological aspects associated with writing are present in preliterate cultures (in visual artifacts), just as orality remains constitutive of culture in literate societies, leading to a blurring of the two presumed phases. Finally, it is not simply the new technology of writing that directly determines the literary field, but rather the programmatic and intratextual definition of literature against other expressive modalities (visual, oral), and other written genres.

The point, in sum, is that the beginnings of literature should not be thought of as a direct consequence of a single media-historical shift, but rather in relationship to a wider, complex, and multidimensional transformation. Literature is enormously dependent on literacy, but it is not simply a linear function of literacy; it is simultaneously a matter of its competition with other components in a complex society and culture increasingly marked by internal differentiations. Literature participates in this process by underscoring its own autonomization and by contributing to the cultivation of autonomous subjectivity, modeled on the concepts of author and reader, as well as in the depiction of character, initially especially in the heroic epics. Asserting the distinctiveness of literature, the epic therefore underpins the emerging distinctiveness of the individual. The force of individual integrity, which we saw in Flaubert's social-critical judgments, the adversarial relationship of the autonomous writer to society, has its ancient roots in the heroism of Gilgamesh, Odysseus, and Roland. The strength of literature springs from the same soil, as does the strength of character. What is it that imbues literature with this heroic capacity? The constitution of heroic literature is the key to the heroism of literature and autonomy in general.

4

Literacy and Autonomy

IN DEBATES OVER the emergence of literate cultures, profound differences over the course of human history are at stake: At times, the transition into writing is seen as a fall, a loss of some initial stage of greater innocence and collectivity, at others the acquisition of writing is treated as the unambiguous and unique key to all subsequent social and economic development. In response, others deny the very standing of some "great divide" between the oral and the literate. Important matters of politics and policy follow from these various positions. If literacy were to be accepted as the *sine qua non* of developmental progress, then education would become an overriding priority; but it would also imply a perhaps triumphal or even "Eurocentric" denigration of nonliterate social formations. These background concerns are very much at operation in discussions of literacy, its origins, and its social-historical significance.

The concern here is in one sense narrower: not the consequences of literacy in general, but rather the consequences of literacy for the history of literature and, in particular, for the constitution of the autonomous literary work of art. Nevertheless, I simultaneously make a bolder claim as well with wider ramifications: that the autonomization of literature, grounded in the nature of language as such but specifically dependent on the practice of writing, contributes to social development through the cultivation of imagination and innovation and by providing a powerful model of autonomous individuality. This individuality becomes the motor of Western civilizational progress. Yet to get to those consequences of autonomy, one must first examine the origins in greater detail.

Earlier I traced Donald's account of the three phases in human evolution leading to the emergence of modern consciousness: mimetic, mythic, and theoretical, the latter dependent on the development of the external memory storage associated with writing, while the mythic phase entails efforts to generate global accounts of the cosmos through the newly acquired behavior of language use. Nothing here is specifically literary: indeed, the mythic constructions entail undifferentiated, global attempts to provide narrative explanations of the natural world — if this anticipates later literary forms, it also anticipates science and therefore adds little to our understanding of the process of literary autonomization. Meanwhile, the later, theoretical turn associated with writing would appear to be, by its very nature, hostile to the literary project. For this reason, the search for literature, within Donald's evolutionary scheme, quickly falls into a trap, which recurs in the work of other scholars as well: The oral world, before writing, does not support literature (for various reasons, including Ong's etymological objection as well as the nondifferentiation of imaginative from referential language use); while the introduction of literacy is claimed to generate a conceptual or philosophical bias for logical thought that is therefore presumed to be hostile to literature: see Plato in the tenth book of *The Republic*. It follows that there might be no place left for literature, incongruous in the world of primary orality and anachronistic in the theoretical-scientific paradigm of literate culture. Literature simply does not fit in: Its distinctiveness is impossible in the primitive unity of the oral world, but it is already too late in the context of an ascendant theoretical thought.

Donald also emphasizes a Darwinian axiom that can prove useful: the assertion that earlier adaptations are carried into subsequent phases. The structures of consciousness are seen as carrying within themselves a record of their own developmental past. This evolution-theoretical claim is fully compatible with the specific temporality of the literary work of art discussed at length in the introduction, that is, the emphatic relationship of the work in the present to literary antecedents of the past. Indeed, the specific character of the work of art includes this anamnestic capacity, which distinguishes it from the other material artifacts of civilization. Because a literary work of significance necessarily engages with prior texts and therefore implicitly carries within itself knowledge of the literary past, one can speak of literature's genomic character, absent in nonliterary artifacts. Donald's schema is useful because it suggests the persistence of the mimetic and mythic forms of consciousness even in the modern theoretical culture. The earlier levels do not disappear, nor do they remain silent. Rather, the culture of literate society includes, as one of its dimensions, ongoing dialogues with the older cultural formations. A modern, differentiated natural science has little need for the mythic accounts of the cosmos; but modern literature, by its very nature, that is to say, its differentiated autonomy, involves a reflection on mythic material as well as on the deeper, mimetic substratum of language. The distinctiveness of literature, extrapolating from Donald, involves less some essentialist identity of the work of art, and more the capacity of literary art to hold on to the profound tensions between the alternative macrohistorical components of consciousness. This implies that in modern society with its external memory storage, where memory is in effect technologically stored (in written documents), literature becomes a very particular kind of memory: those distinctive written documents that draw on deeper strata of consciousness and human existence, precisely those strata that predate writing and that nonliterary writing would tend to ignore as primitive or obsolete.

In their *Psychology of Literacy*, Sylvia Scribner and Michael Cole provide a second approach to the consequences of the literacy transition. This influential study is an attempt to describe the psychological consequences of literacy acquisition through a detailed examination of members of the Vai people in Liberia. The Vai present a particularly interesting case because they developed their own writing system, a syllabary, transmitted informally, that is, without institutionalized schooling, and used fairly widely, at least for personal correspondence. Within the population, Vai writing coexists with two other writing systems: Arabic, taught exclusively in Koran schools and restricted in its use to the religious sphere, and the English of the governmental administration and taught in the official school system. While Scribner and Cole could find certain cognitive distinctions among the various groups—English, Arabic, and Vai literates—in fact, these differences appeared to track alternative schooling experiences, suggesting that it is not literacy as such but the effect of schooling practices that may be most important, at least in a psychological sense. Later, in a retrospective comment on their seminal work, Scribner and Cole affirmed that "Nothing in [their] data would support the statement ... that reading and writing entail fundamental 'cognitive restructurings' that control intellectual performance in all domains. ... this outcome suggests that the metaphor of a 'great divide' may not be appropriate for specifying differences among literates and non-literates under contemporary conditions."[1]

Thus Scribner and Cole tend to downplay the rupture associated with literacy acquisition, at least for individuals. Their position is consistent with the argument above that suggests multiple factors in social-historical development. Thus one would have to argue that it is not just writing that makes the difference, but the institutions that provide literacy acquisition, including the educational structure. Scribner and Cole modify their claim in a number of ways. As psychologists, they concede that they focus on individual cognitive skills rather than social processes or institutions (such as the institution of autonomous literature); in addition, their reference to "contemporary conditions" in the quoted remark indicates at least an agnosticism about the historical role that transitions to literacy may have played in the past, especially in a transition out of primary orality. More specifically, Vai literacy is not simply a matter of a pure literacy, since it is located in a culture where other literacy dynamics are at work. Thus one might speculate that if Vai were the sole writing system in operation, its ramifications might be quite different. Nonetheless, their argument stands in opposition to the assertions that literacy initiates a great divide. For our purposes, the more productive aspect of Scribner and Cole's claim is that the psychological ramifications of literacy are context-specific: They depend on institutional expectations and individual needs. It is, in other words, not literacy as such that makes the difference, but literacy in the context of a differentiated social environment. Literacy may contribute to tendencies toward a social division of labor, but as demonstrated above, it also responded to them. By insisting on the institutional specificity of literacy, Scribner and Cole lend support to the strategy of addressing literacy acquisition in the context of a differentiated society, and therefore the possibility of theorizing the distinctive literary use of language and the recognition of literature as a social phenomenon. As I suggested in discussing Donald, literary autonomy may be less an essentialist matter than a consequence of the competition among factors or sectors of social development.

The foundational work for orality versus literacy studies was Milman Parry's studies of the Homeric epics and his assertion that their formal composition, particularly the stereotypical use of epithets, indicated their original oral composition. Against earlier visions of Homer, which treated him as a paradigmatic author, Parry argued that the *Iliad* and the *Odyssey* were the products of oral performance. As further elaborated in the copious arguments of Eric Havelock, the Homeric epics are claimed to derive from an oral society (between the disappearance of Linear-B of Mycenaean culture and the introduction and transformation of the Phoenician alphabet). Havelock, however, steers the discussion in a particular direction: In the oral society of the Homeric Greeks, the only manner in which cultural memory could be preserved was in oral performance. The epics were structured in a way to allow for memorization through regular verse, stereotypical epithets, and the stark plot lines of heroic action. Moreover, the epics' value was not aesthetic but didactic, insofar as they preserved social knowledge, particularly in the context of the Greek migrations to the islands and to Asia Minor.[2] The Homeric texts that we have, thus argues Havelock, are accurate transcriptions of the oral poems, but it is only later, in the context of literate society, once there are other options for preserving social memory, that the poems are relieved of the obligation to pass on this encyclopedic knowledge. At this point, they are redefined as art, but Havelock's point is less the origin of artistic expectations than the insistence that any aesthetic approach to Homer inescapably misconstrues the original standing of the epics as informational and therefore as specifically nonliterary. As above, the search for aesthetic autonomy is thus again caught in a trap between incongruity and anachronism: before writing, oral performance has a social mnemonic function that is explicitly not aesthetic; but after the introduction of literacy, a conceptual philosophical stance develops that quickly becomes antithetical to literature.

Characteristic of the predisposition of orality studies, Havelock's disregard for aesthetic autonomy is doubled by a fundamental disinclination against notions of individual autonomy. He insists on a description of society specifically as a metaindividual construction that depends on the transmission of tradition. "Society, oral or literate, exists as it succeeds in combining individuals in a nexus, which is coherent. It is not here today and gone tomorrow. By definition it is not a transient phenomenon, as a human being is, though its longevity in historical time has varied."[3] If this verges on a truism, it also displays an orientation toward continuity rather than innovation, collectivistic knowledge rather than individual creativity. The vehicle for the transmission of that knowledge is tradition, which can be conveyed, for Havelock, either visually or through language. Hence Havelock's emphatic statement: "The [second] method is linguistic: you do what you are told to do, in this case by a voice which is collective, a voice of the community."[4]

The transmission of knowledge through language thus assumes an imperative, even domineering character. For Havelock, oral performance communicated the knowledge necessary for the continuity of the culture as a conformist mandate, with no or little room for individual variation or innovation. This is not a dynamic vision of society, to say the least. It is interesting that once literacy enters the scene, literature, which henceforth appears solely as the posthistory of the encyclopedic performance of oral societies, becomes a marginalized activity of apparently negligible importance, overshadowed by the preferred epistemes of literate society, philosophy and science. "Such was the birth of what we call poetry, a performance now relegated under literacy to the status of a pastime, but originally the functional instrument of storage of cultural information for re-use or, in more familiar language, the instrument for the establishment of a cultural tradition."[5] Havelock's denigration of aesthetic approaches to Homer corresponds to his own estimation of the standing of literature in literate society: an atavistic pastime, stripped of its earlier social significance. As a result of his own insistence on the collective character of social knowledge, he misses the role that autonomy, both individual and aesthetic, can play in contributing to the dynamic development of society.

It was Jack Goody and Ian Watt who put forward the strong argument for the developmental consequences of literacy. The transmission of knowledge in preliterate societies, so they argue, depended on face-to-face conversations. "The transmission of the verbal elements of culture by oral means can be visualized as a long chain of interlocking conversations between members of the groups. Thus all beliefs and values, all forms of knowledge, are communicated between individuals in face-to-face contact."[6] As we have just seen, Havelock proceeds from this observation, and, linking it to Parry's work on the putative orality of Homer, draws the conclusion of the encyclopedic character of the epic. For our purposes, his goal is the deaestheticization of the epic. (Thus, for all Havelock's apparent cultural conservatism, he shares the same antiaesthetic standpoint that continues to characterize the left focused on "cultural studies.")

For Goody and Watt, the argument moves in a different direction. Orality does not imply the guaranteed transmission of cultural knowledge through effective mnemonic devices. On the contrary, in their account, orality turns into a vehicle for a flawed memory. Precisely because of the centrality of face-to-face contact, the content of any cultural knowledge is subject to modification through a process they call "homeostatic adjustment": Any speaker or oral performer is vulnerable to the pressures and predispositions of the audience. One can imagine the oral setting as one of potentially lively interchange: not the silenced audience of modern theaters but a source of constant questions, comments, affirmations, or objections. Yet precisely that engagement means that the performer is subject to the possibly intrusive behavior or even threatening pressures of the recipients. While oral performance may mask itself as conservative or traditional, in fact it is always adjusted opportunistically to current needs and understandings. [7]

The principle of homeostasis, the perpetual collective readjustment of memory, corresponds to a further observation by Goody and Watt: the suspicion in oral cultures toward nonconformist individuals. Phrased alternatively: It is only with the transition to writing that texts achieve a certain objectified integrity, and it is within this literate culture that individuality can escape the opprobrium of the judgmental oral community. The two tendencies combine in a profound transformation of consciousness, characterized by a valorization of reason, the sequencing of knowledge, and the development of a skeptical and critical predisposition. Where oral society might be described emblematically by the praise poem, the public panegyric of the leader, literate society generates the sort of critical individuality exemplified by the Flaubert letters cited at the outset of chapter 3. Why can literary authors find the personal integrity to take oppositional positions? Flaubert's critical stance has roots much deeper than the French nineteenth century. Even the epic heroes are problematic, at odds with their surroundings. Even as they appear illustrious and courageous, they are always susceptible to betrayal. This complexity of the epic presentations is further evidence of their literate origins (beyond the intratextual indications of writing, mentioned above: Gilgamesh's tablets, the Bellerophon episode in the *Iliad,* or the competition with chronicles in *Chanson de Roland*). Indeed, for Goody the very structure of an extended narrative, such as the epic, is associated with the sequential thought characteristic of literate cultures (in contrast to Havelock and Ong, who treat the strong narrative plot of the heroic epics as one of the mnemonic functions, symptomatic of performance in contexts of primary orality). [8]

Goody and Watt also identify certain negative consequences of society becoming literate, including the constant proliferation of texts, the professionalization of knowledge, and a growing discrepancy between private lives where orality prevails and the written character of institutional processes. It is, however, in the work of Walter J. Ong that the critique of literacy — "the technologizing of the word" — is carried through most consistently. In fact, despite alternative evaluations, Ong and Goody agree on many aspects of the map of the transition, from the homeostatic character of oral culture to the privatization and objectification of literate culture. Ong even concedes the cultural achievements of literacy, but fundamentally he describes a phenomenological impoverishment associated with the loss of orality, which is, so he suggests, the loss of a vibrant community. "For a text to convey its message, it does not matter whether the author is dead or alive. Most books extant today were written by persons now dead. Spoken utterance comes only from the living."[9]

Ong accounts for the culture of literacy in terms of a reduction of interaction with living humans. This is a negative description of the same phenomenon, which, for Goody, has a positive value: escaping community, overcoming homeostasis, and achieving the objectified integrity of both the text and the personality. The passage into literacy, according to Ong, is a loss of community and a fall into reification. Print shifts culture away from sound, the dimension of authentic human exchanges, and toward visual objections of knowledge as silent. Knowledge becomes thinglike, anonymous, and uninspired. Print emphasizes the inner life of lonely individuals instead of a vibrant communion. The technologies of visual preservation — especially the written word — generate autonomous texts and autonomous personalities. For Ong, this transition represents a profound loss, the silencing of living voice, and the dissipation of community.

The shift to literacy also has important consequences for the experience of temporality. Ong, Goody, and Watt agree on the crucial importance of the durability associated with writing, the permanent record as distinct from the oral transmission of knowledge always susceptible to human error or homeostatic adjustment. For Goody and Watt, the transformed temporality of the visual, written sign generates a greater accuracy, a distinct historical sensibility, and the possibility of text-critical and skeptical attitudes to myth. Yet this capacity to freeze time with the written word also implies a loss of an alternative sense of the passage of time and the standing of words and deeds within a temporal flow. Thus Ong: "All sensation takes place in time, but sound has a special relationship to time unlike that of the other fields that register in human sensation. Sound exists only when it is going out of existence. It is not simply perishable but essentially evanescent, and it is sensed as evanescent. When I pronounce the word 'permanence,' by the time I get to the '-nence,' the 'perma-' is gone and has to be gone."[10] The ramification is consistent with Ong's general treatment of the reified character of literate culture. Orality allows for knowledge of impermanence, of the lability of existence and mortality, in contrast with which literacy presumably freezes experience in isolated moments in time. While writing also allows for a historiographic sensibility, it tends toward a reification of the present, or any given present, rather than a cultivation of the suppler temporality that could convey a sense of individual lives in relation to immortality. It is then only consistent for Ong to attack New Criticism for its very writerly isolation of the text; his own alternative is not a rigid contextualism but rather involves putting the text in relationship to all time and all texts: "One might describe the situation this way: since any given time is situated in the totality of all time, a text, deposited by its author in a given time, is *ipso facto,* related to all times, having implications which can be unfolded only with the passage of time, inaccessible to the consciousness of the author or the author's coevals, though not necessarily absent from their subconscious."[11] Thus, the transition to literacy is not only a loss in the sense of the disappearance of the community of coevals of the present moment. It is also a loss in the impoverishment of the sense of time and, therefore, the loss of the proximity to all texts and interlocutors from all times.

Surveying the various treatments of the transition to literacy, one can note the agreement that profound cultural and cognitive transformations accompany the emergence of writing, although there is also agreement that a stark distinction between preliterate savage and civilized minds is not tenable. The phases are, as argued above, quite blurred. Despite the agreement, there are markedly different valuations and intentions. Goody and Watt propose a progressive developmental history. Havelock shares aspects of that progressivism, although his key argument asserts the encyclopedic, rather than the poetic, character of the Homeric epics. He concurs with the notion that the transition to writing contributes to the development of rational, skeptical, and logical thought. Ong shares the same terrain, with much the same topography, but his phenomenological description tends toward an inverse valorization, condemning the reification associated with literate rationalization.

Of the several theoreticians of the transition to literacy, Ong pays the most attention to questions of literature, characterizing autonomy, as a category for literature, as a consequence of romantic and postromantic aesthetic theory, especially New Criticism and Russian formalism. These paradigms, very late in literary-historical development, separate the work of literature from any larger linkages, especially contextual significance, just as the autonomous personality is separated from the community, both past and present. Ong does allow that primary oral performance implied a certain degree of autonomy, in the sense that the performance itself was distinguishable from quotidian existence. The exercises of the bard or storyteller were distinct from those of other specialized practices, and the substance of the performance included imaginative material, differentiable from empirical reality. Yet the oral epic also entailed an encyclopedic, nonimaginative character, and the relative autonomization of the bard was undercut by the process of homeostasis and the pressure to conform to the respective community expectations. It was only with writing that the autonomy of the work can become a normative expectation, since it is no longer constrained by direct audience pressure. Furthermore, the autonomization of the literary work and the emergence of the epic hero as individual, disrupting the established order, are interlocked. The establishment of the work, as work, and its narrations of heroic deeds are part of the same process.

While Ong attributes literary autonomy to those currents in modern thought that promote a deleterious isolation of the text, I argue that autonomy — in a much longer history — is the vehicle with which literature, and individuals, escape the constraints of a narrow contextualism and community pressure. Ong is certainly convincing in his phenomenological account, the complexity of which surpasses aspects of the linear developmentalism of Goody and Watt. However, his consistent nostalgia for the collectivism of the oral community (reminiscent of Havelock's predispositions for the authority of tradition) distract him from the central drama, the generation of a cultural ability to innovate and change. In the terms of the orality versus literacy discussion, this means the urgency of the capacity to overcome the peer pressure of homeostasis. Indeed, reflection on these arguments point toward the conclusion that autonomy is precisely the opposite of homeostasis. Both for literature and for individuals, autonomy means a pursuit of freedom that transforms the always merely given present context, and it is this ability to surpass constraints that becomes, in turn, the genuine motor of the development ascribed by Goody and Watt to sequential thinking and the other presumed consequences of literacy. As Scribner and Cole have shown, however, it is not literacy as such that generates a great divide. It is rather a competition among differentiated social sectors, for our purposes especially the separation of imaginative language use and its capacity to model adversarial and entrepreneurial individuality. What is it about this distinctive use of imaginary language, or literature, that generates the civilizational project of autonomy?

LANGUAGE USE emerged somewhere between seventy and fifty thousand years ago. It is associated with simultaneous changes in culture, including the first production of visual art as well as ritual burial practices: language, art, and death overlap in a shared epistemology of the symbol. Writing systems emerge much later; there is evidence of the use of pictographs, ideographs, and numerals in Sumerian city-states like Uruk from the end of the fourth millennium B.C. Proto-writing in China and Mesoamerica appear later. If, following Denise Schmandt-Besserat, one derives early writing practices from the use of clay counting tokens, there is evidence stretching back 8,500 years from Iraq.[12] But it is not clear that precursors of writing, developed as aids in counting practices, should be considered as directly relevant to literature or to the dating of writing itself, no matter how they may have been important for early economic practices. Of greater interest is the associated suggestion that abstract counting tokens, rather than pictographic representations, stand at the outset of Mesopotamian writing. In either case, the cuneiform writing that developed gradually took on a phonetic character, until the point around 700 B.C. when Greeks transformed Phoenician script into a consistently alphabetic system. It is from this period that the written form of the Homeric epics is assumed to date. Obviously, they are not the first literature (especially if one includes oral traditions), nor even the first written literature (*Gilgamesh,* parts of the Hebrew Bible, the corpus of Egyptian writing, and numerous non-Western texts all predate them), but the first literature written in a consistently phonetic script. It is here that the logics of phonetic alphabetism and literary autonomy intersect.

Between the transition to language and the acquisition of writing, a regime of primary orality prevailed. Orality studies, beginning with Parry, attempted to dismantle romantic illusions about original authors, such as Homer, by arguing that the epics were the products of oral performance. Those arguments were typically based on intratextual evidence, in particular the assertion that the formal characteristics — stereotypical epithets, regular verse, strong characters, eventful plot structure — functioned as mnemonic devices in a context without writing. In addition, extratextual arguments were mounted with regard to comparisons with contemporary oral performance in the Balkans. Contrarily, Goody and Finnegan have raised doubts about the oral epic thesis. In existing nonliterate cultures, extended epics are rare, and the longer narratives that do exist are not at all consistent in various recitations. Moreover, oral literature, or relatively formalized utilizations of imaginative language in contexts of primary orality, are typically a matter of proverbs, sayings, or short tales. According to Goody, extensive sequentiality and the associated epistemology of linear thought — typical of the grand epics — are precisely products of emerging literacy. The presumably oral features of epics are attributed to the fact of their oral performance; rhyme may well have aided oral performers in the memorization of long presentations, but such a practice is not at all incompatible with the assumption of a context in which writing technology had begun to be available to authors and had therefore already begun to change underlying mentalities. It is these writing technologies that induce the extensive compositional integrity, sequential plot coherence, and continuity of the heroic subjectivity that mark the epic. The mnemonic aspect of Homeric verse is therefore suggested to resemble verbatim memorization and recitation practices associated with the Mishnah, the Koran and the Rig Veda, that is, a secondary orality, a practice of recitation or performance that nonetheless depends on the presence of a written text.[13]

A neat separation of orality and literacy is therefore difficult to maintain: Early literature probably involved extensive oral exertions but only in the context of an incipient, if restricted literacy, and, as Ong points out, the oral performance of literature continued until quite recently, including the reading aloud of novels. The timeline grows blurry for another reason as well. From a media-technological standpoint, it is crucial to insist on the point that prior to the emergence of any writing system, prior to any precursors of writing, what prevailed was by no means a pure orality as the sole vehicle for human interaction, record keeping, or the objectification of the imaginary. Speech may have been the sole medium for words (leaving aside the phenomenological standing of gesture and mimetic expression that accompany speech, with their roots in human evolution, as discussed by Donald), but visual artifacts, whether representational or not, decorative or abstract, are effectively coincidental with the hypothetical dating of the origins of language. At the very least, visual artifacts, such as cave paintings, may have served as memory prompts in oral recitations; they could surely function as records of memory; and in the form of sculptures or paintings on vases, they could be transported to recipients at considerable distance from their point of origin and the artist who fashioned them — that is, the separation of artist and work was fundamental to early art production. Thus visual art, which long predated writing, is characterized by some of the attributes that the proponents of the orality versus literacy great divide ascribe to writing: the relative permanence of textual durability, an objectification, that is, a separation from the artist, and in some cases portability. Furthermore, just as visual art anticipates components of written artifacts, it is also the case that early stages of writing are expressly imitative of the visual representation in pictograms and hieroglyphs. More abstract and ultimately phonetic writing systems develop out of and against that pictorial principle, an archaic opposition that continues to contribute to an underlying entwinement of word and image in modern cultures. Hence Ong's insistence on the association of literacy with sight: Reading is a visual activity. Yet this visuality of literacy is not an unanticipated innovation subsequent to the rupture caused by the invention of writing. On the contrary, it stands in a direct lineage with the artistic artifactual production of prehistoric cultures.

Written literature is not the binary opposite of oral performance. Rather, literature and, in particular, the autonomous literary work, are the heirs to both visual and oral legacies, transforming both and combining them: giving visual presence to verbal art. The visual art of preliterate societies anticipated several characteristics of the literary work:

1. *Durability*. Like the visual work of art, the literary work has an extended temporal existence; it is not evanescent, to use Ong's term describing the temporality of the oral performance. Potentially unlimited in duration, the written word, like the visual work of art, can preserve memory well beyond the immediate moment and, of particular importance, it may outlive its maker. The work, which may last through time, therefore stands in a special relationship both to the artist-writer and to other works. Likely to survive its author's demise, it implicitly poses the question of his death, while holding out the possibility of a poetic immortality, which a writer can pursue through writing. As works of permanence last through time, new works find themselves in direct competition with the cultural inheritance, which may become a canon. The author's effort to outlive his or her contemporaries through works of literature implies a competitive relationship to other works, as written texts proliferate. Just as one might say that oral literatures lacked guarantees of long-term memory, literate cultures lack mechanisms of forgetting.

2. *Portability*. Like sculptures or paintings on jars (but unlike cave paintings), those works of literature that are written are typically portable: not epitaphs on buildings, obviously, but writing on bark, parchment, tablets, and paper. Portability amplifies the implicit separation from the author, inherent in the principle of durability, but it also allows for dissemination. Dissemi-

nation, coupled with the radical reduction of symbols in the alphabet, initiates a teleology of democratization. The democratic expansion of the literary community does not come into its own until the development of much improved technologies (paper and movable print), but it is implicit in the role of scripture in the spread of the axial religions. Literacy is fundamental to modern processes of democratization, but the potential for an exoteric distribution of literacy skills and, therefore, access to texts, is grounded in the standing of writing altogether, particularly, however, in alphabetic writing. Ideographic and hieroglyphic script generate an exclusive readership caste; alphabetic writing, in contrast, implies citizenship. Hence the particularly Western grounding of democratic norms.

3. *Formal integrity.* Not only is the written work, like the visual artifact, durable in the sense that it does not disappear immediately, as does evanescent speech; it is also characterized by an integrity in the sense that, once completed, it cannot be amended arbitrarily. To be sure, a written text can be erased and edited, just as a painting or a sculpture can be modified. Nonetheless these sorts of intrusive corrections are of a different order than the homeostatic transformations that oral performance regularly undergoes. The oral performance is, at every moment, subject to the pressures of the audience; the visual artifact or the written text evidences much greater immalleability. This integrity derives in part from the materiality of the visual work or the written script but, more fundamentally, from the separation of author, public, and work. Homeostatic pressure is possible only because the oral performance necessarily implies the immediate presence of the public facing the author, always subject to community pressure during the act of performance. In the case of the written work, like the visual artifact, the author-artist is no longer necessarily present at the moment of reception. The time gap between production and reception allows for a separation of author from audience and hence prohibits homeostasis, or at least its direct effects. (Of course, one can imagine peer pressure working on the author of a written text in the form of self-censorship or other anticipations of audience response. But even if one recognizes that no author is fully protected from community sanctions, the author of the written text, at a distance from the reading public, is surely safer than the oral performer in front of an audience.)

4. *Semiotic displacement and imagination.* The symbolic character of language as such grounds an imaginative facility, insofar as linguistic activity is predicated on an ability to invoke that which is absent. Language goes far beyond pointing out elements in the speaker's immediate context (an activ-

ity nonetheless not found in nonhuman primates) and includes capacities to recall earlier experiences as well as to discuss hypothetical contents. Because they are both durable and portable, the signifying substance of any work is perpetually displaced from a particular context, especially its point of origin, thereby undermining referential components of a message, while amplifying the imaginary, or polysemous, character. Kafka's initial readers may have associated his city descriptions with Prague, but that is not a necessary condition for his reception by a later international public. (Their fixed locations make cave paintings counterexamples, apparently lodged permanently in their context of origin; however, precisely their frequently isolated location, deep in cave systems, suggests a separation from initial referents. And so the imaginary principle, the invocation of the absent, is relevant here as well, albeit in a somewhat different manner.)

In addition, one can identify certain secondary effects of the visual legacy inherited by the written work. The durability of the visual artifact, be it in the visual artwork or writing as the visual representation of words, allows for a lengthening of the written verbal art, as measured against the oral performance. Long epics are rare in oral cultures, and they are even more rarely recited at a single sitting or even a coherent set of sittings. Writing allows for longer works and the elaboration of more expansive, and more detailed, accounts (and thereby a fulfillment of the mythic cosmological project identified by Donald). Yet the permanence of the written record also allows for the development of skepticism and text-critical attitudes, much less likely in oral settings. By this fact a potential antimythological predisposition emerges. The push and pull between mythological elaboration and skeptical criticism contributes to a cultural division of labor between imaginative literature and historical chronicle. Still, the culture of skepticism may be integrated into imaginative literature as well in the form of irony. While historiography engages in a systematic doubting of myth, irony heightens the imaginative effect of literature by doubting intratextual illusions.

The notional cultural history in orality versus literacy studies tends to move from oral performance (even if it is denied the specific standing of literature because of its orality) through the alleged transcription of the oral epic to the genuine literary work as a late civilizational product. The presumed continuity through these materials involves the claims that oral literature was already narrative and epic, and that epic is foundational for literature; while the latter point is certainly arguable, the former, the narrative, epic character of oral performance, is much less tenable. Nevertheless, one can point out an implicit bias in orality versus literacy studies to assume the continuity and primacy of narrative, which is then projected onto a timeline of technological change, beginning with the new technology of writing. One might just as well propose an alternative trajectory beginning with prehistoric visual art in preliterate societies and moving toward the written work. Indeed, it is none other than Ong, the major proponent of orality versus literacy studies, who underscores the visuality of writing systems, although he strangely tends to ignore the preliterate visual legacy for the written work of literature. In fact, a visual genealogy is all the more credible in light of the fact that the written work, and written literature, retain a visual character through their subsequent history: decorated manuscripts, logographic reading practice, the overlap between the novel and cinema, and so on. Cinematic visualization of literary texts is not a late add-on to literature but rather one further link in a long chain of visual corollaries to the written word, grounded in the visual phenomenology of writing.

Writing and written literature evidently coexist with a visual dimension, but they also coexist with orality (indeed, as argued above, writing competes with and integrates both alternative modes of expression in a sort of constant two-front war). Visuality transforms language, in writing, into the sequentiality that supports narrative, and it gives verbal art, transformed into written works, a permanence absent in the oral performance. Meanwhile writing also inherits the specific verbalism of oral performance. Hybridizing the two phenomenologies—visual-material and oral-verbal—it takes on characteristics of both. The permanence of the visual artifact is combined with the evanescence of orality in the sense that the written work (despite Ong's claim to the contrary) retains knowledge of temporal limitation, although not exactly the same evanescence of content as in the enunciation of speech. The written work of art is subject to and constituted by the passage of time in several ways. First and most obviously, the passage of time defines the literary work of art in the sense that its specific reality is bounded by the limited time of the aesthetic experience: When it is not being read, it falls out of existence. It is dependant on reception, which is necessarily limited in duration. To be sure, a reader can return to a written text in a way a listener may not be able to return to an oral performance and certainly not to a particular moment in a given oral performance. Nonetheless, the duration in time of the written work of literature depends on the schedule of the reader in a more emphatic way than a visual work: A book on a shelf has less standing when it is not being read, than, say, a pyramid when it is not being visited. This difference is an effect of the doubled signification: Literature involves the written signs of oral signs — the alphabetic indication of phonetic utterance — and it is therefore comparable to the written or printed musical score. Without reception or performance they are mute (a term that suggests a reminiscence of orality), while visual art retains a continuous presence in its materiality (as does the calligraphy of writing, but not the imaginative core of written literature).

The written work inherits the evanescence, which Ong restricts to oral performance, in a second way, associated precisely with its presumed durability. This durability is of course only relative: If the written work lasts longer than a spoken word, it too may not last forever. Its materiality is a sort of vulnerability, since material artifacts can crumble away or be destroyed. Moses smashing the tablets of the law, the burning of the collection at the library of Alexandria, and the practice of book burning, culminating with the Nazis (but surely with a longer tradition) all mark the limits of written permanence. Nonetheless, the written work does appear to achieve a permanence, no matter how relativized by these extreme cases. In particular, once written, it appears to be able to survive its author whose death is, in a sense, announced by the work. To this point too Ong is close, citing the Renaissance dictum "Every book is thy epitaph."[14] Yet he operates with too tendentious a distinction between the living community of the oral performance and a pejorative construction of literacy as reified and dead. The written work, as much as oral performance, faces evanescence precisely as it struggles for permanence. The very permanence of the written work poses questions of mortality in ways quite foreign to the phenomenology of the oral performance, but arguably more ominous. Oral literature is exemplified by the praise poem; written literature by the epic in which the hero is betrayed and dies.

Finally, one can add that the permanence of the written literary work through time, compounded by its portability, defines a trajectory of constant displacement from its material point of origin and its initial semiotic context. The written work can move through time and space. A sophisticated criticism, open to the specific condition of the literary work, therefore avoids reducing it to its context, narrowly understood, and instead thematizes the ever growing and irreversible distance between any present reading and the moment of creation. Walter Benjamin referred to this critical view as the "mortification of the work," the recognition of the condition of existence of the work of literature that it is in history and always passing away. Hence his conclusion that the truth content of the work emerges through this historical passage, as the living aspects of the initial context disappear.[15] Hence also the knowledge of the historicity of any given reception of a work of literature and its relationship to previous receptions. Every realization of the written signs in the imagination of a reader retains the evanescence that Ong had restricted to the oral community.

Inheriting phenomenological aspects of both visuality and oral verbality, the literary work consequently combines elements of permanence and evanescence. The permanence of the work of literature, unchecked, would transform it into an idolatrous icon; its evanescence, which is its historical condition, corrects the tendency toward a reification of time while nonetheless permitting a much greater integrity and coherence than what is available to the oral performance. This dialectic opens onto the relationship of literature to religion, discussed in chapter 6. At this point, however, several literary examples can demonstrate the complexity of the relationship between orality and literacy as they pertain to the emergence of autonomous literature. The terrain of the debate is the heroic epic, ultimately a generic effect of the interplay of orality and writing, as chapter 5 shows.

Literacy and Autonomy

The Epic and the Individual

IN ORDER TO make his case, Ong points to the etymology of *epos*, derived from the proto-Indo-European *wek^w*, the source of the Latin *vox* and the English *voice*. This language-historical connection is taken to corroborate the claim that epic poetry is originally a product of oral, preliterate society. Thus he states that "In the West, . . . the epic is basically and irremediably an oral art form. Written and printed epics, the so-called 'art' epics, are self-conscious, archaizing imitations of procedures demanded by the psychodynamics of oral story-telling."[1] The implied denigration of art and self-conscious writing is a telling indication of Ong's bias toward an original innocence attributed to oral culture. More important, what Ong shrugs off as an archaizing style in fact could alternatively be taken to represent a continuity of knowledge, a dynamic conversation between later works and their predecessors, which carries knowledge forward while transforming and adapting it to changed circumstances. Literate culture in the age of writing is suppler and more organic than Ong would suggest. If, however, we dwell on this one point and consider how the late examples of a genre stand in a significant relationship to earlier works, then current literature can shed light on its antecedents. In particular, the contemporary epic can help us answer questions about the origins of the form. This implies taking the literary work of art seriously as a repository of knowledge about the conditions of the possibility of autonomous imagination and not merely, as contemporary contextual criticism would have it, as an artifact of a cultural context or an ideological expression of power. The literary work of art explores the standing of the imagination in general as well as the substance of the historical tradition, especially the genre history, and it is not merely snapshot evidence of the moment of its production.

Ong would, presumably, have to reject as archaizing Derek Walcott's *Omeros*, since it commences with a doubly retrospective gesture: the fisherman Philoctete reporting how great trees had been chopped down in order to build canoes; and the overlapping projection onto that venture of a deep historical process. The foresting activity is imbued with a sense of civilizational transformation, as an ancient polytheistic world gives way to the singular logic of mechanized modernity:

> These were the pillars that fell, leaving a blue space
> for a single God where the old gods stood before.
> The first god was a gommier. The generator
>
> began with a whine, and a shark, with sidewise jaw,
> sent the chips flying like mackerel over water.[2]

The epic begins with an indication of its own epigonic time, the retrospective relationship of its defining subsequentiality to a primitive past. Not just *Omeros*, the epic as genre takes shape by positioning itself as modernity in relationship to a lost age of innocence. The exploits of the hero, indeed his very definition as heroic, involve overcoming the past or, as with Odysseus, resisting the temptations of regression to an earlier condition. Moreover, this historical transition maps onto the very distinction introduced by the invention of writing: It is orality that is overcome. In the first epic, Gilgamesh emerges as a hero and a writer "setting his labors on tablets of stone." In the contemporary epic, *Omeros*, the narration begins with a similar transformation of the mode of language, as an ancient world of orality, projected onto the trees, crumbles before advanced civilization:

> The bearded elders endured the decimation
> of their tribe without uttering a syllable
> of that language they had uttered as one nation,
>
> the speech taught their saplings: . . .
>
> Like barbarians striding columns they had brought down,
> the fishermen shouted. The gods were down at last.[3]

The epic marks the destruction of the former world, but it does so in terms that are far from the triumphalism of a celebratory praise poem, the paradigmatic oral form. The critical and antimythological consciousness associated with writing is evidenced in the genre to the extent that the victorious assertion of a contemporary modernity is revealed as ruthlessly violent. The epic's description of the brutality of the historical progress is, however, as little a matter of nostalgia for the former state as it is a blind celebration of the victory. The complexity of the epic as genre involves precisely this ability to think historically about historical progress, in particular the suffering inherent in the transition from preliterate to literate cultural formations. The violence that Walcott describes in the quoted passage is one with the slaughter at the destruction of Troy or the senseless carnage in the *Nibelungenlied*. The point is not that epics document a violent world, but that as artistic form they capture that violence in order, dialectically, to turn it into an object for reflection and mourning. The antimythological tendency inherent in writing is not simply about debunking the archaic myths of the past; it is equally about directing a critical skepticism toward any mythic self-aggrandizement of the present.

Thus we return to the cultural historical question. Are heroic epics records of oral performance in preliterate societies, as has been argued since Parry's work on Homer? Or are they products of an emerging literacy, recording the dissipation of oral community? *Omeros,* at least, positions the poem as subsequent to the end of primary orality. Yet while Walcott's poem is susceptible to Ong's accusation of archaizing, *Gilgamesh* surely is not, even though it too commences with an indication of the end of orality. The heroic epics, one may conjecture, were specifically written works, even if they drew on some preliterate tales, reorganized into lengthy narratives, and even if they were destined typically for oral performance (in contexts where literacy was still uncommon). We should not read them as records of a way of life in societies of primary orality — that is to say, with an anthropological eye — but rather as explorations of an increasingly autonomous form of expression associated with writing and its corollary innovations, especially the development of a logocentric consciousness, hostile to oral traditionalism: Consider, for example, the affective displacement inherent in the transition from Achilles' mercurial anger to Odysseus's instrumental reason, a historical transformation that structures the relationship of the two Homeric epics to each other and indicates the growing impact of writing on culture. Epic literature is about the heroism of the deed, but it is ultimately driven by that one most innovative deed, writing, just as much as by the civilizational ability to recall and regret the violence that has taken place in the name of progress. One may even presume that that capacity for regret on a grand scale, which requires extended memory, is itself a product of writing. Writing is progress that can reflect on its own cost. It is the genuine heroism, and the epic as form is the record of the cultural and social transition from orality to literacy. The *Iliad* takes note of the duplicity and danger associated with limited literacy in the Bellerophon narrative; and the defeat of poetic orality is enacted in the sirens episode of the *Odyssey*. Similarly, the literate narrator of the *Nibelungenlied* can position himself so as to condemn, retrospectively, the oral poet Volker, associated with a particularly primitive savagery.

Yet we should be cautious not to overstate the rationality of consciousness after the great divide. Following upon the destruction of orality in the foresting passage at the outset of Walcott's epic, writing is established, the names emblazoned on the canoes. Yet writing promptly turns out to be treacherous:

> The priest
> sprinkled [the canoes] with a bell, then he made the swift's sign.

> When he smiled at Achille's canoe, *In God We Troust,*
> Achille said: "Leave it! Is God' spelling and mine."[4]

The passage from the prerational world of orality to the sequential narratives of progressive modernity generates writing and texts. These, however, are neither simple nor transparent. Writing may rationalize consciousness, but written texts develop their own resistant integrity, impervious to the conformist leveling effected by the homeostatic pressure of community. On the contrary, their very autonomy, their distinction from reified language and communication — the distinction between "Troust" and "Trust" — defines a constitutive difficulty, a seclusion, that puts them at odds with other spheres of social development. The misspelling "Troust" in fact stages the hermetic teleology of autonomous literature, the search for a language that is pure language, the adequate linguistic medium for imagination and therefore not contaminated with the communicative alloys of everyday speech with their heteronomous functions. Perhaps more than many other poets, Walcott draws on quotidian language, but he transforms it into a specifically poetic medium, and that difference is signaled by the otherwise superfluous *u* in the name of the boat. The written work is hardly a mirror of quotidian life in literate culture, a transparent account of the process of social rationalization. On the contrary, the key feature of literate culture is the differentiation of spheres of activity, including the autonomization of literature, which — as Kafka puts it in "The Penal Colony" — is difficult to read and therefore "no calligraphy for school children."[5] The transparent rationalization of the social world in the course of progress and development goes hand in hand with the autonomization of imaginative writing and therefore the increasingly hermetic character of literature.

THE FIRST STROPHE of the *Nibelungenlied* establishes the retrospective perspective, the backward glance from the modernity of the moment of composition toward a remembered violent world of the past. This is a memory homologous with the one at the outset of *Omeros*. The gesture of recollection necessarily poses the question of whether that earlier world is better described as pristine or primitive, heroic or barbarian, a golden age or dark ages. The ideologized reception history of the *Nibelungenlied*, sometimes treated as a German national epic, is largely dependent on this antinomy. Does the poem celebrate the age of bloodlust and carnage, or by reporting the brutality does it convey a critique?

> Uns ist in alten mæren   wunders vil geseit
> Von helden lobebæren,   von grôzer arebeit,
> Von fröuden, hôchgezîten, von weinen und von klagen,
> Von küener recken strîten muget ir nu wunder hœren sagen.
>
> ["We have been told in ancient tales many marvels of famous heroes, of mighty toils, joys, and high festivities, of weeping and wailing, and the fighting of bold warriors — of such things you can now hear wonders unending."][6]

The inherent historical structure of the strophe maps onto the problem of the transition from orality. The literate epic poet appears in the modernity of the textual present as an epigone, writing from an advanced civilizational stage, while looking back toward a prehistory, which is judged dialectically: savage in its violence but simultaneously admirable in its capacity for authentic deeds.

The strophe conveys another problematic as well. Beyond the retrospective temporality, the author describes an obstinate tension between himself and his public on the one hand — they are bound together in the first person plural pronoun with which the poem begins, *uns,* and the heroes of the bygone world. This binary suggests a gap between the literate "modern" public and the knightly, heroic, or political sphere: "We" may sing and listen, but they could act. Not only are literature and politics, therefore, defined as alternative sectors of social development; at least from the one side, the literary, which is the discourse of the contemporary narrator, they are placed in a competitive opposition to each other: *vita activa, vita contemplativa*. The heroism of the *Nibelungenlied*, thus the suggestion of the introductory strophe, does not merely concern the historical heroism of the knights of yore (the medieval literature is thus itself already romantic in its imagination of the past; one did not have to wait for the romantic medievalism of the nineteenth century for this sort of nostalgic fiction). It is also a matter of the heroism of the medieval writer, exploring the possibility of claiming a position outside the political sphere: aesthetic autonomy. Through writing, the poet pursues a strategy of independence from political power. By projecting heroism onto the giants of the past, the author is able to have the same glory reflect onto writing as well.

A similar problem recurs in a more complex formulation in the final strophe of *La Chanson de Roland*:

> Quant l'emperere ad faite sa justise
> E esclargiez est la sue grant ire,
> En Bramidonie ad chrestienter mise,
> Passet li jurz, la nuit est aserie.
> Culcez s'est li reis en sa cambre voltice.
> Seint Gabriel de part Deu li vint dire:
> "Carles, sumun les oz de tun emperie!
> Par force iras en la tere de Bire,
> Reis Vivien si succuras en Imphe,
> A la citet que paien unt asise:
> Li chrestien te recleiment e crient."
> Li emperere n'i volsist aler mie:
> "Deus," dist li reis, "si penuse est ma vie!"
> Pluret des oilz, sa barbe blanche tiret.
> Ci falt las geste que Turoldus declinet.

> [The Emperor Charles, once justice had been done,
> And his great anger is finally appeased,
> Has Bramimonde baptized into the Faith.
> The day is over, and in the dark of night

The Epic and the Individual

The king lies sleeping in his highly vaulted room.
Saint Gabriel is sent by God to say:
"Charlemagne, summon your empire's mighty hosts!
You'll march in force into the land of Bire;
You must relieve King Vivien at Imphe
Where pagans hold his city under siege,
And Christian voices are crying for your help."
The Emperor Charles has no desire to go,
"God!" says the king, "how weary is my life!"
He pulls his beard, the tears flow from his eyes.
Here ends the poem, for Turoldus declines.][7]

Even the divine call to continue the war against Islam can no longer inspire
Charlemagne, exhausted by the violence and the suffering that fill the pages
of the epic. Again, the work provides a record of violence, but it is far from
celebrating it (despite ideologically nationalist reception histories). Like the
opening of the *Nibelungenlied*, the backward glance located at the conclusion of the *Chanson de Roland* articulates a retrospective epigonality. Instead
of culminating with a triumphal emperor, the poem gives us Charlemagne
in tears, aged, an allegory of mourning. It is here, precisely in the context
of infinite destruction and the reticence of the emperor before God — is it
treasonous? blasphemous? heretical? — that the author introduces himself,
immodestly, by name at a moment of conclusion: Turold the teller of the tale
ending here. The writer is the shadow of the warrior hero, the opposite and,
at the same time, the companion. Nor should we ignore the slipperiness of
the verbs in the final verse: where Charlemagne mourns is where the history
(*geste*) concludes (*falt*), but the conclusion is in effect a failing: *falt* is the
third person indicative of *faillir*, to fail. It is here that the story fails to continue, where it falters, where it ends in ruin. For the recounting has become a
matter of *declinet*: a word choice with a meaning that stretches from narrat-
ing and writing to declining (as in declining a verb), or more emphatically,
rejecting. It is the record of rejection. While the surface meaning is simple
enough — here ends the story that Turold has been telling — the undertones
of dejection are too powerful to overlook. The foregrounded announcement
of conclusion is undercut by a message of irredeemable failure. The work
ends, but the problem remains open, in a dialectic of permanence and evanescence: What never changes is loss, since fullness is fully absent.

In both epics, the competitive relationship between writer and warrior transforms the author into a fighter in the context of the increasing sectoral competition between literature and politics. At stake therefore is not only the intratextual evidence for literacy and authorship, the appearance of the writer in the text, but the fundamentally agonistic structure of the epic world, which requires closer examination. The evidence of battle and competition in the epic plots is overwhelming, and it consequently plays a major role in the debates on the standing of the epic as genre. How does the topical fascination with violence shed light on the constitution of the genre? For Ong, the oral performance itself implies an agonistic scene, in which the audience can regularly challenge the author (leading to the process of homeostatic adjustment). Moreover, in the context of primary orality — which he claims for the epic — the absence of writing and the alleged reliance on oral transmission as the sole vehicle for memory generate a need for mnemonic devices. These include strong figures and heroic deeds, easier to remember than the sort of subtle details and irony that later come to characterize the genres of writing and, especially, print, such as the novel. Indeed, for Ong it is precisely the alleged disappearance of agonistics, of struggle, in written cultures — that is, the struggle between the oral performer and the audience — that contributes to the disappearance of strong characters in literate culture. Thus, the historical source of the agonistic content of the epic, imagined to be an oral form, is the very character of the interaction between performer and audience.

Ong's claim that the transition from heroic to novelistic figures corresponds to historically changing structures of literary life is no doubt valid. It is not clear, however, why he must also insist that the literary transition has to be separated from other, larger social transformations and grounded exclusively in the media-historical reorganizations through the spread of literacy. If "writing restructures consciousness," must one conclude that consciousness is solely an effect of writing?[8] Is literary history directly and exclusively dependent on technological change, or are there not multiple, relatively independent variables at work in the historical development process? In fact, Ong's argument on the origins of the heroic figure is less convincing than his description of the domesticated character of novelistic fictions. The claim about the interplay between performer and audience is curiously inconsistent. The homeostatic situation can, of course, be described as agonistic, a perpetual challenging of the author and therefore a source of the conflicted content of heroic epics: In other words, the hero as topic can be taken to represent an externalization of the author facing the public. Elsewhere, however, Ong insists on a presumably harmonic and inclusive character of oral culture. Furthermore, we know from other work how much suspicion can be directed toward isolated individuals in preliterate settings as a result of the pressure to participate in community.[9] It appears then that Ong uses *homeostasis* in contrary ways, according to his argumentative needs. On the one hand, he sometimes uses it to demonstrate the harmonious communal integration of oral cultures; on the other, he describes it as a site of contention and a rationale for the embattled heroes and mortal struggle of the epic genre.

Against the dubious claim that it is the homeostatic challenge to the performer that generates heroic figures in oral performance, one can offer more compelling arguments that epic heroism is instead a feature of early literacy. First, Ong's timeline is untenable. It is not the case that an ancient world of violence, heroism, and therefore the epic has been replaced by a universal peace and a total privatization as the context for the novel. Both modernity and the modernization process continue to elicit considerable violence, even if the specific technologies of violence may not be conducive to the epic models of traditional heroism. Recall Marx's dictum on the obsolescence of Achilles in the age of powder and lead. Yet while Achilles is not a modern norm, the examples of modern, indeed contemporary, heroism are not so rare as to declare it incompatible with modernity. Therefore, modernization is not solely a matter of the ironic privatization, devoid of heroes and great deeds, described by Ong, and his relegation of the heroic epic to the premodern, oral context becomes unacceptable.

Second, the empirical evidence on performance in preliterate settings does not support the claim that oral cultures generate heroic epics. According to Goody, oral performance rarely generates the extended and coherent plots characteristic of epics. There is no evidence that heroic epics are generally representative of oral cultures, just as one can easily point to the surfeit of agonistic situations characteristic of modernity, and it is precisely in those situations of conflict that heroism takes place. None of these points proves conclusively the origin of heroism in the context of writing, but it is clear that Ong's neat ascription of heroics to preliterate, oral homeostasis and mnemonic imperatives is not convincing. To explore the question of the literacy of the epic, it is necessary to turn to a closer examination of its textual character and intratextual evidence.

The epic, specifically as a written document, amounts to an imaginary record of a violence that is typically relegated to the past of an anterior age, although the legacy of that violence is frequently shown to continue to haunt the epic present. The violent excess of the past, which is the topic of the epic, is both the inherited guilt of the present and a foil to the modernity of civility. Precisely as a product of written cultures, one of its defining features is the exploration of the relationship to earlier cultural formations, especially primary orality. The epic is therefore a writing about orality, but not merely the written transcription of an erstwhile oral performance.

Meanwhile, further evidence (albeit indirect) for the provenance of the epic from a literate context is implicit in the epic's staging of a dramatic opposition between writing and the powerful world of political action. Specific attributes are implicitly projected onto the practice of writing, as a result of its location as the opposite of the violence, the power, and the heroism that it narrates. The act of writing, so to speak, becomes the opposite of the content of the writing. Consequently, the existential question for this epic writing, and perhaps all literary writing, involves the scope of its pertinence to that real world of brute action that makes up the content of the epic — does writing really matter? At an archaic, but no longer solely oral, moment, Gilgamesh could become hero and writer, but writing subsequently became the *vita contemplativa* defined as the outside to the world of action and political deeds. The anxiety that ensues, expressed so poignantly in the Lamartine verse, is the concern that power may just marginalize the writer, as the eagle drops his plume.

> Comme la plume inutile
> Que l'aigle abandonne aux airs
>
> [Like the useless feather
> That the eagle abandons in the air][10]

Yet the very act of recording that anxiety represents a moment of resistance to the eagle's imperious power. This activist potential in writing, the opposition to unlimited political power, resonates through a further dimension of competition. Because writing is durable, any text finds itself in a race with the plethora of antecedent texts, which threaten to crush it. Any given text has to assert itself against its competitors and predecessors, the longevity of which is guaranteed by writing; but it is the same longevity of written literature that gives it a competitive advantage over the political act. At the conclusion of *Germany, A Winter's Tale,* Heinrich Heine identified this capacity of literature to condemn a political figure in print as the particular

The Epic and the Individual

superiority of literature, otherwise regarded as the weak alternative to state power. The written work of literature, achieving autonomy by insisting on its distance from political power and struggling against the weight of tradition, thrives through competitive engagement, which underpins its basic structures. Agonistics — for which the topic of the heroic epic is the perhaps paradigmatic example — is therefore a result of writing itself and an internally differentiated modernity in which writing confronts the state. The epic is not a relic of an ancient orality, and particularly not if that orality is judged to have been, as Ong sometimes claims, a sort of collectivist harmony.[11]

The need for writing to struggle to justify itself against the presumed greater reality of the political deed has important consequences that define the field of autonomous literature. First, as already noted, the distinction between the literary imagination and the political or historical deed implies a division of cultural labor between fiction and historiography. Both may rely on rhetorical strategies, but they are distinct modes of cognition. The texts of Homer and Herodotus make different sorts of claims on the intelligence of the reader and require different sorts of critical judgments. Even if one were to accept Havelock's antiaesthetic claim about the encyclopedic character of Homer, an accumulation of cultural knowledge that provided for the stability of cultural transmission, and even if one were to recognize literary narrative structures in Herodotus (and in subsequent historical writing), the separation of historiographic writing from fiction is simply not in question. Both modes of writing represent efforts to remember, but the two genres operate with profoundly different norms of evidence and different terms of success. This, as noted above, accounts for the strategy of *La Chanson de Roland* to set its own fictionality in opposition to the historical accuracy of the chronicles. Distinguishing itself from medieval historiography, the literary epic stakes out its claims to a specifically aesthetic autonomy, the distinctively imaginative use of language.[12]

Second, the competitive relationship between literature and politics allows for literature to establish itself as autonomous, while also threatening to undermine autonomy, by highlighting literature's adversariality to the political order. The problem of "aesthetics and politics" is therefore hardly an invention of the ideological conflicts of the twentieth century; it is rooted instead in the fundamental specialization of writing and the distinctive character of the imaginative facility of language. Literary writing is an extraordinarily creative and therefore innovative activity, but literature as an institution retains a fundamental suspicion of political action, despite the fact of the constitutively democratizing component in literary culture, which will be discussed in chapter 7. Thomas Mann's insistence during World War I on his poetic separation from the political sphere went hand in hand with his identification of his literary brother, Heinrich, as endemically political. The terminological distinction, especially in his *Reflections of a Nonpolitical Man*, between the poet and the literary author, *Dichter* and *Literat*, had a particular viability in the context of early twentieth-century Germany that does not lend itself to easy generalization.[13] Nonetheless, it does point to the general problematic of the relationship of literary autonomy to the political sphere: literature's exclusion (or self-exclusion) from politics is itself a political gesture, and one that is the inescapable shadow of the original possibility of literature altogether.

THE EPIC AS GENRE is characterized by an extensive plot structure: not merely a series of episodes or heroic exploits but their sequential organization, with an internal logic and the teleological orientation toward a conclusion. This organization of action is a consequence of the transformation of consciousness associated with literacy. This is not to say that there are no plots or no purposive action in the narratives of oral performance, but it is the case that such goal-oriented narrative, particularly in extended narrative, is rare in the oral context.[14] Evidence of some infrequent narratives in oral cultures does not disprove the key claim that it is the transition to literacy that enables the proliferation of the extended plot structure that characterizes the heroic epic. Literacy greatly increases the frequency of such elaborate narrative plots.

To argue that the presence of extended plot locates the epic narrative in the context of writing does not mean that the nonplot elements of the epic are irrelevant. Havelock, especially, insists that the epic should not be read as compelling narrative but, on the contrary, as the social encyclopedia of community knowledge, the public record in an age without writing. One might even concede Havelock's point on the encyclopedic function (which is not itself necessarily limited to orality, although it would become anachronistic in a literate context, where other forms of record keeping become available and provide greater efficiency). The point is that the narrative, even if it carries other contents, also carries with it that particular organization of time and action, the plot, that is associated precisely with the logocentric consciousness of emerging literacy.

In addition, to argue for the integrity of the extensive plot does not imply a denigration of the status of episodes, the individual event units, the concatenation of which generates the full narrative trajectory. Episodic narrative may well be more characteristic of an oral content. The relative brevity as well as the focus on a single event point toward a limited memory capacity and the time limitation of a single performance. The late residue of this phenomenon is the chapter division in the novel. Yet epics demonstrated an overarching principle of organization. Even if one were to imagine that all the individual events preexisted the epic in the form of relatively independent traditional tales, compatible with the temporal restrictions of oral performance, the specificity of the epic is nonetheless precisely the integration of these tales into a logical whole, whereby that logic can of course assume, of course, different rhetorical shapes — consequentiality, development, decline, and the rest. The probability that some of the material of epics may have circulated orally prior to their integration into the epic is only marginally important to the substantive status of the epic and its composition as a phenomenon of writing. In fact, their oral circulation in the context of literacy, no matter how restricted, still would not disprove the association of writing and epic. On the contrary, an association of epic production with secondary orality is nothing other than the recognition that the epic emerges within the regime of writing, which is after all the precondition for an orality that is secondary.

The tension between orality and the epic is constitutive of an extensive and fundamental genre-theoretical discussion. If the epic is a written genre, what is the status of speech within it? Aristotle praises Homer for his reticence as narrator and his corollary willingness to let his characters speak for themselves.[15] Homer's excellence on this point, Aristotle suggests, stands in contrast to other unnamed epics in which the narrator may be more intrusive, or, in any case, where more descriptive narration rather than direct discourse takes place. This leads to the characterization of the Homeric epics as dramatic, insofar as they stage characters that speak. It is their proximity to the privileged genre of drama that indicates their success.

Greek drama, on the other hand, according to Ong, was the first genre to be solely under the sway of writing.[16] Authors wrote the texts, which were memorized and then spoken. As an aside, one should note that the plays obviously drew on preexisting material, presumably of oral provenance, the various myths that made up their plots. That connection to an archaic orality does not prevent the theoreticians of orality from insisting on the written nature of the drama, and a similar argument could be made here with regard to the hypothetical oral origin of episodes—short, preexisting narratives—later integrated into the written epics. More important at this point, however, is how one is struck by the dialectical tension between the particular linkage of drama to writing, the work of the playwright, and the most emphatic integration of orality as the medium of stage production. The dependency on writing, with its orientation toward a sequential organization of knowledge, is the source of the teleological narrative, the organized plot. *Mutatis mutandis* for the organized and directed activity recorded in the epic. Writing, speech, and plot are intimately interwoven in the epic, with its dramatic character, as much as they are in the drama itself.

The modern recapitulation of the genre problem of the dramatic epic is the Brechtian discourse on epic drama. Otherwise Brecht profiles himself as a critic of Aristotle, particularly the affective theory of tragedy as a framework for the recipients' catharsis. He appears to be much closer to Aristotle, however, in his reflections on the interaction between dramatic and epic elements, albeit with different contexts. For Aristotle, it is the dramatic character of the Homeric epic that is appealing; for Brecht, the goal is the introduction of epic elements into drama.[17] The two arguments overlap in the model of mixing dramatic and epic components, and both are expressions of the same problematic: the existential limitations that any framing context, the so-called epic breadth, places on the dramatic capacity of the individual to act decisively. The ancient epic is not so much about the hero's exploits and victories as about the hero's limitations, his death (Achilles), his misfortunes (Odysseus), or his betrayal (Siegfried). Brecht's epic drama is similarly about the hero's failure to act, or to act adequately. The incapacity of the modern antihero in Brechtian epic theater is the late echo of the death of the hero in the heroic epics. Far from celebrating the hero's deeds, the crux of the epic is the hero's failings and demise.

This melancholic knowledge of heroic failing defines the epic as genre, as with Charlemagne in tears at the end of *La Chanson de Roland*, whose eponymous hero has already died long ago. It is a genre that not only records the passing of a former age, the written imagination of the end of orality, but it also traces the failure of the hero. The epic is thus doubly subsequent. It follows the disappearance of a former culture and it follows in the wake of the fallen hero, whose praises it would sing if it did not also know about the guilt he has incurred, a guilt specifically in relationship to that erstwhile cultural world. This complex epigonality points, finally, to the standing of the epic as written and as autonomous. The double subsequentiality should be understood as a kind of underscored abstraction, since the work is about nothing that is present, and doubly so. It signifies absence in the manner that is characteristic of written symbolization, a sense of evanescence that is constitutive of writing and ultimately much more profound than the impermanence of the spoken word. In its preference for topics that are absent, or which have been destroyed, the epic furthermore underscores its own standing as autonomous literature. It is not a report on the life of the hero, not a repetition of that which is merely the case in the given world, and surely not a documentation of context, but a formalized representation of the negation of its own putative content. The epic is not about the days of yore; it is about their end. It is not about the hero; it is about the hero's death. The integrity of autonomy depends on this logic of abstraction. The work of literature is ultimately about itself, subjecting all positive content to a formal negation. Hence Siegfried's betrayal and Roland's death. This formal integrity grants the literary work a freedom in relationship to the world, and it therefore models autonomy as a desideratum in the civilizational process. The violence of the ancient epic indicates the struggle to break the free work out of the constraints of oppressive context. It therefore anticipates directly the refinement of form and the lability of content in modern poetics.

THE ADOPTION OF the new technology of writing allows for the confluence of verbal art, previously restricted to oral performance, and visual representation. Written literature is the visual representation of the imaginative use of language. It separates the author from the public and thereby puts an end to or, at least, greatly reduces the leveling effect of homeostasis. The author escapes collectivist pressure to conformism, the work gains a formal integrity, and the content of the work comes to include the heroic individual. Individuation, as separation from community, attracts hostile suspicion in nonliterate oral communities.[18] The epic records the exploits of the individuated hero, including his aspiration to achieve and maintain individual standing. The prominence of the epic hero is the diegetic echo of the separation of writing from homeostasis, a double process, pursuing both freedom and loneliness. The isolation of the writer is the enfigurement of autonomy and its emancipatory potential. Without solitude, neither the integrity of the work nor the concentration of the author would be possible, as modern authors well recognize. Thus, for example, Marguerite Duras: "A separation is always necessary from the people around the one who writes the books. It is solitude. It is the solitude of the author, and of the writing. To commence, one asks what this surrounding solitude is. . . . This real solitude of the body becomes the inviolable solitude of writing."[19] As a perpetual crucible of individuality, written literature announces the possibility of integrity and autonomy. It contributes to the dynamism of the civilizational process not only because it is linked to a literacy that participates in the dissemination of technical skills, but because literature — in the figure of the creative author, the paradigm of the fictional character, and the reader in front of the book — is the milieu in which creative and thoughtful individuals are nurtured. Literature is central to the liberal arts curriculum not for reasons of ideological mobilization but because literature has served, in effect, as the liberal arts education of humanity.

The epic hero emerged as a function of writing in the context of social differentiation and the competition among alternative sectors. The phenomenology of the written word determined the nature of the epic, and its hero, who mirrored the author's escaping the pressures of community opinion. The heroic condition reproduces the condition of the author: breaking with norms, asserting freedom, and running risks. The urgency of those risks and the lability of the enterprise of individuation are measured by the likelihood of the death of the hero. Epic writing, like later literary writing more generally, finds itself in a competitive field, besieged by the proliferation of other texts, alternative modalities of expression — visual and oral — and subject to denigration from the standpoint of the active life of political power. Literature struggles to assert its autonomy against these rivals, just as it asserts its own validity against death, the knowledge of which is embedded in the work's very substance. Asserting itself against dissolution, literature becomes autonomous and free.

This discussion of epic heroism was introduced in chapter 3 with reference to Flaubert's adversarial standing vis-à-vis nineteenth-century French society. Whence the strength of character to maintain his criticism? What imbues the author of literature with the capacity to judge his surroundings with such vehemence? To be sure, one could provide specific answers with regard to Flaubert himself, or the romantic definitions of literature current since around 1800. Much more, however, is at stake. For Flaubert stands precisely for the adversariality that derives from literary autonomy, and literary autonomy is a result of a long human history with several components, but particularly the fact of writing itself. Of course, not all writing is autonomous literature. But we are concerned with the imaginative use of language, its transformation into visual signs, arguably amplified by the dissemination

The Epic and the Individual

potential associated with alphabetic scripts, and compounded by religious, political, and democratic parameters that will be addressed in the next chapters. In the meantime, it is the transition to writing that we have isolated, for argumentative purposes, all the while trying to underscore the fact that writing never operated in isolation.

Nor did it ever operate without deleterious results as well. Goody and Watt qualified their insistence on the developmental consequences of literature by enumerating the disadvantages, the never-ending production of texts, the professionalization of expertise, and the alienation of the specialized elite from the general public.[20] Yet the hesitation about writing is already evident in Plato, as is well known, in *Phaedrus*. The reflection on the trivialization of memory through the dissemination of dubious texts represents one of the most strident critiques of the new literate culture of Athens. It stands at odds with the attack on poets in *The Republic*, which was ultimately an attack on the culture of orality. Insistent on the thesis of Plato's advocacy for the transition to writing, Havelock remarkably ignores *Phaedrus* in his otherwise comprehensive *Preface to Plato*. At the very least, one could attribute Plato's ambivalence to the transitional moment in Greek culture between orality and literacy. Yet, when we look more closely at *Phaedrus*, it is not simply nostalgia for orality that we find. True, the dialogue (itself a written imitation of an oral setting, mixing genres and therefore structurally comparable to Aristotle's account of the dramatic quality of the Homeric epic) dwells on the deleterious effect of written texts, but it cannot wish them out of the world. Therefore, it implicitly reaches toward a new norm. The point is not to banish writing because it is harmful, but to expect it to meet the standards of oral criticism. For it is in speaking and listening that an authentic truth is attained. This still is consistent with the oralists' description of the superiority of preliterate communication.

Nonetheless, Plato has Socrates suggest, only seemingly in passing, a point at which orality and literacy meet: "the principles of justice and goodness and nobility taught and communicated orally for the sake of instruction and graven in the soul, which is the true way of writing."[21] Orality is the proper vehicle of instruction and criticism, and there is no doubt that writing can impoverish knowledge by separating it from the vibrancy of exchange and reducing it to external possession. But Socrates identifies a higher goal of "the true way of writing," a writing in the soul, that establishes the integrity of a personality, imbued with interiority, and thereby an access to a philosophical truth. The argument may have little to do with the specificity of the imagination and imaginative literature, but it has everything to do with the consequences of literacy for individuation. Even in the context of *Phaedrus*, the classical site of the oralist anxiety over the proliferation of writing, a promising constellation of writing, individuality, and autonomy breaks through. "Writing in the soul" is Plato's designation for this autonomy project. The next chapter, which includes further discussion of *Phaedrus* and its relationship to liturgy, turns to the question of the soul, or more specifically, the sacrality of the word in religion and its particular consequences for the construction of literary autonomy.

The Epic and the Individual

Religion and Writing

THE PREVIOUS CHAPTERS examined the ramifications of writing technology for the constitution of literature. As significant as this materiality of writing and literacy practices remains for understandings of literature and the expectations internalized in literary works, it is nonetheless not the case — as will be shown in this section — that the acquisition of the new technology of writing alone provides a sufficient explanation for the phenomenon of literature. To be sure, literature is dependent on the media that transport it, but it is not fully determined by such media-technological conditions. Autonomous literature presumes writing, but it cannot be reduced fully to an effect of writing. If that were the case, one might then proceed to wonder whether different types of script — hieroglyphic, ideographic, alphabetic — generated distinct logics of literacy leading to necessarily different types of texts: Chinese literature an effect of ideographs, Hebrew literature a result of Hebrew script, and so on. Similarly, one would necessarily place considerable emphasis on the ruptures in the history of writing itself as pivotal events in literary history: the "history of the book," the spread of paper, Gutenberg's printing with movable type, and the more recent technological innovations, particularly in the electronic media.

These could be fruitful lines of inquiry that might form the roadmap for a possible field within a genuine discipline of comparative literature. Yet this examination would also force a distinction between the technological history of writing and the poetic history of literature. The material technologies of writing — including the specific script as well as the material tools themselves: pens, papers, printers — are after all not sufficient explanations for the character of literature. The media-technological approach to the history of literature is fundamentally inadequate because something else enters the mix in order to constitute literature and our expectations of the literary work. This supplement involves the specific spiritualities of transcendence that defined the Western tradition and that established the distinctive Western understanding of its sacred texts. To be sure, the West of Judeo-Christianity is not the only culture organized around the sacrality of texts; the cultural transitions associated with the spread of axial religions is a nearly universal phenomenon.[1] Yet it is in the West in particular, and in a particularly important way, that the mantle of sacrality has come to define the field of literature and the expectations around a literary work. It is not writing technology alone that constitutes the phenomenon of literature; literature is also a consequence of deep cultural expectations about creation, faith, and redemption, all of religious provenance, which enable literature in the sense that it has developed over the past millennia. Without transcendent religion, no literature, and certainly no literary history.

Of course, literacy acquisition and associated technologies have had a profound effect on society in general. The more narrow focus at this point in the argument, though, is the historical emergence and development of literature as autonomous literature, that is, as structured utilizations of imaginative language, rather than wholesale social change. This specifically literary process of autonomization cannot be accounted for solely in terms of the paradigm of a transition from orality to literacy. The inadequacy of the media-technological approach becomes evident in two problems: first, the foundational critique of literacy in *Phaedrus,* and second, the hypothetical derivation of the heroic epic examined in the previous chapter. In both instances, one finds the media-technological or orality-versus-literacy approaches unable to account for core literary phenomena, which presumably have another source. There must therefore be more to the story of literary origins than alphabetization and its consequences. This additional component is religion, to which we will turn after a discussion of the two revealing cases we have cited.

BEYOND THE BINARY opposition of orality and literacy, a third component emerges in the foundational analysis of the transition to literacy, *Phaedrus.* Despite his dismissive contempt for existing literate culture, Socrates nonetheless points to a potentially true writing, a writing in the heart or in the soul. This Archimedean point of authenticy stands opposed to the

Religion and Writing

false writing, or the falseness of standard writing, associated with Lysias and with Phaedrus, and which is the very motor of the dialogue. One can only guess whether an authentic writing would stand opposed to the inadequacies of orality, or whether the appeal to a true writing indicates a potential to retrieve something approaching the integrity of orality in a later and very different historical era.

In addition, however, that appeal to an authentic interiority is followed by a sudden transition in the nature of the dialogue's speech. (In this dialogue, speech is a topic of writing, and one faces a structural crossing of orality and literacy in the genre itself.) The transition occurs when Socrates abruptly concludes matters by reaching to prayer. Why this sudden demonstration of piety and the shift of linguistic register? Prayer certainly surpasses both the degraded dimension of mendacious writing, as well as the perhaps admirable give and take of oral discourse that, we know, Socrates values so much. Instead, as a sort of resolution to the dispute between the two principles, Socrates enacts another linguistic principle altogether, when he moves into prayer at the conclusion: "Beloved Pan, and all ye other gods who haunt this place, give me beauty in the inward soul; and may the outward and inward man be at one. May I reckon the wise to be the wealthy, and may I have such a quantity of gold as a temperate man and he only can bear and carry."[2] As Catherine Pickstock has argued in her critique of Jacques Derrida's reading of the dialogue, Phaedrus and Lysias are associated with the city as a site of commerce, power, and deception. Socrates's appeal in his prayer for modest wealth represents a counter to the avarice of the world of exchange, while simultaneously invoking a model of harmony: a harmony of the inner and outer man, to be sure, but also of the one and the many. Hence the reference to the one god, and then the others, anticipating the immediately subsequent exchange between Socrates and Phaedrus. Just as Socrates has commenced with the one, and then opens to the plurality and difference of other deities, he turns to Phaedrus to ask if more should be added to the prayer. Proceeding from the supplementarity of additional gods, he moves toward the possibility of addition from his interlocutor. This is the very structure of prayer. The liturgical moment is the point where difference and addition can enter a world that is open to transcendence. Plato cleverly allows Phaedrus to reply in a way that captures the complexity of difference and identity in the eros of friendship: He asks Socrates to ask for the same for him, insisting that "friends should have all things in common."

The assertion that friends should share common things does not amount to an agenda for social policy. It is after all a claim about friends, a private category, and not about citizens as members of a state. Something quite different is at stake: the questions of singularity and plurality, the one and the many, repetition and change. What is the relationship of identity, a given identity, to the possibility of difference: both to a different identity (a friend, for example, but also a god) and to becoming different? The prayer appears to resolve the tensions of the dialogue, the binary opposition of writing and speech, by adding the dimension of liturgy. It is only in the context of the appeal to the gods — more precisely, to the one god, and to the many — that the dialectical stalemate between orality and literacy opens onto a wider field. Rather than approaching the question of literary history or, indeed, the larger question of civilizational development with a single-minded focus on communicative technologies, we find this seminal analysis of orality and literacy pointed toward the role of religious experience and transcendence in the human condition.

Phaedrus traces the social and cultural consequence of writing, as Pickstock has amply demonstrated.[3] Literacy implies greater accuracy, as evidenced by the exchange over determining spatial location. Phaedrus insists on determining the "exact spot" (266) where Boreas carried off Orithyia, while Socrates is satisfied with much less accuracy and also displays a greater suppleness of thought. The precision made possible by written records carries with it the risk of a reified reductionism, the narrow-mindedness, endemic in the processes of bureaucratic state-building for which writing was central. The Socratic resistance to writing is therefore not at all a nostalgia for a lost paradise of orality but a penetrating recognition of a cultural impoverishment that can accompany the indisputable progress of writing. For writing, despite the pretense of accuracy, is also associated with concealment and misrepresentation — Phaedrus carries Lysias's speech hidden under his cloak — in contrast to the forthright face-to-face interchange with Socrates.

Moreover, the carrier of writing, Phaedrus, resorts to threats of violence against his interlocutor Socrates: "I would have you consider that from this place we stir not until you have unbosomed yourself of the speech; for here are we all alone, and I am stronger, remember, and younger than you: — Wherefore perpend, and do not compel me to use violence" (274). Thus Phaedrus's model combines a simplistic notion of accuracy coupled with brute domination. It is not that the psychological orientation toward accuracy, provided by writing, is simplistic. Rather this particular version of accuracy entails a diminished definition of the world simply as it is, rather than how it changes. This diminishment furthermore implies a propensity to violent manipulation of a brittle cosmos, without nuance or malleability. In contrast, Socrates explores possibilities of being that allow for flexibility, innovation, and openness: an openness both to others and to the divine. Thus Pickstock: "Socrates maintains a suspicion of all violent or insidious exteriorities, those which, it would seem, merely affirm the division of interior and exterior. The modes of exteriority which are given a positive account are those which do not violate the boundary by force, but which inspired a willing opening of the inside to receive or commune harmonically with the outside, whether divine or earthly. . . . [F]rom the myriad stimuli in which the philosopher-lover is immersed one should derive . . . an account of the self as constituted by its opening to receive its environment, both physical and divine."[4]

It is therefore prayer that concludes the dialogue as a corrective to the violence of writing. Plato suggests that writing reduces the human condition, and, in the same vein, he associates that reduction with violence. This is surely much the same as Ong's insight into the deleterious consequences of writing for community. In this way the historical process becomes considerably more complex than the binary suggested either by Havelock, with his relatively positive assessment of the world of orality, or by the developmentalists such as Goody and Watt with their emphasis on the acquisition of literacy. The two sides in that debate share the basic division between orality and literacy, albeit with different valorizations. In *Phaedrus* one finds, however, that a critique of literacy does not necessarily imply a return to the orality of myth. Beyond the narrow choice of myth and a demythologizing conceptual thinking, the dialogue introduces a third position, a liturgical moment, and therefore points to the possibility of transcendence. No matter how this transcendence may have always and everywhere represented a human possibility—as it evidently did for the pagan Socrates—it is nonetheless not in the philosophy of Athens but in the spirituality of Jerusalem that this defining component of Western culture develops most vibrantly.

THE RECOGNITION OF the cultural standing of religious transcendence also invites a revision of the account of the constitution of the heroic epic. As argued in chapter 5, the heroic epic merges the exploits of an emerging individuality with the adversarial task of the writer, asserting himself against his own mortality. Gilgamesh is both political hero and writer, and in both capacities he does battle with death. Yet if the epic is the first crystallization of writing and literacy, then precisely the question of battle, that is, of the violence that characterizes heroic epics takes on a new significance in light of the above reflections on Phaedrus's threat. His readiness to harm Socrates, as an expression of the degraded culture of writing, is fundamentally one with the violence that defines all the epic heroes, themselves effects of the new technology: Achilles, Odysseus, Siegfried, and Roland. Writing elicits heroism and violence. This claim follows from a concatenation of the arguments in chapter 5 with the analysis implied in *Phaedrus*. The more interesting question now, however, is why those accounts of violence, the extensive descriptions of heroic brutality, are not simply "accurate" (in the reified sense of Phaedrus's positivism as in his search for an exact location), nor simply celebrations of brutality, but in fact also entail deeply anguished records of suffering and therefore a protest against violence. It is precisely that capacity for an empathetic solidarity that is intimately linked to transcendence and to its expression in liturgy. Where does this solidarity come from?

The durability of writing confronts the writer with the question of mortality, leading to the obsession with death in the epic, as written genre, as well as to violence. It is moreover the capacity of writing to separate the author, as individual, from the community, protecting him from the physical threats of homeostatic pressure. A consequence is the constitution of the hero as, ultimately, an outsider who challenges the status quo: Odysseus's ability to flout the decrees of deities, or Siegfried's intrusion at the Burgundian court. Nonetheless, it is impossible to read the heroic epics as unambiguously affirmative accounts of heroic violence. Perhaps the case for a mitigation of violence is most difficult in the Homeric texts. To be sure, Adorno claims that the account of the slaughter of the women of Ithaca, punished for their prostitution (Book 22 of the *Odyssey*), suggests a denunciation of violence, despite the absence of an explicit voice of condemnation.[5] That critical distance derives, presumably, from the very logic of an autonomous aesthetics, rather than from any tendentious intent, for which there is no evidence. It is not, however, clear how one could demonstrate that such a reading derives from the character of the text itself, rather than from the sensibility of the reader. Is it the *Odyssey* that conveys this caring, or is it Adorno, the reader? Still, even if we concede that the Homeric recording of the slaughter rescues the violence from oblivion and preserves it for posterity, and even if we overlook the potential counterargument that precisely such recording might be intended as an admonition to servants to be loyal to their masters rather than some insistence that servants' suffering has as much claim on poetic representation as do the deaths of heroes, it is nonetheless the case that this sort of putatively critical stance is quite muffled. One need only compare the silent objectivity of Homer in the face of these deaths or the destruction of Troy with the eloquence of Jeremiah in response to the destruction of Jerusalem in *Lamentations* or the insistence on transcendence in Christian accounts of martyrdom. Whatever natural aspiration to redemption and transcendence might be evidenced in the written document simply as written, or in the pagan work of art, takes on a qualitatively different character after the spiritual revolution inherent in the axial religions of Judaism and Christianity. Accounts of violence and human suffering cease to be acceptable as facts of human life, given the admonition to "choose life" (Deuteronomy 30:19) or the primacy of love (1 Corinthians 13).

We have already looked at the conclusion of the *Chanson de Roland*, where Charlemagne sits in tears at the destruction and loss, while the author appears in counterpoint confronting the end of his narration and an end of history: not some ultimate peace but the full recognition of catastrophe. Charlemagne's tears imply an aspiration to a lost completeness and divine redemption, even as he refuses the archangel's request that he carry the battle further. He displays his faith, paradoxically, through the rejection of the divine demand for a continuation of the holy war. Mourning similarly defines the end of the *Nibelungenlied*, significantly in a way that crosses the battle lines and obscures the hierarchies of the feudal order.

> Ditrich und Etzel   weinen dô began,
> Si klagten inneclîche   beide mâge unde man.
>
> [Dietrich and Etzel began to weep, and
> deeply they lamented both kinsmen and vassals.][6]

Their tears are inclusive, mourning all: Kriemhild and Hagen, relatives (or equals) and troops. This unrestricted field of death is then allegorized into an emblem of the frailty of all existence and an ineluctable passage from happiness to sorrow. Word choices refer back explicitly to the open strophe of the epic, indicating the composed and written character of the text, underscored by the element of self-reflection at the very conclusion.

Ine kán iu niht bescheiden, waz sider dâ geschach:
Wan ritter unde vrouwen   weinen man dâ sach,
Dar zuo die edeln knehte   ir lieben fruinde tôt.
Hie hât daz mære ein ende: daz ist der Nibelunge nôt.

[I cannot tell you what happened after this,
except that knights and ladies, yes, and noble squires, too,
were seen weeping there for the death of dear friends.
The story ends here: such was the Nibelungs' Last Stand.]

The narratorial subject also confronts his own end and the limit of his incantatory power, although well aware that mourning, indeed a collective mourning, will continue. Yet the story, the *maere*—a singular, in contrast to the plural *maeren* of the first strophe, suggesting a transition from the textual indeterminacy of orality to the accuracy of written versions in the very course of the epic—here comes to an end.[7] The fact of ending, the story and the lives, is what elicits the sorrow, but such sorrow makes sense only on the assumption that this sort of violence should not happen—on the basis of what ethical claims?—and that a redemptive transcendence might be imaginable, beyond the conclusion of the recitation.

The sorrow at the end conflates the author's regret at the conclusion of his story, the observers' mourning of the death of the figures, and the familiar affect of the reader, sad that a good read has come to an end. In all these variants, a melancholy implies the counterfactual expectation of a continuation beyond the arbitrary limits of the work and the ends of existence. The lamentational moment points to a sense of an infinite, denied in the terminations faced by mortals, but nonetheless undeniably promised. The self-confidence of the Homeric narrator, his so-called objectivity, in contrast, suggests a thorough acceptance of an ultimately closed world: Even the gods are fully continuous with men. In the melancholy epics, however, lamentation is directed not only at the narrated deaths but also at the inadequacy of the narrational voice itself. The narrator can doubt himself only because of the internalization of a norm of transcendence and redemption.[8]

The spiritual sensibility that implies recognition of the possibility of transcendence points in multiple directions. It transcends the limitations of the individual hero in order to imply a human solidarity, a community that is open, rather than exclusive, allowing for the ability to mourn for all dead, including the enemy. It also suggests the limitations of the individual narrator and therefore the inadequacy of his isolated voice. For Pickstock, this "narratorial dereliction," the internalized sense of inadequacy, defines liturgical performance and derives from the characteristically prophetic resistance to speech: "the same 'slow tongue' of Moses, the 'unclean lips' of Isaiah, the demur of Jeremiah, and the mutism of Ezekiel." Both points stand in contrast to the model of the Homeric epic, whose purpose is "to glorify the deeds of men," understood as conclusive, while transcendence implies a constant openness beyond that which is already given.[9] Yet precisely that openness of transcendence also implies the inadequacy and incompletion of the given reality: context and contemporaneity are not enough.

Plato has Socrates suddenly move beyond the critique of literacy by breaking into a prayer. Similarly, our reconsideration of the epic indicates that as much as its violence and heroism are grounded in the phenomenology of writing, its mournful character is informed by a sensibility that cannot be described plausibly as simply an effect of writing. Therefore this inquiry into the foundations of a history of literature and its entwinement in the civilizational process cannot help but recognize the definitive and central standing of an element beyond writing, religion, especially the sacrality of scripture, in the historical constitution of the literary work of art. Neither the binary opposites of orality and literacy, nor their presumed corollaries, myth and demythologization, are adequate without reference to this third and independent variable, which involves the human possibility of participation in the divine. While the transition to the new technology of writing affected the imaginative use of language in the multiple ways described in the previous chapter, particularly the independence, autonomy, and isolation of the writer, the distinct experience of transcendence allows for the capacity to escape that isolation, without a regression to mythic formulations. Religion, therefore, in the emphatic sense used here, is not somehow an effectively mythic "before" to writing and philosophy. It is, on the contrary, "after writing" — the title of Pickstock's volume — in other words, very much a corrective to the trivializing and violent potentials of writing described so trenchantly in *Phaedrus*. This civilization-historical significance of faith is therefore enormously important for the constitution of the work of literature in several ways. This chapter explores these connections: if faith, then fiction, as fiction inherits the redemptive mantle of faith.

THE DUAL FOCUS on language origins and writing origins is intended to suggest both genuinely chronological phases — major transitions in civilization history took place fifty thousand years ago, and three thousand years ago — as well as logical aspects in the constitution of the literary work. Those distant pasts therefore remain present in the contemporary work of literature, insofar as they persist as functions both of language itself and of the specific dynamics generated by writing technology and the associated tensions between writing and speech.

These two claims are joined by a third: the history of literature undergoes a further and similarly definitive rupture with the establishment of the world religions. Judaism/Christianity as well as the spread of Buddhism, Confucianism, Hinduism, and Islam fundamentally restructure the cultural articulations of the human condition in ways that are both comparable and profoundly different. In most instances, the spread of the new religions establishes a central set of canonized and sacred texts, the dissemination of which is crucial. It is writing (although surely not writing alone) that allows the world religions to spread, and the religious transformation is to a large extent a matter of asserting the supremacy of certain texts. To what extent the consequences of Buddhism, Confucianism, Hinduism, and Islam included a redefinition of texts in general, and in particular literary texts, is a possible project for a genuine field of comparative literature. To be sure, the general cultural consequences of literacy in China and India were dissimilar from each other, and certainly from the West.[10] Understanding the particular literary consequences (as opposed to general social or cultural ramifications) is a more precise question. Yet it is certainly the case that the religious revolutions of Judaism and Christianity are foundational to Western cultural definitions and — this is our concern here — the character of the literary work of art. Without reflection on the particular cultural history of Western religion, the character of Western literature remains incomprehensible.

For Pascal, in the fourth of his *Pensées*, the alternative to fallen nature is writing or scripture, *écriture*. For Coleridge, scripture, the Bible, represents the "living educts of the imagination."[11] At stake for both is an act of faith as imagination in a relationship to texts. We approach the question of religion certainly not as ideology, not even in the sophisticated Feuerbachian form as a projection of human desires. Rather, the counterfactuality of faith stands behind and permits the imagination of literature. Heir to the religious tradition, literature inherits the sacrality of the holy word. Because no work of literature is a holy book — except the holy books themselves, which may be literature but which are certainly not only literature — and that difference, the insurmountable distance between the holy word and the epigonic work, contributes to the melancholy of the narrator, always falling short of the sacred norm. The literary work of art does not achieve the perfection of its implicit model. Yet it is more importantly the case that no work of literature, at least in the Western tradition, can escape that imitative competition with the sacred word and is therefore always implicitly measured in terms of its relationship to transcendence and redemption. The autonomy of the work of literature, or rather the autonomy to which a genuine work aspires, is an imitation of the divine word. The creative mandate of the author, called upon to generate that which is genuinely new (no matter how one necessarily draws on inherited material) invokes the model of the creation. Such relationships are much more substantive than questions of dogmatic belief, religious affiliation of authors, or the literary deployment of biblical or other sacred material in secular fiction. Well beyond such tracings of specific religious identity in literary works, literature and religion interact to the extent that the Judeo-Christian legacy redefines the value of texts. Furthermore, their core precepts of transcendence become normative expectations throughout the culture and, especially, in literary works, no matter how ostensibly secular and devoid of explicit religious reference. The categories of modern literature are, fundamentally, religious.

To suggest that the constitution of literature derives from a religious legacy is counterintuitive. Histories of literature typically attempt to lodge literary autonomy in a modernity defined by the marginalization of religion, relegated increasingly to a private sphere. As a result, the heroic story of modern art, and literature in particular, typically involves its struggle to escape the control of traditional religious authority. Indeed, it is fully parallel to the same story that is told for modern science. Galileo's battle with the church is one with the emancipation of literature from censorship and the *Index Librorum Prohibitorum*, and it is a battle for freedom that continues in the contemporary conflicts between religious institutions and instances of postmodern art: The acts or threats of censorship elicited by abrasive representations in turn call forth appeals to the need for poetic license, freedom of speech, and the separation of church and state. Ultimately the standard accounts of cultural modernization, whether they pertain to art or science, carry with them the hostile Enlightenment evaluation of religion that culminated in Voltaire's judgment: *Écrasez l'infame!*

Yet this liberal account of autonomy as the separation of the individual and cultural formations from the control of religious and political authority misses the very grounding of those claims to autonomy in a longer tradition of authoritative Judeo-Christian norms. Secularization is of course hardly irrelevant to literary history, yet neither is it irrelevant to religion, as any reader of the prophets quickly recognizes. But the relevance of secularization to literature is not a matter of the necessity of an escape from religion. Religion is not an outside to literature, a prehistory to be overcome and repressed. On the contrary, the very elaboration of the expectations of transcendence inherent in Judaism and Christianity enables the Western literary tradition. Precisely because of the religious constitution of literary autonomy, its dependence on sacred norms to elaborate its own agenda, the historical process of secularization, and the ontological condition of the distinction between the sacred and the profane are indispensable to literature and its history. Conventional wisdom describes a modernization in which fiction can free itself from faith. What such wisdom misses is how both faith and fiction depend on a valorization of counterfactuality, which can be socially productive by providing the institutional frame for a cognitive freedom. Religion and literature permit, indeed depend on, the capacity to surpass the reality that is merely given. The marginalization of religion through dogmatic secularization, like a degradation of imaginative literature, undermines that freedom.

The transition to writing was the precondition for epic poetry. Alphabetization initiated a specific process of rationalization in Platonic Greece, and that rationalization produced a differentiated sector of reflection on literature that was called "poetics" in ancient philosophy. Yet both the transition to writing and this rationalizing differentiation are insufficient to explain the aspiration to literary autonomy; that was the point of our earlier examination of *Phaedrus* and the *Nibelungenlied*. The promise of redemption, which literature inherits from religion, resists the reduction of the world to the heroic isolation of the epics or to Phaedrus's positivism. Moreover, this redemptive pathos, the promise of another world, reinforces the imaginative potential in language as such. The linguistic use of symbols presumes imagination, but it is in the institutionalized language usages of literature and religion that this imaginative capacity is consistently cultivated. This realization evokes Coleridge's pairing of scripture and imagination. The following sections of this chapter examine three distinctive, if overlapping, aspects of the literary work of art as it depends on the religious legacy.

THE SCHOLAR OF religion John Milbank has pointed out how Aristotle retained considerable hesitation about the notion of poesis, somehow always in the shadow of praxis, particularly in the *Nichomachean Ethics*. Because praxis contains its end in itself, it provides the Aristotelian model of autonomous activity, while poesis, which brings forth an object — and an object, moreover, that imitates a real world object through mimesis — slides dangerously close to the degraded realm of techne. Is the artist perhaps only an artisan? Aristotle "is wary of poesis because a shadow of techne hangs over it which Aristotle's categorical equipment is not altogether adequate to banish. For only the 'internal' act of praxis was conceivable by him as entirely outside the manipulative anticipations of technique."[12] At stake is the judgment on poesis: Is it a degraded craftsmanship or an innovative creativity? The case for the former could point to the standing of the product as a secondary expression of an otherwise complete subject, and very quickly such a productive subject — productive because poetic — might find himself lost among a surfeit of these externalizations, strange and estranged. By making more and more things, the subject engaged in poesis in this sense reduces the world to things and thereby threatens to become little more than a thing himself. If he is assumed to be initially complete, then the products are either superfluous or deleterious, in this Aristotelian theory of alienation, echoes of which linger in subsequent hesitations about art as mere ornament and therefore superfluous. To argue, alternatively, for a poesis that is genuinely creative (rather than merely productive), the Aristotelian understanding of the human subject has to undergo an anthropological reassessment, involving a recognition of human incompleteness in the world. In turn, the standing of the results of poesis could be reevaluated, once there is room for surplus, change, and gift. But this nonartisanal understanding of poesis and its outcome requires moving outside the Aristotelian ontology in order to find a richer treatment of creativity.

If the work of art as an imitation of nature is conceived only as a repetition of the already given, it is not new at all but in effect redundant and creative only in the limited sense of having been realized in material. It may document the intention of the artist, but it lacks any significant relationship to the future except as a durable record for future recipients.[13] If, however, the work, not merely the end product but equally the process of its fashioning, is seen as a site of genuine innovation, then creativity takes on a different character: the introduction of the radically new and unexpected into the world as an unencumbered and consequently free process, a gift. Therefore, the work of art becomes a cipher for aspiration and freedom, and this is precisely the line of division between the classical Greek conceptualizations, both Platonic and Aristotelian, and the implications of biblical spirituality.

The Hebrew assertion of the unqualified newness of creation is not limited or restricted in the manner of the Greek mythologies, which are always burdened by earlier generations of gods. Genesis describes a radically new beginning, foreign to the Greek mind. Furthermore, the biblical accounts of divine intervention into human history are emphatically innovative in a way quite distinct from the Greek gods' perpetual reestablishment of the already given, when they meddle in human affairs but never profoundly transform them. This innovation implies that creation is constantly renewed, just as it is always new, in contrast to the inescapable epigonality of the Greek sense of time. Hence the assertion of Christian time as prefatory in contrast to the closed or epilogic character of pagan temporality.[14] The distinction is quite obvious in terms of the characterizations of personalities in representative texts. Homeric use of epithets implies an unchanging stability of the person, in effect regardless of experience and with no room for transformative reflection. Whatever the vicissitudes of life, whatever may have transpired, whatever challenges he faces, Odysseus is always cunning, but of course never cunning enough to be able to change. In contrast, the laughter of Sarah, when she learns that she will give birth — laughter that is inscribed in the name of Isaac or Yitzhak — has no epithetic value at all; it does not reduce Isaac to a one-dimensional character trait, as is Odysseus. Not only is Isaac not constrained by a singular descriptive term; he like other figures in both Hebrew and Christian texts undergoes profound internal changes. The completeness of the Greek world, by definition, has no room for the possibility of creativity, and therefore innovation described by the Bible.

This distinct view of the possibility of change in the world inspires the expectation of innovation that comes to inform the work of art. The work of art is not a derivative of the given but rather itself an indication of the potential for an innovative gift, endowed with the capacity to surpass any existing state of affairs. This distinctive innovation underlies the critique of idolatry: "The critique of idolatry always involved something more than the natural suspicion of one religion concerning others, but implied that the true God was most neglected by the 'religious' tendency to make absolute and alien some valued object within culture which is always humanly engendered."[15] Pagan idols limited the infinity of openness in a way homologous with the attributive epithet in Homer: an assertion of the past instead of the possibility for the future. The critique of idolatry is therefore, in a sense, an anticipation of the modern critique of alienation: the effort to emancipate humanity from a self-limitation by its own products. As the work of art inherits the legacy of that critique, through the antirepresentationalism of the biblical prohibition on images and later through a Christian aesthetic of dereliction — images of abjection rather than completion — and allegory, it can move toward the center of cultural expression and self-definition. If Aristotle ultimately kept the artist near the artisan and therefore marginal, the Jewish-Christian redefinition of creativity allows for a crucial centrality to the work of art: It becomes the appearance of the new in the world, and therefore the promise that the world can always be renewed — not restored to some *status quo ante* but fundamentally reopened to innovative freedom.

This magnified urgency devolves upon the work of art and becomes constitutive of the expectations directed at art and literature in the West; to designate art as merely entertaining or ornamental always implies that it has somehow failed to fulfill its mandate. Two further factors compound this importance of art. The first involves a profoundly different anthropology. The aesthetic of dereliction involves representations of suffering, especially the crucifixion, which cannot be more different from the paradigmatic celebrations of human form in classical Greek sculpture. Suffering becomes a preferred subject matter, hence the slave mentality to which Nietzsche dismissively objected in Christianity. A latter-day review of this conflict between a pagan humanism and Christian suffering stands at the core of the debates between Settembrini and Naptha in Thomas Mann's *Magic Mountain*. Of course human frailty and anguish pervade the Hebrew Bible as well, notably in the anxiety of the Psalmist but surely also in the narrative of enslavement in Exodus. For Greek philosophy, the freedom inherent in praxis and, as we saw, presumably absent in a technical reduction of poesis, applies in particular to the citizen and not to the slave. Those category distinctions preclude one of the defining features of biblical spirituality, which is the blurring of the line, the possibility of the slave to become free and, by extension, the dialectic of abjection and redemption: Suffering humanity can participate in divine grace. This is the point of continuity between Jewish and Christian accounts — but obviously also the definitive point of rupture as well — the account of God as man. A corollary for Paul, and later for Luther, is the dialectic of slavery and freedom. These transformations, emancipation from slavery or redemption to grace, indicate a historical dynamism largely absent in Greek anthropology that accepts a natural distance between slave and citizen.

This religious and anthropological distinction between pagan and Hebrew-Christian accounts is pertinent to the history of literature as art, second, because art henceforth becomes the vehicle for an expression of a critique of suffering and a promise of happiness through redemption. Indeed, it is primarily through the refusal to celebrate the merely given (the critique of idolatry) and the dwelling on suffering (the aesthetics of dereliction) that the work of art can lay claim to the status of truth. This holds for all art: the fact that art in the West develops in the context of religion and through the support of the church, is not primarily sociological evidence of patronage structures or the availability of material resources (although these are not at all irrelevant), but rather an indication of the spiritual substance at the core of the project of Western art as such.

This is especially the case for literature, in the wake of Christianity's narrative of the incarnation of God as Word. As Henri de Lubac wrote: "Christianity is not, properly speaking, a 'religion of the book.' It is a religion of 'the Word,' but not uniquely, or principally, of the Word in either its written or even oral form. It is the religion of the Word, 'not a mute, written word,' says St. Bernard, 'but of a word incarnated and living.'"[16] This passage does not only suggest a distance from the media-technological determinism of the orality-versus-literacy project, but it also indicates the expectation directed at the Word: its capacity to intervene in life, whatever its medium, oral or written. Here de Lubac and Bernard are notably close to Jewish liturgy, which similarly asserts an ambivalence about the medium of transmission — the Torah is "from the mouth of God in the hand of Moses," that is, it is both oral and written, and it is a "tree of life for those who grasp it." The Word is redemptive not because it is either oral or written; indeed, the question of technological medium is surpassed. The Word is redemptive, instead, because it is divine. In both Jewish and Christian versions, the message of divine transcendence, which one might think of as the "content" of the pertinent texts, is ultimately inseparable from the interventionist or world-transformative consequences of the Word. And precisely this transformation is itself a compounding of transcendence: To use the standard spatial metaphors, the vertical transcendence toward God allows for the horizontal transcendence toward humanity, and thus the perpetual potential for transformation in the world. The human or natural world is incomplete; the word of God promises a transformation toward completion.

To demonstrate the enormous difference in the literary imagination effected by transcendent spirituality, one might examine some of the specifically religious literature, such as parables or saints' lives, as examples of transformations. Yet the claim here is not the narrow one that a new devotional literature develops that one could place multiculturally next to classical Greek literature in the framework of a cultural relativism. Rather, In the wake of the spiritual revolution, the literary imagination is so deeply transformed that subsequent writing, even ostensibly secular writing, becomes informed by a vision incompatible with pagan views, even where the specific textual projects might be construed as proximate. All literature now aspires to a spiritual journey toward redemption. Consider for example a comparison of Ovid's *Metamorphoses* and Kafka's *Metamorphosis*, the latter surely not a Christian text and whose arguable relationship to Judaism is in any case not an orthodox or doctrinal one. Both ancient and modern authors, of course, describe transformations, but with deep distinctions. The plural of the Greek title should not be taken as a magnification of the potential of transformation, a radical lability in existence; on the contrary, it has the effect of reducing every particular case to an instance in a repetitive series, each thereby becoming nearly casual. The imbalance in the world, always resolved by the metamorphosis, is typically of a limited character, and the transformation is above all physical. The physical resolution corresponds to an inner intent, with harmony ultimately reestablished. Change takes place in the world, but in a reassuringly conservative manner, perpetually restoring a natural, nearly animistic order. Kafka's singular metamorphosis, in contrast, serves to underscore the uniqueness and incommensurability of the event, its strangeness and particularity, even if, by implication, that strangeness may be universal (the subsequent changes in the family and the growth of the sister point to the ubiquity of transformation, but in equally disquieting ways). The metamorphosis, of course, is not the harmonizing result but the unmotivated outset and the source of irresolvable anguish. The desire for a resolution — Gregor's efforts to come to grips with his condition, the sister's offers of help, the family's rearrangements — stand at odds with the elusiveness of any satisfaction. Even Gregor's death brings nothing to conclusion. The world remains open; the abjection of the work of art holds open the possibility of redemption that Ovid's idolatry forecloses. Ovidian creativity is epilogic, showing how the world became what it always was, and why it must be so; Kafka's prefatory poesis demonstrates the openness of the world and how transformation, as degradation and hope, may still transpire within it.

WHILE THE ESTABLISHMENT of any given canon typically entails debate and conflict, the late twentieth century witnessed bitter polemics within academic literary scholarship over the character of a canonic project altogether. The protest expressed an understanding, or misunderstanding, of the canon as solely a vehicle for the expression of political and social power through the medium of literary selections. This resulted in the calls to direct a hermeneutics of suspicion toward canonic and curricular selections, as well the calls to revise them, along the lines of alternative aspirations for political power.[17] In this view, then, canonization appeared effectively inescapable, although the adjudication of quality shifted from the aesthetic to the political terrain. Alternatively, connoisseurs of the canon, appreciating the putative high quality of masterpieces, insisted on their importance and, especially, on their standing as a resource, a trove of materials for later writers. Robert Alter, for example, underscored this latter point, while also trying to calm anxieties over ideological agenda: All texts are richer than their dogmatic defenders, which allows later writers to reuse classic texts in heterodox manners.[18] Diachronic intertextual referencing does not indicate ideological stability (as the anticanonic camp would have it), but on the contrary, for Alter at least, it points to the possibility of differential reception patterns.

The opposing sides could frequently share a fundamentally postmodern assumption about temporality: the absolute availability of former texts, among which one (or the author) can choose arbitrarily. Yet suspicion, in a negative manner, and connoisseurship, positively, render the relationship to the past nearly ornamental, in no way limited by parameters of historical obligation. Not that either position is devoid of legitimacy: political opinion has indisputably influenced and continues to inform literary reception, and creative authors do draw on traditional material in unpredictable ways. Nonetheless, both perspectives remain strangely uninterested in the particular relationship to the past, that particular historicity of literature that defines Western textuality that emerged after the religious revolution.

As noted above, Pickstock characterizes pagan temporality as epilogic. The present always stands in the wake of a past, and completed, act of creation. Her point is to distinguish this pagan temporal structure from the prefatory anticipations she locates in the Roman rite, as the paradigmatic expression of a Christian phenomenology.[19] But it is not only the relationship to the future that is changed by the promise of redemption; the relationship to the past is changed as well with equal profundity, and hence also the relationship to the past texts. The very promise of redemption is itself a linguistic act and therefore part of the linguistic character of creation; it is always prior to the present, in the form of covenant and revelation. Retrieving that promise involves a process of literary memory, which has no corollary in the pagan world. Of course, the Greek playwrights recycled myths inherited from the past, and Latin literature draws on Greek antecedents. None of this, however, approaches the dynamic necessity and historical teleology inherent in scripture, particularly the retrospective gestures of later texts toward earlier ones: be it a matter of the prophets' references to the early history of Israel, or the New Testament referencing of the Hebrew Bible.[20] The later text does not merely allude to or restage a predecessor (as with pagan literature), but it engages with it in complex ways within a historical process, thereby opening a conversation that continues to shadow the core texts: in the form of Midrash for Judaism or the Christian exegetic tradition that begins with the Church Fathers. To read a text does not merely involve deciphering the written words but also exploring the reception, the notionally *oral* tradition. This is presumed in the critique that Luther's doctrine of *sola scriptura* rips the text out of historical layers of interpretive context: the ultimate anticanonism.[21] Yet precisely those layers are necessary to recognize the objectivity of the historical legacy.

The claim that the past text makes on the present — and this is precisely the question of the canon — is undercut, if the bridge of community between past and present is denied. This is the case where experience is reduced to an exclusively empirical and mathematical world, without the transcendent dimension that defines the revolution of the axial religions. The problem is not empiricism as such but the reifying suggestion that the human condition is adequately accounted for as an accumulation of facts without spiritual aspiration, without a desire for the supernatural. With reference to Peter Ramus (who also figures largely in Ong's work), Pickstock describes this predicament as a reification of memory when "memory becomes a matter of simply a retrieval of objects, merely a kind of stocktaking or enumeration, thus vastly reducing the reach of memory. . . . For when things are 'available' in such a way, epistemological activity becomes purely speculative, and memory is simply a matter of repeating the 'glance,' rather than an act which testifies to the temporality of knowledge and which facilitates the judgment of analogy between instances, ensuring the continuity of the knowing subject."[22]

When the rationalization of the world defines existence exclusively as an accumulation of facts, it renders them ultimately incomprehensible. Interpretation becomes impossible because hypotheses, which require conceptual imagination and which are therefore, by definition, nonfactual, are prohibited. At stake then is an effort to preserve the realm of imagination through the temporal structure associated with faith: Only because of the promise once made are there options to envision the future alternatively. This is not a denial of facticity but a recognition that powers of cognitive creativity are required to grasp it and transform it. It is precisely here that literature, as the privileged vehicle of imagination, coincides with religion as faith and with history as the opportunity for humanity to fashion its own world, not in order to achieve a definitive closure but because of the promise, inherent in transcendence, of infinite openness. Milbank's eloquent characterization of this concatenation might be taken as a summary of the agenda of the theological politics of the movement of radical orthodoxy: "Reason orientated only to a beatitude supposedly within its grasp dispenses with hope, only to land up as without hope, and at best resigned to its condition. . . . What *faith* proposes as reason, then, is taken as hermeneutic keys to reality. First *hope*, and then *charity* which is the erotic lure of the other and our giving ourselves over to the other."[23]

How does this condition define the canonic dimension of literature? The phenomenology of writing as such, with the durability of texts, necessarily poses the question of the author's mortality. The written text will probably outlive its author. The same durability, but of others' texts, confronts the author who, with equal necessity, faces a growing body of existing work, which threatens to overwhelm him. Hence the condition that Harold Bloom designated as the "anxiety of influence," rooted in the very condition of writing. To this characterization, we must add the particular legacies of biblical spirituality: the definition of the act of creation as linguistic and therefore a model for literature as creative and prospective; the insistence on the priority of a revelation, eliciting literature's retrospective vision and its particular relationship to the past. Literature is anticipatory and anamnestic simultaneously, but this capacity for memory is complex, insofar as the literary tradition and the religious tradition intertwine. The author stands in competition with predecessors (even if he mines them, as Alter suggests) and the Bible may at times become one more prior text, another competitor. Yet whereas the epigonality of any writing threatens the writer with obscurity and death (from the power of earlier writers), the promise of transcendence remains a source of consolation. More generally, to the extent that a spirituality of transcendence defines the foundational temporality of the broad

Western cultural tradition within which the work appears, that spirituality is also, ultimately, a source of inspiration. The historicity of the work of literature includes both a resourceful drawing on its past and a rebellious effort to transcend it.

In order to illustrate the character of this temporality, in particular the relationship to the past, and the relevance of transcendence, a specifically nonreligious writer can serve as a useful example. Surely the Marxist Bertolt Brecht is a strange choice with whom to demonstrate the operations of religion in the constitution of the work of literature. Nonetheless a poem such as "To the Burned Poets" clearly thematizes a relationship to the tradition and a fear of obscurity on the part of the poet, just as the well-known programmatic "To Posterity" can easily be read as an exemplification of Brecht's concern with the relationship between past and future. Yet a more concentrated example, the laconic "Hollywood Quatrain" permits an inquiry into the nature of canonicity, within the field of issues described above:

> Jeden Morgen, mein Brot zu verdienen
> Gehe ich auf den Markt, wo Lügen gekauft werden
> Hoffnungsvoll
> Reihe ich mich ein zwischen die Verkäufer.[24]

> [Every morning, to earn my bread
> I go to the market, where lies are bought.
> Full of hope
> I get in line among the sellers.]

The poem no doubt invites the reader to engage in biographical considerations: an expression of Brecht's despair in his California exile during the Nazi era. Indeed, the choice of Hollywood in the title underscores the particularity of the reference, as the German author invokes the American location, and moreover a location with unavoidable cultural connotations. It is obviously not the California landscape or meteorology that is implied by Hollywood but rather film production, the culture industry, which corroborates the intratextual location of the "market where lies are bought."

The laconic lexicon is characteristically Brechtian (although oddly reminiscent of what would come to be considered the typical postwar West German poetic vocabulary of sparseness, the so-called *Kahlschlagliteratur*). Strangely, it also has an archaic ring. The phrase "to earn my bread," particularly in juxtaposition with "every morning" suggests a notion of "daily bread" and points to the German rendering in Luther's translation of the Bible, perhaps particularly to the Lord's Prayer, although here, in the poem, the daily bread is explicitly to be earned and not given. Indeed, three of the four verse lines are dominated by terms that point to an economy of exchange: earn, market, sellers. The singularity of "hopeful" or "full of hope" in the third line stands as an exception, an enfigurement of a donational alternative to the rule of exchange and identity logic: Gift and commodity stand at odds with each other. The *Hoffnungsvoll* marks semantically and structurally a moment of anticipation, breaking out of the lexical consistency of the other verses.

This anticipatory hope embodies the counterfactual principle in the empirical world of exchange. As such, it might be taken as the moment of promise in the poem. That hope at the same time retains an undeniable similarity to the overriding object of economic desire: lies. The poem describes the point where mendacity and fiction overlap, an intersection necessarily problematic for the project of literature. While the term can be taken as an ideologically critical characterization of the activity of Hollywood, particularly in the judgment of the culturally critical German exiles, its resonance is much larger. In terms of poetic sonority, Hollywood and *Hoffnungsvoll* are linked by alliteration and syllabic structure; a deeper connection begins to emerge. "Lies" signify everything that is not true in the sense of the reduced facticity discussed above, the merely empirical world without the openness of transcendence. Lies have in common with hope an incongruence with the merely given: It is the lie that can challenge the ostensible permanence of a bad reality by offering hope. At the very core of this fallen world is a desire to go beyond itself, to find something else that then necessarily cannot be regarded as true in an empirical sense. Indeed, it is the very opposite of the empirical. The lies of literature are revealed to be closer to the hope of faith than to the hopelessness of the historical context.

It follows then that "lies," like "hope," indicate an anticipatory dimension, fractures in the oppressive present of *Jeden Morgen* (wherein the morning is bitterly ironic, insofar as the term tropologically refers to a new beginning). This aspect of the text exemplifies a poetics of creativity, variations on the capacity to articulate qualitatively new alternatives to the status quo: the nonfactual character of the literary imagination is the very basis of its ability to articulate innovation and difference. Against this background, however, the defining moment of the poem, its invocation of canonicity, stands out all the more starkly. The grammar of the poem consists of two simple sentences. The first involves the going to the market, wherein the verb presumably indicates a moving forward and therefore both a spatial direction and a minimal sense of future. The second sentence, however, turns on the reflexive and prepositional verb *sich einreihen zwischen*: to take one's place among or to insert oneself among. While the primary connotation of the verb is spatial, in the sense of squeezing oneself in, there is also a temporal suggestion: entering into the series, taking one's place in a timeline. The ambiguity of the poem depends on the notion of the *einreihen*. Either the desperate and destitute poet is forced to join ranks, with even military connotations, since he has no other source of sustenance, or the subtly triumphal poet is now standing shoulder to shoulder — with whom? — and is therefore hopeful. In the latter case, he grows hopeful against the degraded regime of lies, but hopeful, as well, thanks precisely to the counterfactuality of literary imagination. Surely the others with whom the poet joins are also sellers of lies, producers of fiction, and therefore the authors of the literary tradition, his own predecessors in writing. He joins the canon (of course, this is simply one moment in Brecht's extensive efforts toward self-canonization). The very act of joining the tradition, entering into the ordered series, and taking his place in a literary-historical line is the source of hope. The poem underscores this point through the doubling of semantics with visual, that is, typographical, representation. Grammatically, it is the *I* of the fourth verse that is modified by the hopeful of the third: I am *hopeful* as I join ranks. Yet the *sich einreihen* suggests intruding between existing rows or columns. He is joining in rather than, for example, joining on — *sich anschließen* — which might indeed suggest a mere appendage. This distinction is important because the *Hoffnungsvoll* ideographically inserted between the rows of words represents the very act of intrusion visually. It carries out the function named in the next line. Squeezing oneself in between the lines of literature, or the literary tradition, renews a hope, no matter how futile or mendacious it may appear.

"Hollywood Quatrain" is evidently an exploration of the process of joining a literary tradition, and the associated, complex process of impoverishment and enrichment. His abjection in literature, rather than the economic situation of the exiled poet, stands as a precondition for consolation and hope, which he finds in the tradition. As much as the poem may draw on Brecht's personal experiences, the core of the poem involves the poetic condition as such, and, in particular, its second half names canonicity as a source of poetic strength. It is interesting that, here at least, Brecht is not at all at war with the canon, not competing for greatness, but identifying the tradition of literature, as a source of hope, precisely in its counterfactuality, its nontruth. The tradition carries the message of redemption, the promise of happiness, and, as de Lubac insists, it is not merely a fiction but part of a real history, albeit a reality that involves transcendence.[25] Brecht's four lines, devoid of doctrinal religion and, if anything, marked by his ostensible leftism, are surely far from what might be taken to be examples of religious, devotional, or pious literature; the example is therefore all the more instructive. Despite the presumed secularity of this poem and of Brecht's work in general, the consequences of Judeo-Christian spirituality demarcate this poem and the character of the Western work of literature in general. Just as Kafka's "Metamorphosis" demonstrates the structure of transcendence with regard to creation and innovation in contrast to the pagan immanentism of Ovid, "Hollywood" demonstrates the powerful tug of canonicity as an indebtedness to the past that is inescapable, even for the ideologically nonconservative poet. The poet joins the "rows" (*Reihen*) of authors as a result of his own weakness and isolation in an adversarial situation, but he also joins them in solidarity and compassion. The free act of the gift that is creation is also present in the plenitude of hope in joining the past. The poet does not only wage a battle against the canon; in "Hollywood," Brecht accepts it.

THE PHENOMENOLOGY OF future and past, creativity and canonicity, grounded in a human condition of language, receives a distinctive consecration through religion. Those two dimensions of literariness retain a structural centrality as a result of their sacred articulation, even in presumably secular contexts. The Judeo-Christian experience of sacred transcendence structures subsequent literature (in a way similar to the argument that Max Weber made about the framing and foundational relationship of a Protestant ethic to later, secular, and presumably postreligious capitalist behavior). Yet beyond the programmatic openness to the future and the past (in contrast to the closed character of the pagan world, fraught with its epithetic limitations and its epilogic temporality), there is a third sacred legacy: an openness to imagination. The very mandate for faith, in its counterfactuality or absurdity, is foundational for the standing of fictionality.

As discussed earlier, the crux of the prehistoric acquisition of language was the development of a distinctive capacity to manipulate symbols. Utilization of symbols itself implies a capacity to refer to absences and hence implies an imagination. Not all language use is primarily imaginative (consider referential or communicative instances), but all language nonetheless does presuppose an imaginative capacity, by virtue of its symbolism, and therefore leaves room for the specialized activity of imaginative language use, the distinctive terrain of literature. This predisposition is intensified in writing, particularly in the gradual development toward phonetic script, insofar as the written symbol becomes, in effect, doubly symbolic: a written cipher of a vocal utterance, a visual symbol of an aural symbol. This implies an even greater potential for imagination, as confirmed by the emergence of the initial great works of literature, the heroic epics, in situations of writing (no matter how uncommon the de facto literacy may have been).

This imaginative capacity, the very core of literariness, was amplified by the religious revolution. It is a crucible for genre history: the psalms as models for lyric poetry, the narratives of the patriarchs or Jesus as models for developmental biography, the standing of the parables as short fiction, or the religious ceremony, itself, as the framework for the development of dramatic representation. Yet prior to these specific lineages, a different aspect comes into play, the very foundational relationship between literature as imaginative and religions of faith. The characterization of fiction as requiring a suspension of disbelief, a willingness to accept the counterfactual, points to a religious genealogy. Suspension of disbelief is nothing if not a double negative on faith: that is, the capacity for belief is posited as initial, then doubted by an empirical skepticism facing the counterfactual, which is then, in a final move, retracted by an act of suspension. The result is not a psychotic hallucination, since the rationality of disbelief is merely held in abeyance. For similar reasons it is not ideological: the reader does not succumb to "lies" (Brecht) or partisan misrepresentations but instead entertains them for a limited duration during which a disbelieving doubt remains suspended, held back but never gone, a threat in the form of an absent presence. Fiction and literature, therefore, are not — as the modernist history of secularization would have it — somehow opposites of religion, which have finally become autonomous and free from the inquisitional constraints of parochial doctrine. On the contrary, literature is heir to religion: not only with regard to the structures of creativity and canonicity but, with equal importance, its core characteristic of imagination. The literary imagination, the willingness to dwell in the counterfactual, is a psychological capacity nurtured and sanctioned in the history of faith. In that sense, even the two temporal dimensions — creativity and canonicity — insofar as they reference counterfactual conditions, future and past, are themselves basically variants of imagination.

In what specific ways does the literary imagination derive from Judeo-Christianity? Are there precise aspects that can distinguish between this religion legacy, with its literary consequences, and non-Christian classical literature? And can these arguments be made without recourse to particular and possibly merely contingent genre-historical features? Milbank provides a useful perspective when he turns to a set of eighteenth-century theologians and their efforts to provide a Christian account of language origins. From them he tries to develop a theory of language that is neither positivistic nor "fideistic" — that is, grounded in dogmatic assertions of faith — but which, while recognizing the metaphoricity of language, does not fall into the linguistic nihilism he attributes to deconstruction. For our purposes, it is not that full argument that is crucial but the reference to the eighteenth-century debate on the linguistic character of ancient Hebrew literature. Of particular interest, thanks to Milbank's work, are the literary-critical arguments made by Robert Lowth, bishop of Oxford and then of London, when he published, in Latin, his *Lectures on the Sacred Poetry of the Hebrews* (1758).

Milbank draws our attention to Lowth's discussion of ancient Hebrew "poeticality," which is to say, the specific language use, which, however, he treats as intimately connected to the religious vision. In other words, religion does not figure as a set of doctrines external to language but as the metaphysical presumptions inherent in the modes of poetic expression themselves (which informs Milbank's reference elsewhere to a "linguistic turn" in theology). Lowth identifies two particular aspects of Hebrew rhetoric that are germane in this context: the "oral repetition and redundancy" of pleonasm, and the brevity and identification with nature associated with apostrophe. In both cases, he asserts that the Hebrews achieved a greater poetic quality than did the Greeks. Thus, for example, the contrast of Isaiah's (12:15 – 16) "direct comparison of armies of men to a corn-drag with Homer's much less unnerving comparison of horses trampling men, with horses trampling down the corn."[26]

Pleonasm, the "repetition with difference" that characterizes the poetry of the Hebrew Bible, displays a particular structure with both literary and religious-metaphysical ramifications. The repetition of particular topoi from national history made them available for metaphoric application to new situations — they were both particular and universal. New circumstances could be put into relation with prior ones with the help of a concrete language. While in Greek allegory—for example, the allegory of the chariot in *Phaedrus*—there is clearly a true "content" somehow wrapped in a fictional package; in Hebrew poetry, Lowth describes a literary form that he labels the "mystical allegory," in which both terms are understood to be concrete, historical, or natural and therefore true. It is a rhetoric of pleonasm that puts them in a suddenly dynamic relationship.

Moreover, for Lowth, Hebrew poetry is concrete in its imagery, but it also thrives on the dynamism and ambiguity, indeed obscurity and hence mysticism, of the allegories.[27] This eighteenth-century poetics involves a breaking through the continuum of history, the sudden proximity of that which is temporally separate, to which reference was made in chapter 1. Here the point is that Lowth identifies a feature of biblical rhetoric, clearly implicated in the religious metaphysics but by no means doctrinal, which combines a natural concreteness with an openness to unexpected connections. This is quite at odds with the pagan allegory in which a figure would be deployed to illustrate a philosophical point or, quite similarly, myths would be reread as, so to speak, proleptic enfigurements of philosophical points. Thus de Lubac cites Jean-Baptiste Dubos on the pagan allegorizers: "They wrapped up in fictions almost all the secrets of theology, morality, and physical science."[28] Lowth's biblical rhetoric, in contrast, points to a perpetual openness to the new. Where pagan allegory illustrates prior philosophical points, fully complete in themselves, biblical allegory is understood to be deeply creative, indicating the potential and freedom inherent in history. It is therefore presumed to be true, while the pagan allegory remains merely fiction, or rather a fictionalization of prior knowledge.

Pleonasm as repetition generates a chain of references in an open world; it allows for discussion and reinterpretation (Midrash), which is precluded by the pagan philosophical model of the external fiction concealing a single inner truth. Like pleonasm, apostrophe also entails a doubling, but specifically in the form of interlocution. It is not a description of the cosmos but a call to God. The epilogic structure of pagan time implies a repressive structure of belief, since what is has been established by a prior act; the apostrophic modality of Hebrew poetry allows room for response. Thus Milbank, in a gloss on the philosopher Johann Georg Hamann, elaborates how the recognition of a metaphoric (rather than referential or instrumental) origin of language allows for quite distinct instantiations: a rhetoric of personification, in which the natural world is, in effect, imbued animistically with human features, as in polytheism, or, alternatively, the figurality of apostrophe that places humanity in discussion with a god of the universe and, hence, a monotheism.[29] Both cases demonstrate how religion can be understood as a consequence of the metaphoricity of language (and not as an ideological deception), but it is the specifically apostrophic rhetoric, coupled with the pleonasm of mystical allegory, that defines the biblical legacy. In sum, Milbank's reading of Lowth suggests a general linguistic turn in theology, but it also points to the particular language of Biblical spirituality organized around pleonasm and apostrophe.

One might call this point in the argument the Maccabean moment: the competition between an epilogic aesthetics of polytheism and the rhetoric of redemptive emancipation. Yet surely the result cannot be an either-or, to the extent that the literature of the West has been profoundly defined by both Greek and biblical legacies — although not always equally so, and with varying consequences. The conflict comes to a head in de Lubac's engagement with the Christian exegesis of the Hebrew Bible. To what extent does the older, historical text have relevance in the light of the subsequent revelation? Buried in the hermeneutic question lie centuries of the relationship of the church to Judaism and the Jews.[30] De Lubac takes pains to maintain a dialectic between the possibilities of historical approaches, that is, explorations of the standing of the Old Testament in its context, and allegorizing readings, the specific texture of a Christian reception. Hence his need to enter into considerations of allegory as such: when does the nonfundamentalist, nonhistorical reading uncover an authentic spiritual meaning? When is it — and this is the concern that haunts every speculative interpretation — merely arbitrary? Inspiration runs the risk of becoming idiosyncratic and eccentric. This motivates his need to dwell on the distinction between pagan and Christian allegorical practices; while both surpass the literal meanings, they are, ultimately, diametrically opposed in a manner that grounds the Christian allegory, the search for the spiritual meaning of the text, in the objectivity of a divinely sanctioned historical process.

Ancient allegorists, to repeat the useful characterization, wrapped fictions around the secrets, or truths, of knowledge: theological, philosophical, or scientific. Bracketing the distinction between such secular ancient knowledge and the sacred substance of a Christian faith, we can examine the alternative structures of allegories. In the pagan model, the representation, the allegorical image itself, is a fiction, a useful construct, perhaps a pedagogic device used to illustrate the underlying claim. The allegory at stake for the early

Christians, and for de Lubac, however, is the Hebrew Bible, redefined as the "Old Testament," whose historical truth is not doubted, even if the Christian reader sees its meaning ultimately only revealed elsewhere, that is, in the message of Christ. In this way, not at all unlike Lowth's model of the mystical allegory embedded in biblical language, with its doubling of concrete referents, the Christian allegory is "true" in both its terms; neither is a fiction, in particular, the former end—the Hebrew referent. "In Christian exegesis there is neither myth, on the one hand, nor naturalistic thought or philosophical abstraction on the other. What is proposed here is to 'introduce through figures'—the events and the laws of the Old Covenant—'to the view of Truth,' which is nothing other than 'the fullness of Christ.' In this way we really are going, at least taking a first step, from history to history—although certainly not to history alone, or at least not to the mere exterior of history."[31] Not merely exterior, because it is leading to the historical fact of redemption. Strikingly, this Christian account and the Jewish rhetoric of the mystical allegory, including Benjamin's messianic variant, share the entwinement of figural representation and redemptive history, the dual themes of literariness and historicity discussed in the introduction to this book, in contrast to the merely fictional or arbitrary standing of the pagan allegory.

Yet if we identify pagan allegory as primarily fictional in contradistinction to the redemptive-historical underpinnings of biblical and patristic rhetorics, why then insist on the specific religious dimension in the construction of literature? It would, after all, appear that the classical legacy of the fictional allegory could suffice to account for subsequent and modern understandings of fiction and imaginative literature more broadly. The conclusion is tempting, but wrong: The pagan allegory, precisely when it is fictional, is ultimately a philosophical and pedagogic project. It projects a sophisticated truth into a rhetorical figure, in order to convey the truth via the instrumentalized image. But the image is thereby rendered heteronomous and, ultimately, false, an external shell, in contrast to the true philosophical message it has been utilized to convey. While this allegory may be useful for philosophy, it is deleterious for the literary imagination: instead of reading Homer, one looks for the philosopher behind the epic. In contrast, the mystical allegories of Hebrew poetry as well as the allegorization of the Bible in Christianity are themselves operations of a historical truth, perpetually open, whether due to the nonclosure of Hebrew pleonasm or the perpetual newness of Christ. "When they looked everywhere in Scripture . . . for prefigurations of everything which goes to make up Christianity, the Christian exegetes were not attempting to harmonize, as has rightly been said of many 'allegorical' interpretations of Homer, 'myth' with 'reason,' that is to say, with the knowledge, the feelings and the ideas which were current in a later period. . . . What they wanted to construct was something else again. It was, to use a formula which first gained currency at the time of St. Gregory the Great: 'the edifice of faith.'"[32]

Faith, however, is nothing other than that suspension of disbelief that also constitutes literary fiction — in contrast to the degraded fictions of pagan allegory, even if they are understood as little more than mnemonic devices for philosophical schools. Literature is, particularly in its imaginative character, much more than an allegorization of philosophy, more than an encyclopedic compendium of cultural knowledge, more than the reifications of epithetic stability or didactic fables. It is the openness to the unknown (not a pedagogy for convention) — but an unknown that operates in history with a promise of historical happiness. Literature is the vehicle through which readers can aspire to another world, an imaginary world, in a pursuit, beyond doctrine, of transcendence. Yet transcendence is, as we have seen, not only vertical but also horizontal: the capacity to transcend a restrictive individuality in order to recognize others and to open oneself to them in desire, solidarity, and love. It is precisely here that the religious dimension transforms the literary tradition that begins not simply with the violence of epic heroes, but also with the capacity to mourn: Charlemagne's tears. In sum, the work of literature not only gives expression to ideas — philosophically — as well as to the condition of the writer, but, inheriting the mantle of sacrality, it enfigures transcendence, the imagination of surpassing the world as it is, or more emphatically: recognizing that surpassing that informs the world.

7

The Democracy of Literature

PREVIOUS CHAPTERS have traced an extensive argument through three preconditions of literature: the acquisition of language and the associated capacity for symbolic thinking; the transition to writing technologies; and the impact of the religions of transcendence. These three events represent both chronological transitions in the emergence of literature and logical components of literature as such. Each transition enabled an increasingly articulate skepticism toward the surrounding world. Language itself involves a symbolic capacity to invoke that which is absent, and hence a facility for imagination. Writing, in turn, expands the room for critical contents by minimizing the conformist processes of homeostatic adjustment. Religious doctrines of otherworldly norms of justice provide a powerful archimedian point from which to question any given state of affairs. This ability to call the present into question, be it through invocations of an imagined past, aspirations for a future, or, more fundamentally, the very capacity to articulate counterfactuals, has profound consequences for the relationship between literature and history. Indeed, it is only partially an overstatement to claim that without this literary overreaching of existing conditions — the human capacity to represent — history would not take place. To the extent that history is a result of human intention, teleological projects to change the conditions of life — no matter how those plans may never be fully realized or go astray — it depends on an ability to envision alternative futures. It therefore involves imagination, and imagination depends on the evolution of literary culture. It may have been accidents of weather that protected Elizabethan England from the Spanish Armada; but it was the corpus of Shakespeare's works that contributed centrally and indispensably to the articulation of models of humanity and individuality that shaped Anglo-American culture. It is the amplification of imagination through the experience of literature that has motored the cumulative human aspirations realized as developmental progress.

The special relationship between literature and history has several dimensions. Most immediately, it implies treating literature as a reflection of history, the presumption that history marks the real process or structure of experience, which then takes on a secondary afterlife in the perhaps ultimately superfluous dimension of literature. This reflective model suggests that literary works testify to the social world in which they emerged: *Lucien Leuwen* tells us something about France under Louis-Philippe, *Effi Briest* is a reflective document on life in Bismarckian Germany, and *Native Son* serves as a report on race in the America of the Great Depression. Historians may therefore choose to make use of literary texts as evidence for their claims about historical social or cultural contexts. This conversion of the literary work into a document for historiography, however, necessarily avoids its aesthetic specificity. As a document, it is precisely not a work of art in any emphatically literary sense; as a reflection of its context, it is not an object of aesthetic reception. Indeed, from the documentary approach to the work of literature arises this key question: Why should this piece of writing continue to interest us, or those of us who are not professional historians of Orleanist France, Bismarckian Germany, or American race relations? One can further ask why the literary document should be preferred over alternative textual accounts of the particular social settings, such as journalistic descriptions or other sorts of evidence. Literature, after all, is probably not always the most reliable witness to historical events.

There is a cognate configuration of literature and history that is of some interest: not, as above, the literary document as an illustration of history but literature as the medium for historiography. At stake here is the utilization of literary form, including elements such as figurative language and narrative structure, for more or less professional or specialized accounts of history. Thus, one can read some great historians as great writers, and one could well inquire into the standing of writing in the training of professional historians. But the hypothetically strong relationship between historiography and literary form has a different, more problematic significance: the related claim that historiographical writing, because it uses figural language, is indistinguishable from fictional literature. This postmodern argument is

The Democracy of Literature

even more familiar in philosophy — because philosophers use metaphors, there are, so some have claimed, no epistemological grounds on which to separate them from poets, hence the study of philosophy and the study of literature merge as one.

This claim is untenable. It is merely an enormous overstatement of a truism: history and philosophy both operate with language, and figurality is constitutive of language, and therefore — this is the incorrect extrapolation — historical or philosophical language is presumed to be identical to that imaginative use of language that is literature or, more precisely, literary fiction. To claim that the expression of nonfactuals in language — the use of metaphors by historians or philosophers — is therefore merely fiction would imply that any other nonfactual, a lie, for example, would also have to be regarded as fiction and therefore literature. Yet there is surely an ontological distinction to be made between the story that an apprehended criminal might tell in order to concoct an alibi and the story that Henry James writes as an exercise of professional authorship, even though both stories make claims that are not empirically true. Moreover, this argument, made with reference to the figurality of language in historiographic texts, applies as well to the language of historical figures, for example, politicians. Their use of language may be, more or less successfully, literary, but they are therefore not truly generating literature, no matter how metaphorical their speeches. Thomas Mann made just this point in his essay "Brother Hitler." Both he and Hitler, his political adversary, utilized mythic, and therefore literary, components in their language but with quite distinct intents: not solely the distinctions between their substantive goals, but in the sense that Hitler's use of metaphor was oriented toward a real-world operationalization — real, no matter how bizarre and fantastic — while Mann's claims, in his literary writing (as opposed to his political speeches) were intended for the aesthetic conventions of a specialized literary culture.[1]

These two cases — literature as historical document and the figurality (or "literariness") of historiographic writing (or political exhortation) — are the inverse of each other, the former collapsing literature into history, the latter history into literature. Let us put them both aside. In contrast to both these reductions, one should insist on holding onto the distinctiveness of the two components in the sense of the earlier discussion of sectoral competitions, while nonetheless attempting to define the relation of literature to one particular field of social life, more narrowly drawn than history, that is, politics. However complex the connection between literature and history may be, the involvement of literature with politics is the central concern of this chapter.

Politics involves the articulation and pursuit of transformations in the conditions of the life of the community. This civic project depends vitally on the capacity for imagination, the ability to articulate alternative ways to live. Furthermore, this force of imagination is precisely that element of the human mind that literature most cultivates. The human ability to imagine counterfactuals and, therefore, to pursue change preexists literature, but the human power to imagine alternatives, which is the precondition of making choices, would surely not be as vibrant without the resources of literary fiction. Literature is political not primarily when it puts forward a political thesis, but by virtue of its literariness, its autonomy, its call to the reader to put the given reality in brackets long enough to begin to reflect on alternatives. Because the reader, understood as the addressee of literature, can entertain a fiction, suspend disbelief, and allow for imaginary alternatives to the status quo, this is a reader called to freedom. Literature, as literature, becomes political because it is an appeal to the freedom of the reader; because literature addresses a public, it constitutes a public sphere and therefore contributes to the institutionalization of democracy.

THE IMAGINATIVE character of literature establishes a relationship between author and reader, implicated in the pursuit of freedom, the reader's as well as the writer's. This pursuit of freedom is furthermore inscribed in the literary text itself, in complex ways and at various levels. This political resonance of literature, and particularly when that literature is at its most literary or poetic, is best explained by returning to two texts already discussed.

Chapter 2 examined a stanza from Lamaratine's *Pensées des Morts* in order to pursue literary resonances of the problem of language origins, particularly with regard to the phenomenon of the persistence of rhyme as a defining aspect of poetry. In chapter 6, Brecht's "Hollywood Quatrain" provided an opportunity to examine questions of transcendence, especially canonicity, in an ostensibly nonreligious text. A different issue is at stake now: the attempt to identify the specifically political component of their aesthetic autonomy. How does the poetic being of a literary work implicate it in the life of the polis? Of course, both Lamartine and Brecht led active political lives in their respective contexts. Lamartine played a prominent role in French politics in the first half of the nineteenth century, while Brecht's biographical trajectory is tightly intertwined with the political vicissitudes of twentieth-century Germany and the conflicts of the early Cold War. Neither case has to be reviewed in detail here. Suffice it to note that both poets led lives open to politics, and they reflected on that involvement in their own writings. Yet it is not that political biographical feature that is of determining importance. Of course, there is no reason to avoid or suppress the biographical engagements of the two poets, but one would be hard put to claim that such engagement is either a necessary condition or a consequence of poetic writing. It may be the case that poets are in fact frequently comparable to Lamartine and Brecht, involved in public affairs; but there is an equally compelling image of the poet as withdrawn and disengaged. Indeed, one should add that for most poets attracted to politics, the experience is rarely a happy one. Poets may be drawn, for whatever reasons, to political movements, but an eventual disillusionment characteristically follows. The fact that writers frequently drop out or move away from political movements is as telling as their initial attraction to them. But the argument presented here is prior to these matters of career choice or pronounced allegiances; it involves instead the insistence that literature as such has political implications, regardless of the poet's biography or his or her subjective intentions.

As we turn to the poems themselves, let us also focus the argument by bracketing those elements in the texts that might be taken as directly thematic references to political conditions, defined broadly. To the extent that the work is primarily about such referencing it becomes tendentious. Even Marx and Engels were suspicious of such *Tendenzliteratur,* preferring literature of quality to literature marked by ideological purity.[2] Yet while they (and a legion of critics in their wake) tended to imply a distinction between two bodies of writings — here tendentious writing, there literature of quality — it is more useful to identify tendentious moments in any text, even if that tendentiousness is not significantly determinative of the overall significance of the work at hand. Indeed, tendentiousness may be more in the eye of the beholding reader, rather than in the author's intention. Therefore, in order to make the strict argument that is the topic of this chapter, the political character of literary autonomy, it is crucial to refrain from relying on evidence that might be regarded as the specifically tendentious points in the two poems. In particular, this means that it will be necessary to identify political ramification of Lamartine's stanza that do not involve the claim, for example, that the poem's eagle is somehow a symbol for the monarch. Similarly the argument should not depend on rediscovering Brecht's anti-capitalism on the basis of the market references in "Hollywood Quatrain."

Clearly, if a full reading of either poem were at stake here, that sort of referentiality would certainly play a role (as would the biographical vicissitudes of the poet-politicians). Practical criticism need not be as methodologically ascetic as I propose here. This asceticism, however, reflects the recognition that the important claim about the political significance of autonomy cannot be sustained by drawing on evidence that involves precisely the most non-autonomous elements in the two works. Nor can it be based on biographical idiosyncrasy, the respective authors' empirical predilections. To make the case for a political substance in aesthetic autonomy requires avoiding short-cuts and focusing instead on the poetic mission of literature as such.

Where then is the political reverberation in these texts, if not in the royal eagle or the venality of the market, the references to state and economy? How does the establishment of an aesthetic autonomy, rather than through such referential moments, render these works relevant to the life of the polis? Meanwhile, another potential objection requires consideration. By examining these two texts, one runs the risk of inviting the criticism of arbitrary selection. Demonstrating a political logic in poems by writers who were themselves, we know already, politically engaged might be regarded as effectively tautological. In light of this concern, the following analysis is directed at the least engaged and referential moments in the texts. Yet the potential objection goes further: even once the political component in the works is teased out, we have not necessarily proven anything about literature in general, but only about the predispositions of two particular authors. Any claim about the social standing of a work of art, in its singularity — which is the condition of serious art — is susceptible to the criticism that elite opinion, in this case the worldviews of the individual authors, is being confused with larger phenomena. No examination of any limited body of works, it would seem, can ever prove a claim about the standing of literature in the social world. In one sense, there is ultimately no way to answer this concern and to bridge the gap between the intense, hermeneutic, and critical examination of single texts on the one hand and the generalizing quantification of the social sciences on the other. In another sense, however, precisely this tension, between aesthetic singularity and social formation, turns out to pervade the poems themselves, and this binary points to the location of politics in literature.

Because the phenomenon of literature is constitutively linked to language, any work of literature, hence any poems, and these two, as particular examples, exist through language with the multiple implications for hominization, symbolic thinking, and imagination. Language use, as a general phenomenon, necessarily implies using a particular language. No one speaks, or writes, in language in general, but only in the one (or perhaps several) available to the speaker: Lamartine writes in French, Brecht in German, and therefore each has to be understood as staking out a position within the field of possible statements in each of those languages. Yet any linguistic particularity — the use of French rather than German, and so on — is not a function of the specific linguistic characteristics. Lamartine's poetry cannot be reduced to the syntactic features of French (use of subjunctive, rules of conjugation, and so on), nor does it make sense to say that Brecht chooses to write in German because of some particular attraction to its patterns of verb placement. These basic points underscore their more interesting corollary: that to write in French or German indicates an involvement in the respective language communities, the social formations where French or German is the lingua franca. This does not imply a closed and isolated nationality: A French author is surely also susceptible to influences of various national provenance. Nevertheless, writing in language at all necessarily means writing in the language of some particular community, no matter how open, and the author therefore participates in a certain shared condition: Writing in German does not only carry with it the German intellectual tradition and literary canon but also the social condition, replete with the historical legacies of the German past.

A parallel argument becomes pertinent now. Just as any language use implies the use of a particular language, it also implies the invocation of a particular content. The utterance as such, through the use of words, implies a semantics and hence a topic, even if, as in the case of linguistic self-referentiality, the topic is language itself. This is not to say that the utterance, or the particular type of language use in literature, is solely a matter of its semantic content; other dimensions become prominent, perhaps more so in poetry than in other genres or in nonliterary language use. Yet the semantic function of language is inescapable, which accounts for the invocation of conditions of being, as it happens, in the initial words of each text: Lamartine's "It is the season" and Brecht's "Every morning." That these are both temporal conditions amplifies the similarity between the poems but is not crucial to the argument here. The point rather is that each poem establishes a condition by naming it, and by naming it, it makes it accessible to the critical scrutiny of the reader. Because the poetic utterance does not rely on the claim of an indicative referentiality — that is, it is not assumed to be true in a directly empirical sense — a different sort of reception is evoked, a focused curiosity in the possible resonance of the imaginative language use. Consequently, the condition necessarily invoked by the use of language encounters the scrutiny of the reader; the poet's imagination invites the reader's imagination, and therefore the possibility of envisioning a transformation of the named condition.

In these cases, then, Lamartine's season and Brecht's mornings, conditions are both unavoidably named (of course, other conditions might have been possible, but some condition is always necessarily consequent to the character of language as semantic) and—such is the result of the poetic functioning of language—they are called into question as well. Literary autonomy invokes an imagined world but also holds it in permanent suspense. Just as fictionality entails the suspension of disbelief, the willingness to accept the unreal for the duration of the reception of the aesthetic object, so too is the imagined world also in doubt, recognizably ephemeral, never available for confusion with the empirical world: It is, after all, merely a literary enfigurement. There is therefore a double negation in play, the retraction of empirical skepticism (suspension of disbelief, on the reader's part) and the recognition of the fictionality of the imagined world, whereby the first is precondition of the second. To accept the poetic invitation requires credulity and then results in the apprehension of the possibility of alternatives. The imagined world itself is always subject to the possibility of change precisely because of its imagined and therefore unstable character.

Lamartine and Brecht do not simply make statements about instances of temporality; they invoke them and, in effect, protest against them. This protest is achieved through the irony of affect in Brecht, implicit in the use of "hopefully," and in Lamartine through the metaphor of abandonment, and each suggests an alternative political strategy for the poet. For Brecht, the critical hesitation implied by the single verse of hope—a pause in the rhythmic unfolding of the discourse—precedes a prescription of integration, his participation in the collective of the sellers, against which he had registered the protest of the second verse, with the designation of the lies that are for sale. While we read this earlier as an act of canonic integration, it is also a horizontal transcendence, the recognition of a commonality with other human beings, even in their degraded condition of seriality and reification: seriality insofar as they are standing in lines, and reification as indicated by their reduction to their economic function. This is a solidarity that requires imitation. The poet becomes like the others, thereby risking the loss of the singularity and difference that is the precondition of the poetic

The Democracy of Literature

situation. The politics of the poem therefore address the necessity and risks of participation in the collective social situation. In light of Brecht's biography, this topic involves the proximity to communism and the force of the culture industry, commercialized mass cultural production in the twentieth century.

In contrast, Lamartine's romantic politics point in a different direction: a separation of the individual, justified in the poem through metaphors of natural processes, the seasonality of winter or the ornithological imagery of molting feathers. The separation of the individual from society, the fate of the poet, becomes a matter of regret, even as it is described, ironically, as resulting from natural processes. As different as Brecht's collectivism and Lamartine's individualism may seem, they share categorical structures — individuality and collectivity, abandonment and solidarity — despite different nuances in the suggested balances. Indeed the differences are ultimately less important than the shared dynamic, which is indicative of the political problematic of the poem.

Standing as the extreme case of the literary work of art, the poem focuses attention on the autonomy of the poet or, more precisely, the poet's independent subjectivity in the context of collectivist social pressures. The poem stages the possibility of individuality altogether, threatened by the pressures of social constraint, yet nonetheless fully dependent on the social condition for the very possibility of language use. The result is a peripatetic moment in both examples, the single verse of "hopefully" on which Brecht's quatrain turns, and the structure of Lamartine's rhyme pattern, when the couplet that rhymes *mille* and *inutile* effectively names the implicit social-theoretical program. Facing the growing force of mass society and the political structures that it engenders, the poet appears to grow useless. Uselessness is the accusation, however, that is directed not only at poetry for its autonomy, but at every nonconforming aspiration for individuality, even though such initiative is the very source of dynamism in any society. In this sense, we can locate the politics of poetry not in the biographical engagement of the poet, nor in the tendentious message (Lamartine on the state, Brecht on capitalism) but in two dovetailing configurations: first, the appeal to the imagination of the reader, who is thereby called into a relationship with the text and the author, defined by the freedom of interpretation; second, the objective structure of the poem, concerned with the condition of poetry, as free speech, vis-à-vis the conformist language of social pressures. In both cases, however — poetry as an appeal to the reader and poetry as the encoding of social theory—literature is about the defense of individuality in society and therefore, fundamentally, a vehicle for a process of liberal democratization.

One needs to proceed carefully. For the goal cannot be a mandate, an authoritarian, normative expectation that literature must be democratic or that it must advocate particular political positions intentionally, even the position of democracy. One can easily imagine a deleterious outcome, a dogmatic insistence that literature maintain a politically correct line in a mechanical manner that would however in itself be inimical both to the fragility of literary autonomy and to the processes of liberal democracy. It does no good to envision a pursuit of freedom in a manner that destroys the same freedom. In this context, it is useful to recall that even communist literary politics claimed to operate in the name of democracy, while National Socialism, despite its avoidance of that specific term, also defined itself as an expression of the people, or folk. An attempt to understand the significance of autonomous literature in a civilizational process that includes a democratic teleology has to avoid falling into the trap of generating just one more prescriptive aesthetic that would in fact be incompatible with the genuinely democratic substance of literature asserted here. Literature is democratic not because it propagates a party-line message or articulates an ideology; in fact, it might very well display both those features and even have ostensibly undemocratic or antidemocratic contents, as in the case of Ezra Pound's *Cantos,* and nonetheless participate in the democratic teleology of literature. Rather, literature is democratic because it calls forth a reader as an imaginative and thinking individual, invited into a process of interpretive freedom and reflection and because the literary works themselves carry within them, constitutively and formally, reflections on the problem of imaginative individuality facing the social pressures that work against independence. Literature provides an aesthetic experience that contributes to the suppleness of mind of the democratic citizen, while also displaying the inherent tension in democracy between individual integrity and community pressure.

Lamartine's poet fell out of the good graces of the social order, or was pushed out by the growing competition, while Brecht shows the poet in desperation, choosing to reinsert himself, via imitation, into a literary order, be it of canonic continuity or conformist alignment. Either the poet is isolated, in a gesture against society, or the poet intervenes in society. These alternative missions of poetry are not arbitrary functions. On the contrary, they represent positions constitutive of the very standing of literature in society. This frame, however, hardly means that literature faces the impoverished choice between propagandistic tendentiousness and mute quietism. The previous account of literature as foundationally involved in a process of democratization, neither as propaganda nor as quietism, continues to hold, but now with a caveat. We should understand the democratic standing of literature as always only a potential, while remaining susceptible to alternative degradations, either toward an excessive politicization or just as much as toward apathy and nonengagement. Overpoliticization and depoliticization are the extreme temptations for literature, inherent in the very condition of literariness, and, perhaps more so, they are temptations for literary scholarship as well. Even if we posit a necessary political horizon for the autonomous work of literature, in particular in its capacity for imaginative freedom and the community of a democratic public, there is nevertheless no guarantee that any given work of literature will successfully aspire to that democratic horizon, and certainly none that all works will do so equally well. If literature is inherently and constitutively democratic, that does not exclude particular cases where antidemocratic formations become determinative, be it either in the form of repressive politics or the adamant refusal of politics. For this reason, it becomes crucial to define exactly what it is about literature in general that is under examination when one raises the question of politics or political literature. This sort of clarification will be useful in navigating between the distorted forms of politics that threaten the democratic teleology. Literature participates constitutively in the democratic teleology of humanity, but literature and democracy both can succumb to destructive forces.

The political question for all literature cannot be limited to the topicality of politics in some subset of literature. Autonomous literature — whether narrowly political in its subject matter or not and, perhaps, even more so when not ostensibly political — turns by virtue of its constitution and not because of any thematic choices toward politics. By appealing to a public, literature contributes to the establishment of public life. By enacting the possibility of creativity, which necessarily means creation of the new, it asserts the possibility of freedom. By calling on the reader to participate in a process of imagination, it liberates the individual toward choice. It is as literature, autonomous and imaginative, that literature is most political, and not, by way of contrast, in the moment of advocacy of particular political contents. Moreover, the process of literary reception, even as it invites the reader into an imaginary world, also establishes a relationship with the author, or narrator, and therefore an ethical world: The reader of imaginative literature should not be thought of as somehow escaping from a real world. On the contrary, it is through the aesthetic education of reading that the individual cultivates a capacity for imagination, for criticism, for alternative sensibilities and therefore for an amplified, not a lessened, ethical participation in the world. Literature therefore democratizes. On this, the lesson of the twentieth century is clear: Literature may not disappear entirely in totalitarian contexts, as the brilliant example of Soviet dissident writing shows, but there is no such thing as a successful totalitarian literature, that is, a literature that, in the pursuit of aesthetic quality, simultaneously promotes totalitarian structures of personality or behavior.

The history of literature overlaps with the history of democracy because the categories of the autonomous work of imaginative literature imply a teleology of freedom. Entering into the work of literature, the reader participates in a cognitive transformation that amplifies the potential for freedom and autonomy while at the same time underscoring the social relations, the realm of ethics, and politics, in which the reader as part of the public becomes a citizen. Yet to the extent that the work of art, and literature in particular, is assumed to be able to provide an aesthetic education or carry a truth or enfigure or enact emancipation, what is it, specifically, about the work that explains this quality? A satisfactory answer will necessarily go deeper than particular contextual relations: the relationship of French classical theater to the power of the absolutist court, or the proliferation of the novel in the nineteenth century and the implications for democratic liberalism. Indeed, such historicist case studies, as useful as they might be for historiography, miss the very particular diachronicity that informs works of literature: not just Homer in his time, but Homer in our times, our continued ability to immerse ourselves in his fictions and the significance of that capacity for literary history.

The alternative to this reductionist historicism entails a simultaneous insistence on two points. First, it is urgent to retain a strong insistence on literary autonomy, the self-setting and self-defining character of the work of art in order to separate out moments of tendentiousness or biographical engagement from the discussion of the politics of literature. The discussion of the politics of literature is not primarily about the heteronomous mandate of the absolutist patron to represent aristocratic power, nor should it be about the extent to which a twentieth-century author displays obedience to a particular party line. Second, however, the autonomous work of art is at the same time fundamentally political, inescapably involved in processes of political transformation, but beyond any explicit tendentiousness. Now one comes to focus on the core issue, the overlap of autonomy and politics, but this odd couple is only tenable as such if one recognizes the causal relationship between the two, that is, literary autonomy as a determinant of liberal democratic politics. The challenge of the rest of the chapter therefore becomes, ultimately, to explain that causality. What is it specifically about the autonomous or (following Walter Benjamin) auratic work of art, the work of literature that is not primarily referential but imaginative, that is not primarily conventional but self-defining, and that is not tendentious or otherwise thematically political, which somehow nonetheless implicates it in the ongoing transformation of literate societies toward democratic forms?

YET THE CLAIM that literature has a significant relationship to politics may face stiff resistance. Is not all this talk of the political character of literature simply a function of the overpoliticized humanities, the politically correct pursuit of race, class, and gender, or the poststructuralist obsession with power? Or perhaps, even worse, it may represent the last residue of the twentieth-century totalitarianisms, especially a communist aesthetic that, defunct everywhere else, continues a grotesque afterlife within universities. In response, one could easily cite earlier examples of the politicization of the literary vision, such as the role of concepts of national literature in nineteenth-century Germany as part of the process of nation-building, which had a clear resonance in the scholarly world, as academic criticism became the handmaiden of Prussian state formation.[3] Still, pursuing the infinite regress of politics and literature to even previous cases can hardly counter the argument that the politicization of the literary-critical vision might distort the genuine character of literature, understood to be most literary when it is least political. The skeptical question directed at politicized literary criticism ultimately asks why we should not simply think of literature as entertainment or recreation, refined at times perhaps but nonetheless ultimately inconsequential for public life. A successful book may reap profits for the publisher and author, and it may distract readers, granting them hours of repose, but why should we think of it as having a significance that can be reasonably called political? Political processes take place in the public sphere and in government institutions, not in imaginative literature.

The most obvious answer to the challenge is the circulation of ideas. Literature thematizes certain ideas, be it directly in the mode of advocacy or symbolically, stridently or subtly, and thereby distributes them to a readership. We need not assume that those readers are simply passive receptacles, blank slates onto which literature writes new ideas. Yet new books do bring ideas, whether they are rejected, accepted, or modified by the reader. New ideas are made available, old ones are reinforced or criticized. This process is clearest in the case of a tendentious text. Richard Wright's *Native Son* makes the case for racial justice, even if the very rhetoric of making a case limits the scope of literary expression, as James Baldwin famously argued.[4] The same process, in a different generic register, has to do with the anti-Semitic imagery in T. S. Eliot's poetry. It is possible to say the poems are "about" those images, but it would be hard to make the case that the imagery, or the thematic anti-Semitism, is the sole substance of the texts, and surely not the sole aesthetic substance. Nonetheless, the public function of these literary texts involves the circulation of offensive imagery, arguably with political consequences. The point is not to argue individual culpability: "hate speech" is a dubious enough notion, and it becomes even less tenable as a credible concept in the context of literary writing. Nor does it make sense to reduce a complex work to one troubling image. Nonetheless, the very circulation of denunciatory images cannot be neatly separated from consequences in public life. Literature can have a brutal impact. As Sartre put it in *What Is Literature?* with regard to authorship, "If he speaks, he fires."[5]

Yet this model of the political character of literature, reducing it to specific referential comments or images and their presumed consequences, is the least interesting way to approach the question of literature in politics. It may work well for the study of crude stereotypes, but it is blind to the aesthetic specificity of literature. It levels the difference between literary and nonliterary texts (and thereby elicits the question of why look at literary texts at all, if the same prejudicial contents might be found more clearly and more explicitly in other forms of expression, for example, party platforms, newspaper editorials, and so forth). Still, this result, the occlusion of the literary character, is inevitable if one foregrounds the presumed message and minimizes the significance of the imaginative use of language, which, after all, defines literary form. If the question involves the politics of literature as literature (rather than just any dissemination of political allegiance through language), then it is indispensable to pay attention to the specifics of the type of language usage that distinguishes literature, and in particular the ramifications of autonomization. An analytic model is required that does justice to the literary character of literature in its relation to politics, and not just to the political message that may be contained in a literary work.

But we also need a model of politics that does justice to the fundamental logics of civic life, in its relationship to literature. In order to investigate the pairing of literature and politics, it is crucial to develop a more thoughtful approach to the latter term than to treat is as a simple bundle of ideological claims. More than any local message, politics traces an ellipse around two focal points: decisionism as a precondition of any action, and dispersion, as the limiting distribution of power in order to thwart a tyrannical concentration and allow for a free and democratic participation in the life of the political unit. Political leadership involves the power to decide, in exceptional circumstances, but the perpetual temptation to corruption inherent in power warrants its dispersion in order to guarantee freedom.[6] These twin components stand in a productive tension with each other: the use of power to act and the limiting of power to protect.

The polis needs to be able to bring discussions to a conclusion in order to decide on a course of action. Now, the very management of a discussion and certainly the prospect of concluding it, as well as the realities of executing any decision, require an apparatus of administration. To vest that apparatus with authority is an unavoidable precondition of the execution of its mission, but precisely that authorization runs the risk of turning the apparatus of government, be it the single leader or the subaltern agents, into a goal in itself in the forms of tyranny or bureaucracy. The existential need for any political community to conclude discussion in order to decide to act is foreshortened, radically, in a tyranny and becomes repression. The point is not to justify repression as an ontological necessity but to underscore how the very need for decision, in any and every political setting, is susceptible to degenerating into a repressive outcome. In contrast, with regard to bureaucracy: Any action of the polis requires realization, therefore organization, and hence an apparatus of offices, but that institution, with its inherent inertia, may take on a life (no matter how slow) of its own.[7] Excessive bureaucratization is not an unavoidable outcome of politics, but it is a constant possibility in any political community. Moreover, the expansion of bureaucracy with its own innate resistance to action may ironically undermine the very possibility of political decision and action.

To consider the core question of how literature opens onto politics requires reflection on politics at this level, rather than focusing solely on the presumed ideological message of this or that text, the particulars of an author's biography, or claims about the internal politics or the revolutionary character of political language: Did Sartre resist the German occupation?

Were the texts of Louis-Ferdinand Céline's novels somehow fascist? For an adequate theory of politics and literature it is necessary to delve to a much deeper level. If politics is about choice and decision as the preconditions of action, then the political character of literature involves its innate processes of posing choices and enabling action as steps toward the construction of a vigilant citizenry. One can think of Brecht and Sartre as models of engagement here — not the specific positions they took on particular issues but their expectation that the work of literature model and elicit the decisionism of the activist recipients.

Yet if activism as a virtue can mean civic responsibilities, it can equally degenerate into forms of ideological mobilization or self-destruction, when political obsession takes over all other dimensions of being. The same range of options applies to literary texts, running between the value of an invitation to act (as opposed to an enervating quietism) and a numbing assertion of the absolute priority of a particular allegiance (as in propaganda). Yet politics is not only the appeal to action; it is equally the call for a prior, thoughtful consideration of matters of public life. Such vigilance represents a check on the state apparatus and therefore causes a dispersion of power. When, however, the mandate for reflection grows to a point that politics is effectively excluded (because deliberation goes on forever), quietism ensues. Dramatic literature, in its convening of the community, tends toward decisive activism, while the novel, with its focus on individual interiority among a polyphony of characters and addressed to the private reader, tends toward a dispersion of power. The former resonates with democracy per se, the mobilized public, the latter with liberalism and the lives of individuals.[8]

The teleological orientation of literature toward the formation of a public implicates it in politics. The literary public sphere paves the way for the political public. Politics in turn is structured around the polarities of decision and action, on the one hand, and the dispersion of power, on the other. As a consequence of the constitutive connection of literature to public life, the varied character of politics — decisionistic, activistic, centralized, federal, bureaucratic, whatever — reflects back into literature and literary history in important ways. The assertion that the orientation toward the formation of a public informs literature with a political substance remains an abstract generality unless the specific historical character of political institutions is taken into consideration. Literature addresses both an ideal public, implicit in the texture of the works, and its contemporary public, as limited by existing structures of the state and general social conditions (such as literacy rates). While literature, fundamentally, involves the interpellation of the autonomous recipient who has the potential to become the autonomous citizen, this process can only unfold within the empirical possibilities for civic life. The phenomenological potential of literature therefore stands in a complex relationship to the history of public spheres and structures of the state. The changing relationship of individuality to the state, the development of modern state structures, indeed fundamental redefinitions of politics, community, and action, pose different challenges to literature as the crucible of public individuals. The question of literature and politics is consequently a function of the changing character of politics altogether.

The emergence of the modern state fundamentally revises relationships among individuals, public life, and political institutions, and hence also the orientation of the work of literature toward the generation of a public.[9] This rupture in political structures — the transition from the distributed powers of traditional society to the centralized state of modernity — has deep implications for the character of the literary public toward which the work of literature is directed. All the same, it is important to keep in mind the profound distinction between the temporal structures of the work of literature and those of the political institution. Literature maintains emphatic relations to the canonic and traditional past, implicitly preserved in the work, and an aspiration toward the future — at the very least toward the future reader, always invited to read, reread, and understand anew. This specifically poetic temporality, which intertwines past, present, and future, stands at odds with the imperative of the present that defines the modern political state, as Edmund Burke suggested in his critique of the revolutionary regime in France.[10] The goal of the state is to maximize benefits now, regardless of long-term resource consequences and, of course, regardless of the past, which appears to any contemporary politician only as an irrational restriction on action. Of course, certain political figures may invoke a heroic past or pursue policies with what they see as a progressive orientation toward some glorious future. Nonetheless, the action of the state takes place in the moment of the present, in contrast to literature's more complex temporality. To the extent that literature can transmit its complex relationship to time to its public and exhort the public to recall the past or reflect on the future, it may generate a political resistance to the tendency of the state toward presentism.

The intersection between literary and political spheres is archaic, as the opening of *Gilgamesh* documents. Both emerged through the invention of writing, in order to preserve narratives, for literature, and in order to maintain records, for the administrative state. This shared origin in script was turned into a rivalry by scripture: the prophetic and later Christian insistence on an emphatic distinction between the state, as worldly, secular, and fallen, and an alternative expectation of holiness that, as we have seen, the work of literature inherited, if ultimately in secular form.[11] This rivalry, with its theological grounding, was compounded by the sectoral competition, driven by the existential consequences of the distinction between *vita activa* and *vita contemplativa*: the writer came to look on the politician, an actor in an allegedly realer world, with a mixture of longing and disdain. Recall the conclusion of the *Chanson de Roland* and the counterpoint between the melancholy emperor and the departing author. Finally, the dialectic between literature and politics is compounded by that core political category of decision: Writing is also about a series of decisions, down to the very process of choosing, word by word, the next term. Writing is therefore the perpetual state of exception in which the author as sovereign must decide, and it therefore also models decisionism.[12] The overlap is undercut by a fundamental distinction as well. It is in the character of writing to hold decisions in suspense, the sentence can be rewritten, or the content, only realized in the imagination, can be rethought. The political act, in contrast, once taken is irreversible: It can elicit others, it can provoke opposition, but it cannot be retracted in a way that a literary draft can be reworked. As powerful as the impact of fiction may be in politics, the existential dimension of imagination is ultimately less consequential and less unforgiving than the world of political deeds.

Nonetheless, literature remains involved in politics and thereby plays a specific civilization-historical role. Literature democratizes: The effect of literature includes the proliferation of democratic categories by calling forth thoughtful readers, allowing for political action, and generating an imagination skeptical of the present and potentially critical of the omnipresent (and always presentist) bureaucratic state. It does not democratize (primarily) though an explicit loyalty to specifically democratic institutions but rather by recreating them through the constitution of the readership. No doubt, some authors may hold antidemocratic allegiances, and these positions may even make their way into their literary works. It is doubtful, however, that such texts ever convinced anyone of the virtue of an antidemocratic political position. Reading *Voyage au bout de la nuit* probably never turned anyone into a fascist, at least if one assumes a genuinely literary reading (as opposed to a propagandistic deployment) of the text. In this sense, Sartre could claim that, because the teleology of a work of literature is toward liberty, there is no such thing as a good anti-Semitic novel.[13] That claim is not a political proscription, denouncing certain texts because of their politically incorrect values. Rather, the very nature of literature includes the promotion of freedom, and successful literature will therefore be constitutively incapable of establishing structures of oppression. The phenomenology of literary reception is emancipatory, even against regressive values inherent in a work's content.

Literature democratizes; autonomous literature elicits autonomous individuality. Both processes — one democratic, the other liberal — are grounded in foundational aspects of writing. Literature, as writing, contributes to the spread of literacy and the development of an increasingly inclusive public. The principle of dissemination, rooted in the portability of the written text and heightened by mechanisms of reproduction (especially the printing press, a watershed aspect of modernity), implies a challenge to arcane and centralized power. Furthermore, literacy includes an implicit reorganization of cognitive structures toward a rational sequentiality and, hence, a principle of criticism. Because writing puts an end to the regime of homeostatic adjustment, a critical individuality emerges, the ability to stake out positions against the state and the community, while the endemic suspicion of individuals directed at nonconformist individuals, which is a trait of preliterate cultures, is reduced. It is finally, however, the autonomous character of literature, its difference from the empirical world, and hence its relationship to the imagination that most defines its political consequences. Literature is the spiritual exercises of the democratic citizen, the training ground for a capacity to imagine alternatives and to reflect on their possible realization. Literature is the democratic distribution of the right to imagination. While it may contribute in extreme cases to escapism, its genuine goal involves building a public that can be imaginative in the management of its own affairs, individually and socially. It asks its readers to suspend disbelief and decide on other worlds, it encourages a suspicion toward the given, and, by appealing to all readers — potentially to everyone — it disperses power and resists the tendency of the bureaucratic political apparatus toward its own expansion. The rest of this chapter examines examples of politics in literature, reflecting two moments in the political history of modernity: *Hamlet* and the emergence of the modern state and Goethe's *Wilhelm Meister's Apprenticeship* in the age of the democratic revolutions.

AESTHETIC EXPERIENCE enables deeds. Any human action requires imagination, but aesthetic experience enhances the possibility of action, in particular innovative action, and therefore a political praxis. While much contemporary literary criticism has directed its overpoliticized attention to the representation of identities in literature, the argument here does not concern cultural membership (an ultimately anthropological question). On the contrary, the argument is about facilitating innovation, decision, and action. The politics of imaginative literature is not about maintaining communities, as cultural studies would have it; on the contrary, it is about changing them.

Hamlet provides intratextual reflection on the transition from illusion to practice. It is a sustained study of the possible relations among appearance, imagination, and action. Rather than dwelling on Hamlet's inaction (the traditional German reading of the play), one can recognize the text as, on the contrary, a call to action, directed to the reader, through the process of imagination. Thus an initial state of passivity or enervation is posited, even though Hamlet is above all an appeal to an engagement mediated by appearance. The first scene poses the problem, as the two sentinels, Bernardo and Francisco, meet in the existential dark, engaging mutually in an appeal to recognition, which, however, is established only through the mediation of the invocation of a third and absent party and the credo of "Long live the King" (I.1, 3).[14] The figures emerge out of obscurity by invoking the life of the king, although the topic of the scene will swiftly turn to the king's death and his ghost. Whatever value for theater history or drama technics the ghost material may have held at the opening of the play as an appeal to the sensationalism of popular taste, it simultaneously poses the problem of apparitions and appearance.[15] Through the recognition of the appearance, the image of that which is absent, the viewer, and ultimately Hamlet himself, are directed toward an action that does not involve ghosts but, on the contrary, has very real-world consequences. Illusion is preface to action and, hence, literature to politics.

The issue is not that the appearance of the ghost is entwined with the political crisis of the state, as indicated by Horatio — "This bodes some strange eruption to our state" (I.1, 69) — or in the subsequent analogy to the death of Caesar. While the ghost is overdetermined as political, with its relationship to the royal household, this obvious connection concerns only the topical material. What is truly at stake is the consequence of the illusion as such: not the king's ghost, but any ghost at all. The play traces how the phenomenology of reception, viewing the illusion, suspending disbelief in order to accept the presence of the ghost, is in fact the first step toward action. It is therefore precisely not the royal venue, the household of the sovereign, that concerns us but the trajectory from illusion to deed. Illusion is not yet the deed, but neither is deed possible without the prior process of aesthetic experience, so the play suggests. For the dramatic figures' encounter with the apparition is evidently a reflective staging of the audience's encounter with the whole dramatic illusion, the play *Hamlet* itself.

The second scene confirms this passage from illusion to action, as we first encounter Hamlet. In his introductory speech, in response to the queen's question, "Why seems it so particular with thee?" (I.2, 75), Hamlet launches into a reflection on the relationship between appearance and essence, the external signs of "seeming" sad, and his putatively genuine state. He insists on the actuality of the melancholy, while conceding that the appearances might be only superficial trappings, that is, they stand in contrast to his true material condition. The naturalism of the account, with its suggestion of the semiotic arbitrariness of the appearance, is undercut by the power of the dialectic, since the two poles are entwined inextricably, and even more by Hamlet's own characterization of the relation of the signs of affect to action:

> "Seems" madam? Nay, it is. I know not "seems."
> 'Tis not alone my inky cloak, cold mother,
> Nor customary suits of solemn black,
> Nor windy suspiration of forced breath,
> No, nor the fruitful river in the eye,
> Nor the dejected 'haviour of the visage,
> Together with all forms, moods, shapes of grief,
> That can denote me truly. These indeed "seem,"
> For they are actions that a man might play.
> But I have that within which passes show —
> These but the trappings and the suits of woe. (I.2, 76 – 86)

The last two verses set up a naturalist antinomy. On the one hand, that which "passes show" and goes beyond appearance toward some materiality, as opposed to the superficiality of trappings. The question of the passage from illusion to politics is embedded in the construction of the phrase "passing show," which, taken at its word, indicates that the real is not some radical otherness to appearance, or to imagination, but rather that which passes through illusion and therefore beyond it. In this sense, the trappings themselves are not ornamental and external to substance but signposts on the way to the reality of affect or of action. Indeed, we learn just prior to this conclusion that the presumably secondary, even deceptive "trappings" are themselves already actions, that is, they are very much real, even if real only in the mode of play. In the context of an overall assertion of the material reality of the melancholy, against the queen's efforts at consolation, Hamlet's theory of semiotics and affect is oriented toward action. Even where he is most passive and moribund, the thesis of an inactive Hamlet is not supported by the text.

Illusion is discovered as action, and as a vehicle for further action. The trajectory commences with the encounter with the ghost, who functions as a muse for the vengeful prince. The enactment of illusion becomes the inspiration for productive action. This logic then passes through the discourse on the appearance of affect, until it leads eventually to Hamlet's double strategy: first his plan to feign madness, and thereby become himself a vehicle of deceptive illusion, and, second, the production of the play, organized literary deception. With regard to his acting mad — "actions that a man may play" — it is crucial to recall how he presents this plan to none other than Horatio, who, returning from his studies in Wittenberg, represents a figure of knowledge, albeit of an evidently limited character. It is Horatio who, after all, sets himself apart from Hamlet's acceptance of the ghost, attributing it, in effect, to an excess of fantasy: "He waxes desperate with imagination." (I.4, 87), which reveals Horatio to be the prosaic carrier of a less imaginative reason, as confirmed by his subsequent baffled response to the ghost as "wondrous strange" (I.5, 164). In contrast, it is poetic Hamlet who appropriately rejects prosaic Horatio's lack of imagination and calls upon him to accept the strangeness: both the strangeness of the apparition and the strangeness of the behavior that Hamlet intends to adopt as his intentional strategem of entrapment and revenge.

Hamlet's strategic simulation of madness is a political act, a step in his efforts to avenge his father's death. Yet the lynchpin of his program lies in that other production of illusion, the performance of the players. It is therefore again action through play, playacting as ludic illusion that provides for a transition to political praxis. To be sure, the character of the relationship of play to political action is fundamentally mechanical and forensic. The text is rewritten to include the murder as reported by the ghost in order to allow Hamlet to observe whether his uncle shows signs of guilt. The mousetrap is ultimately just a polygraph test, but it registers a direct and foundational connection between literature and politics: "the play's the thing / Wherein

The Democracy of Literature

I'll catch the conscience of the king" (II. 2, 602 – 3). Nonetheless, in combination with the discussion of the ghost, the theory of semiotic affect, and the dissembling of madness, the interpolated drama further underscores the fundamental concern with the role of illusion and imagination in the generation of political deed, which unfolds in the closing act of the play. It is through the process of imagination, the willingness to accept illusion, that a capacity to act matures.

The autonomous and aesthetic character of the play — not *The Murder of Gonzago* but *Hamlet* — also gives evidence that the work of art remains less than political action. If literature clears the way for action through the phenomenology of imagination, it also refrains from carrying out that action, except in the imagination, and it consequently maintains room for reflection on the possibility of the action. Literature articulates action and immediately defers it. While *Hamlet*, in one sense, traces the course of the prince from some initial immobility to action and revenge, it is not the case that the play blindly celebrates that revenge or gives its imprimatur to action for the sake of action. The conclusion of the play is too bloody, and the Danish state too devastated, for *Hamlet* to be misunderstood as a celebration of an unproblematic passage to political violence. On the contrary, having allowed for the imagination of action, the work of literature also insists on a consideration of the consequences of these potential deeds in all their gore. While this consternation is implicit in the melancholy tableau of the stage strewn with corpses, it is anticipated earlier in Hamlet's reflective comments on his sighting of Fortinbras's army. At first, the presumed willingness of these soldiers to face death confronts him with his own inaction and therefore provokes him to opt for a course of violent action: "Oh, from this time forth, / My thoughts be bloody or be nothing worth." (IV.4, 65 – 66). Nonetheless, precisely in counterpoint to this rationale for action, he expresses a contrastive denigration of the rationale for battle: the premonition of the carnage pursuant to a profoundly irrelevant cause.

> while to my shame I see
> The imminent death of twenty thousand men
> That for a fantasy and trick of fame
> Go to their graves like beds, fight for a plot
> Whereon the numbers cannot try the cause,
> Which is not tomb enough and continent
> To hide the slain? (IV.4, 58 – 65)

Hamlet's manifest shame is that for his much greater cause, the murder of his father, he has not yet taken up arms. Yet the deeper recognition of the senselessness of the imagined battle indicates the pointlessness of violence. An analogy follows: Hamlet at Fortinbras's army, imagining the death of twenty thousand, and the audience of *Hamlet*, suspending disbelief in the viewing of the killings on stage. The aesthetic illusion operates with a complexity that allows for the imagination of action and simultaneously a hesitant reflection on its consequences. In other words, the aesthetic experience is not activist in the sense of a mechanical mobilization to engagement or the approbation of any and every deed as poetic. While it allows for the possibility of action, precisely though the amplified capacity of imagination, it is also that same imagination that can pause to ponder the consequences of the deed and therefore choose to refrain from carrying out in reality the counterfactual it has considered. To exclude that reflective moment from the processes of imagination, in the name of protecting action from the burdens of Hamletlike conscience, would ultimately mean a repression of imagination and therefore, counterproductively, a reduction of the capacity to act at all. Autonomy involves the ability to act, but equally the strength of character to decide to refrain from action that might be senseless.

GOETHE's *Wilhelm Meister's Apprenticeship* involves a similar itinerary, a development from complex modalities of illusion (theater, adolescent infatuation, religion, and the ideologies of the *ancien régime*) toward a capacity to act in a modern and posttraditional society. In contrast to the Shakespearean world of the emerging modern state as Leviathan, Goethe's novel describes the construction of subjective individualism in the age of the democratic revolutions. In this sense, Friedrich Schlegel famously grouped this novel together with the French Revolution (and Fichte's philosophy) as a fundamental tendency of the age at the end of the eighteenth century.[16] The novel is barely political in any thematic sense, but it is a description of an aesthetic education, a development through art and beyond art into a civic life of productive activity, and the novel is certainly also intended as a vehicle of a similar education for its readership. The political subjectivity that emerges from aesthetic experience has little to do with the terrorist state structures that emerged in the French Revolution, especially the expansive Jacobin regime. Rather, the individualism that is constitutive in *Wilhelm Meister* and that serves as a model for the novel's public has much more to do with the individualism and dispersion of power associated with the American Revolution, to which the text makes important and multifold reference. The politics of *Hamlet* culminates in the eternal return of the state and its sovereign as the agent of decision, in the closure provided by Fortinbras; the politics of *Wilhelm Meister* are marked by the disappearance of the state and the emergence of a wide social space available for free and creative activity. Where Hamlet's motivation was, ultimately, revenge at court, Wilhelm's is ambition in an increasingly complex society. The novel models this new individuality.

While the novel is typically regarded as the paradigmatic *Bildungsroman*, tracing the developmental path of the eponymous hero, it is hardly reducible to a narrative of Wilhelm's education understood as a passage from error to truth. On the contrary, it traces a passage from a simplistic to a complex epistemology, appropriate to a society characterized by growing individualism, initiative, and mobility. It is less a journal of the hero's subjectivity than a journey into posttraditional society, and so we need to pay attention to apparently formal questions of the novel's constitution, including the relationships among statements or thoughts belonging to Wilhelm, statements by the narrator, and the statements of the growing number of characters in the novel. This constellation of claims serves to highlight the extent to which Wilhelm is trapped by his own illusions, corrected only by the narrator's irony.

The novel undergoes a significant change in the final two books, as Wilhelm surpasses the limitations of his youthful fantasies. Leaving the life of the theater behind him, he becomes much less the central actor of the plot, turning instead into an observer, one among many figures in an increasingly complex world of competing interests and points of view. It would be a misreading to see in the final chapters a victory of the panoptical Tower Society, for the members of the society are themselves relativized by the perspectives of other figures. In addition, the activities of the tower are, at least at one point, described as leftovers of former aspirations. They point toward a closed world of control rather than the open society of the novel. To be clear: This is not *Bildung* in the sense of a progression from illusion to truth, but an expansion of the horizon from a self-enclosed subjectivity to a wide world of competing individuals, without an overarching feudal order. The formal corollaries include the displacement of Wilhelm from the center of the novel in the concluding books as well as the relative silencing of the narrator, replaced by a multiplicity of voices. As it reaches its conclusion, much more of the novel transpires through reports by individual figures or in their conversations than as narratorial discourse. Hamlet's epistemology, in his opening speech, involved a contrast between that interiority of melancholy, which was authentic, and the outward trappings, the "passing show." Wilhelm too passes beyond the merely ornamental or illusionary, from theater to new horizons of engagement. Yet while Hamlet found his engagement in the violent and destructive deed, Wilhelm discovers the social world in which productive deeds are possible in a pursuit of individual happiness. The conclusion is an ironic world without closure.

In order to enter that world, Wilhelm must reexamine and revise his own dogmatic prejudices, as expressed especially in book 5, chapter 3, in the letter to his friend Werner. Wilhelm dwells on what he describes as fundamentally incompatible ways of life, at least in Germany. For him, these differences "are not due to any pretentiousness on the part of the aristocracy or the submissiveness of the bourgeoisie, but to the whole organization of society."[17] A full and rounded personality is possible, according to Wilhelm, only for the aristocracy. The nobleman represents simply through his presence; he is born with standing, and so he appears. In contrast, the middle class, the carrier of commercial activity, is tied to business activity. "The burgher should not ask: 'Who am I?' but 'What do I have? What insights, what knowledge, what ability, what capital?' The nobleman tells us everything through the person he presents, but the burgher does not, and should not. A nobleman can and must be someone who represents by his appearance, whereas the burgher simply is, and when he tries to put on an appearance, the effect is ludicrous or in bad taste. The nobleman should act and achieve, the burgher must labor and create, developing some of his capabilities in order to be useful, but without it ever being assumed that there is or ever can be a harmonious interplay of qualities in him, because in order to make himself useful in one direction, he has to disregard everything else" (175).

The passage weaves together two distinct claims. First, Wilhelm suggests that, while the aristocrat can cultivate a full and cohesive personality, the bourgeois tends toward a one-sidedness, reflecting the exigencies of the social division of labor. This image, consonant with much of classic-romantic philosophy and subsequent critical theory, points toward the social construction of personality: not a natural given or an abstract essence but an internalization of forms of social organization. Furthermore, the economic forces of specialization, from which the aristocracy is allegedly shielded, force a concomitant specialization of the individual as alienation or as professionalism. Wilhelm believes not only that he might escape this one-sidedness by an aristocratic path to totality but also that there is something fundamentally urgent about avoiding such a one-sidedness.

The pursuit of totalization takes on a particular significance in light of the debate over the *Bildungsroman* as genre. If one adopts the model of a linear movement from illusion to truth, or from the puppet theater to the Tower Society, then Wilhelm's cultural criticism, the critique of particularity as one-sided, has some plausibility, since the desideratum would be deemed to be the holistic vantage point of an all-embracing conclusion. The structure of *Wilhelm Meister's Apprenticeship* hardly supports this argument. The Tower Society does not offer an apodictic conclusion. Instead, it is just one among several pedagogic, economic, and rhetorical possibilities in the closing books. Indeed, the evidence provided by the form of the novel would suggest that Goethe was predisposed to demonstrate the salutary significance of individualistic particularity, what Wilhelm denounces as one-sidedness, precisely as a vehicle of creativity. The multiplication of individual possibilities allows for competition and innovation, in the way that a single and unambiguous truth, such as dogma, would only constrain. Reason is not understood as the voice of ultimate authority, inescapably valid for all and for all times, but as the dynamic and reflective capacity of individuals. One might even speculate that Wilhelm's desire for totality, as suggested in the letter to Werner, indicates a repressive nostalgia for the protective confinement of his middle-class childhood, no matter how much he attempts to imbue it with an aristocratic sheen. In that case, however, his desire to enter the nobility ought to be recognized just as his own, particular, bourgeois career, masked as a pursuit for totalizing completion.

While the first claim inherent in the letter to Werner maps the duality of totality and particularity onto class differences, the second claim involves the interplay of being and appearance. In order to escape the mere facticity of bourgeois life, determined by the degraded categories of achievement and possession, Wilhelm aspires to the higher truth of illusion, where theatricality and aristocracy overlap. The novel partially corroborates Wilhelm's concerns. Although the critique that he directs at Werner is overstated and not at all the last word on the bourgeoisie, the novel does attribute to Werner a limited, commercial *Weltanschauung* from which Wilhelm would understandably try to distance himself. Yet out of the fire and into the frying pan: The theatrical world, with which Wilhelm hopes to correct the failings of his own bourgeois provenance, is itself beleaguered by the pressures of commercial exigencies. Aesthetics aside, theater directors cannot escape problems with contracts and meeting the payroll. In general, the argument of the letter nonetheless suggests that the transition from *Sein* to *Schein* represents a progress in conceptual abstraction, a recognition of the complexities of representation that escape Werner fully. Werner's crude positivism of being lacks the complexities and nuances of Wilhelm's capacity for illusion (an opposition that recalls Phaedrus's narrow accuracy and Socrates' capacious imagination).

All this speaks for the perspicacity of Wilhelm's claims in the letter. Yet the text of the letter is, at the same time, deeply flawed. It is flawed, first, in the class compromise that it suggests, and it is here where it is most German and emblematic for the *Sonderweg*, the presumed underdevelopment of a bourgeois culture in eighteenth- and nineteenth-century Germany. Because he, as bourgeois, cannot rule, since political power is reserved for the aristocracy, Wilhelm chooses to imitate aristocrats. Theatrical representation is the vehicle through which the bourgeoisie succumbs to the illusion that it might lay claim to political power, and much subsequent German history follows from that particular self-deception. In place of liberal democratic institutions of governance, it was satisfied with a vibrant theater life. Yet Wilhelm's association of aristocracy and appearance is, more importantly, false in its core claim, that is, the description of the aristocracy as solely concerned with appearance and hostile to genuine achievement. This caricature is belied emphatically by the encounter with the nobility around Lothario in the final chapters. Indeed, if there is any single illusion that Wilhelm, in the course of this presumed novel of development, overcomes, it must be the deeply bourgeois fantasy of the indolent aristocrat, since we find, by the novel's end, that the German aristocracy is nothing but the better bourgeoisie: rational, acquisitive, and entrepreneurial.

Wilhelm Meister's Apprenticeship traces a repositioning of subjectivity, from a simplistic opposition of illusion and truth to an ironic integration into a competitive multiplicity of interests. At the same time, it explores the very constitution of an emerging modern society in which the ideals of the Enlightenment are pursued — or, at least, Goethe would wish it so. We know of Lothario's engagement in the American Revolution, and his decision to return to Germany and pursue those revolutionary ideas there. "*Here or nowhere is America*" (264), he had written to Jarno, announcing that it would be on his own estate, in Germany, that he would pursue the liberal democratic revolution. The call to politics could not be clearer. "It is quite apparent to me that, in many matters concerning the management of my estates, I cannot do without the services of my farmhands, and also that I must rigidly insist on certain rights; but it is also clear to me that certain dispositions, though advantageous to me, are not absolutely essential, and some of them could be changed for the benefit of my workers. One doesn't always lose by giving up something" (263). Here one finds the reform-minded aristocracy very much engaged in the affairs of the world — hardly the theatrical aristocracy of Wilhelm's letter — and nonetheless unimpeded by the closed-minded middle-class avarice that seems to characterize Werner, at least in Wilhelm's hostile description of him.

The aristocracy that Goethe portrays is evidently prepared to pursue revolutionary changes in the interest of economic and social progress. Challenged by Werner, who, typically, expresses concern about the rate of return on a capital investment, Lothario replies unambiguously: "That will not be adversely affected if the State, in return for reasonable and regular tax payments, allows us to give up the feudal hocus-pocus and thereby grants us a complete right of disposal over our property, so that we would not be obliged to maintain it in such large units" (311). Goethe has Lothario express a clear hostility to the feudal system, the "hocus pocus" of vassalage relations. He calls for unencumbered property rights, and he subsequently proposes that individuals be able to marry freely, without feudal restrictions. That the novel itself concludes with three "mixed marriages," marriages of inclination between the bourgeoisie and the aristocracy, provides a diegetic corroboration of Lothario's reformism.

Wilhelm Meister's Apprenticeship investigates the opportunities for individuality in the context of an accelerated modernization. While Wilhelm himself, temporarily at least, treats the aesthetic opportunity of the theater as a vehicle for an illusory integration into the aristocracy of the *ancien régime*, his own understanding of that aristocracy and society as a whole was severely limited, as the novel demonstrates in detail. His maturation requires overcoming his theatrical adolescence. From aesthetic experience to public reason, from puerile fantasy to private property: This is the developmental trajectory implied by the novel and to which it invites the reader. The goal is not an ultimate reason, some definitive conclusion (Friedrich's irony at the end prevents that) but a vision of rational individuals, whose capacity for freedom has been cultivated through aesthetic experience and realized in an emerging market economy.

Wilhelm Meister's Apprenticeship concerns the standing of reason in the human condition, the emergence of rational individuals in the process of modernization, and the role of aesthetic autonomy, especially the pleasure of illusion, in that development, which is both civilizational and personal. Social progress is a matter of rationalization, but not in an authoritarian sense of a reason imposed from above. The novel describes free individuals learning to use their reason to make their own choices. The ability to grow into that reason depends on a maturity for which the aesthetic experience is an indispensable passageway. Literature, therefore freedom.

Hamlet finds his way from the experience of appearance and illusion to the possibility of action in the context of the emergence of the modern state and the decline of medieval networks of power. The individual faces administrative power and responds with a search for a praxis mediated by fiction. Two centuries later, in the age of the democratic revolution, Wilhelm Meister discovers the social world of action through an aesthetic education. He must work his way through illusions in order to overcome them, just as the illusions of the *ancien régime* are being surpassed. Indeed, precisely that democratization of the world, as sketched in the reform plans discussed above and modeled on the American Revolution, has as its precondition the capacity of imagination, as well as the oxymoronic process of imagining a realization: the challenge of a transition from the counterfactuals of the imagination to achievement in the world. That the ghost from *Hamlet* reappears in the theater passages of *Wilhelm Meister's Apprenticeship* underscores the continuity in the emergence of a liberal democratic modernity through the institutions of aesthetic autonomy.

8

Imagination and Economy

LITERATURE GIVES expression to the imaginative excess that freely surpasses its moment of production. While the literary work is surely colored
by its time and place, what makes it specifically literary is precisely its ability
to escape the constraints of context. It is this same freedom that defines the
role of literature in civilizational history. Understood as the formal structure of imagination organized into linguistic symbols, literature engages
with the human condition by generating a profound and dynamic predisposition toward social development, not only by promoting literacy (with
all its media-specific consequences: rationality, sequential thought, critical
culture, democratic dissemination of texts) but also through its inherent
valorization of the new. Heir to the axial religions of transcendence, autonomous literature has become, in effect, their greatest missionary, proclaiming
to the world the urgency of creative originality and the redemptive promise
of happiness. Constantly representing possibilities that surpass the present
reality, literature invites consideration of alternatives to any given state of
affairs. At the same time, addressing the reader as a member of the public, literature lays the foundation of a polis; it thereby takes on a political
character and provides a pedagogy leading toward democracy. Indeed, the
implied audience of literature, the reflective individuals of the literary community, corresponds with the characteristically democratic structure of a
political community, the public sphere, a collective form that is nonetheless
made up of decidedly uncollectivized individuals, each with a distinct subjectivity and aware of that singular distinctiveness. The elaboration of the
autonomous work of art as a centerpiece of Western cultural history is there-

fore inseparable from the normative standing of autonomous individuality and, consequently, the political structures appropriate to that individuality. To speak, with critical theory, of an emancipatory character in the work of art, and especially in literature, can only mean that literature is, in its very essence, a democratizing force: not through any democratic *parti pris* or tendentiousness on the part of the author but through the literary-aesthetic experience itself. Whatever the political affiliation of the author of a work of literature, the dissemination of literature, like the spread of literacy, is democratic. A similar dynamic operates between literature and economic processes, to which we now turn.

MULTIPLE OVERLAPS between economy and literature indicate a deep affinity between the two social sectors. Some of these intersections are not significant to the argument pursued here. Where one sector simply remains topical for the other — representing economy in literature, or inserting literature, as an industrial sector, into the economic system — we identify these variants only in order to note their limited import in this context. For example, the question of economy and literature might be reduced simply to programmatic economic positions propounded directly and intentionally by an author, in a sense similar to the possibility of tendentious advocacy as a version of the presence of politics as a topic in literature. Frank Norris can be read as a critic of late nineteenth-century capitalism, Pound integrates economic doctrine into the *Cantos*, and one can surely derive positions on market exchange, international commerce, and contract law from the *Merchant of Venice*. But these historicist investigations — the standing of the authorial voice in its treatment of contemporary economy — are unlikely to generate fundamental insight into the character of Norris's novels, or Pound's poetry, or the enduring fascination exercised by Shakespeare's drama. Whatever we might learn about economy as topic in these works would remain largely incidental to their literary substance. (Needless to add, what we would learn about the dynamic of the economy itself from literary sources is not likely to add significantly to what an economic historian would be able to derive from other sorts of data.)

Economy may be represented more subtly in literary works, where it is less a matter of authorial advocacy and more a function of generic conventions or aesthetic form. In the course of the eighteenth century, theater was transformed by the gradual displacement of the aristocracy from the stage and its substitution by bourgeois figures in the French *mélodrame* and the German *bürgerliches Trauerspiel*.[1] This is arguably more a sociological than a specifically economic phenomenon, if not for the significance of the middle class that automatically poses the question of the market economy. Gustav Freytag's *Soll und Haben*, a best seller of the German nineteenth century, is instructive on this point. For the authorial intent is made quite clear by the choice of epigraph, a citation from Freytag's friend and collaborator, Julian Schmidt, calling for literature to present the German people at work. In fact, however, the substance of the text hardly shows manual laborers or any events in a sphere of activity that could possibly be described as productive; instead, this *Bildungsroman* treats the private affairs and public concerns of the merchant hero. The representation of economy shows a contrast of this sphere of circulation with twin foils: anti-Semitic imagery of Jewish acquisitiveness and similarly antiaristocratic figures of noble indolence (the latter clearly the opposite of the productive aristocracy we discussed in *Wilhelm Meister's Apprenticeship*).[2]

In the above two cases, exemplifying authorial intention and the tropes of generic convention, economy is little more than a topic for the literary work. Neither construal necessarily tells us much about literature as an autonomous creation, and therefore nothing about a necessary connection between literature as such and economy; in other words, the economic material remains merely a topical choice and therefore only one among many such possible choices. Pound's eccentric economic theories may be read, indirectly, as an interpolated aesthetics, shedding light on his own poetic self-understanding. Still, this too remains at best an indirect connection, insofar as the economic material would act only as a metaphor for literature. To think through the mediation of economics in literature in reverse: One would hardly turn first to the economic passages in the *Cantos* as evidence for the character of economic life in the early twentieth century.

The corollary to economics as a topic for literature is literature as an object of the economy, for example the publishing industry and the literary marketplace. But treating literature as a commodity in the economic system would hardly differ from an economic study of any other distinctive commodity. One can certainly consider trends in the publishing sector, just as one might study the energy market or the automobile industry. Literary objects might plausibly be recognized as having some particular character. Nonetheless, it is surely also the case that other commodities have their own particularities as well; the distinctiveness of literary works therefore tends to disappear and become a matter of the noise associated with any local area of the economy. The number of references to commodity aesthetics in contemporary literary criticism make it surprising that so little serious attention has been paid to real economic data on literature and its production: rates of book publication and sales, income data for authors, or capitalization in the publishing industry. All the same, such matters are not of immediate concern here.

There is one aspect of the economic frame around literature that is of particular pertinence to our study of the standing of autonomy in history. As Émile Zola insisted, "Money has emancipated the writer, money has created modern letters" and Pierre Bourdieu cites this testimony on the historical emergence of the principle of autonomy.[3] Both for literature and for the other arts, the development of a market economy allowed for the emancipation of the author and artist from dependence on aristocratic, state, or church patronage. The ability to attempt to sell one's works on an open market separated the producer from subordination to the wealth and therefore the immediate will and taste of the patron. What followed was hardly self-sufficient independence, however, since market imperatives are far from irrelevant, even if they are more mediated than a patron's commands.[4] Nonetheless, a significant if not unlimited range of flexibility emerged, within which the author's creativity could come into play more effectively than under the regime of patronage. The market economy is, in this sense, most definitely a precondition of artistic freedom.

It does not follow that autonomy is solely an effect of the market as it develops in the emerging capitalism of postmedieval modernity. As we have seen, autonomy—far from simply a function of the market position of the author—depends on several dimensions deeply rooted in the long-term civilizational process. These include the symbol usage in prehistoric language acquisition, the reduction of homeostatic pressure writing developed in the ancient world, and the integrity of creativity that derives from Judeo-Christian theological concepts. This complex background predates modernity in the standard usage of the term. Market mechanisms themselves are not solely a modern phenomenon, no matter how much their consistent and rational expansion is unique to the modern economy. Zola's emphatic insight into the interaction of market and freedom may be symptomatic of the nineteenth century and its developed and self-conscious capitalist economy, but the phenomenon of market exchange itself has deeper roots in economic history. The very fact that works of art might be bought and sold, even in antiquity, contributed to the constitution of the autonomous work of art and

Imagination and Economy

therefore to its emancipatory character: the dynamism of market exchange imbues the work of art with its own spirit of freedom. The availability of the work of art for commercial exchange is one consequence of the portability, discussed earlier.

Against Marxist strategies of describing the work of art as a commodity and therefore degraded, the neo-Marxist Theodor Adorno argued that the work could retain a certain standing outside economics. He insisted on the point that no genuine work is solely a commodity, thereby shielding it from the hostile judgment otherwise implied by Marxist anticapitalism. Yet this insistence on the noncommodity character of the work — as important as it was as a response to an antiaesthetic reductionism that treated the work solely as commodity — is itself insufficient. Instead of defending the aesthetic object on the grounds that it is not (or not fully) a commodity, it is worth considering the real taboo in Marxist and post-Marxist literary criticism: the thesis that the integration of the artistic production into a capitalist system may in fact be salutary and a source of its emancipatory substance. Commerce, ergo culture? This line of argument would lead quickly to the assertion that artistic freedom is an effect of capitalist relations. Were it not for the marketability of art, the very phenomenon of adversarial art would be impossible, since the crushing weight of the patron would be felt constantly (as typically remains the case in subsidized public art). For this reason, without rejecting the notion of commodity aesthetics, it is productive to think through the character of the commodity status of the work of art and the benefits it implies. The question of literature and economy should be pursued precisely with regard to a notional interdependence of literature and the capitalist economy, the one autonomous because of the market, the other mediated through literature. If the phrase *commodity aesthetics* has any use, it is as an indicator of how the development of the market for literature and art contributes significantly to the democratic implications of aesthetic autonomy. It is, at least in part, the force of the market that drives artistic progress, and it is that same force that can make art and literature progressive, in the sense of an association with processes of democratization.

More important than representations of the economy within literature, be it in the sense of authorial intent or generic convention, we need to explore where and how economic parameters operate structurally within the work itself. Such a project runs immediately into considerable resistance. The typical critical account of the impact of the market economy on aesthetic production is largely hostile. On account of the widespread apprehensions about the market common in the contemporary humanities, the commonest manner of addressing this topic uses the denunciatory term *commercialization,* suggesting that artistic integrity is sacrificed in order to render the product more marketable. This anxiety about commercialization itself derives from a long tradition from early nineteenth-century romanticism. Moreover, this charge of venality presumes a context of competition between a beleaguered high culture of authentic works and an irresistible and insatiable demand for a degraded popular culture. Consequently, market influence on the internal structure of the work is normally regarded solely in pejorative terms, particularly with the underlying assumption that the writer compromises creativity and hence the authenticity of the work whenever he or she takes public taste or consumers' habits into account. The dismissal of commercialization in literature is, in the end, an expression of a hostility to market mechanisms by an appeal to a vague but implicitly elitist assumption about culture.

Without denying the possibility of that destructive scenario — some mass-market products may indeed be of low quality — one should still reserve considerable skepticism for this received opinion, which reflects the biases of a cultural elite toward both popular culture and the marketplace. The term *culture* is turned into an instrument with which to attack the market. Alternatively, one ought to ask how the market is in fact conducive for aesthetic production. One can surely argue that all new writing takes place in a context characterized not only by the durability of previous writing — hence the pressure to engage with the tradition, whether as rebellion or as adoption, as discussed in earlier chapters — but also by the presence of other contemporary writing. No writer is the sole writer in the present. The problem of influence can be examined in terms that go beyond historical inheritance, for example, Shakespeare's influence on Brecht, but also in present forces of competition, as in Brecht's influence on Sartre. Moreover, most writers do not stop at the production of one work but continue to produce; hence they can gauge the public — and market — responses to their own previous work, as well as the response to the products of their contemporaries. It follows that a literary scholarship prepared to consider competitive strategies among contemporary authors ought to be able to trace any individual writer's next move as part of a market dynamic influencing the character of ongoing writing. The logic of the market as integrated into the work is not only a matter of accommodating the public, and certainly not merely a matter of reducing the work to the presumably low level of the public (as an elite criticism would have it). The market consequences for literary production are at least as much a matter of competitive actions vis-à-vis professional contemporaries. This aspect of literary history is largely ignored because of the overwhelming hermeneutic bias to interpret individual works, rather than larger trends, as well as the academic bias against serious accounts of the productivity of competition.

THE PROPOSAL TO examine how writing is in part a function of competition in the literary marketplace is one example of how literary history might systematically pursue the presence of economic categories in literature, without restricting the discussion to the superficial topical representations of economic material within literary works. Marketplace competition is an integral component in the history of literature. There is, however, a related topic, a second nontrivial overlap of literature and economy: the manner in which autonomous literature itself generates character predispositions that are relevant to economic behavior. In order to focus on this connection between literature and economics, it is useful, again, to reconsider the model of the connection posited between literature and politics. In the previous chapter it was argued that the appeal of literature to a public necessarily implicated it in a political discussion, as does the obligation to choice that is inherent in the constant decisions of the writing process. From this came the claim that literature is inherently political (because directed at the public sphere) and, furthermore, this politics is inherently democratic (because literature addresses reflective individuals who maintain their independence even as they participate in a public). Yet just as literature opens onto the political sphere, so too does literature, precisely through its autonomy and aside from any topical preferences or ideological message, generate structures of thought and behavior that are pertinent to the economy, specifically a capitalist economy. To demonstrate this claim demands an adequate discussion of literature and economy that can consider capitalism as more complex than the narrow Marxist reduction of capitalism to a system of commodity production. Therefore, though an inquiry into the economic virtues inherent in literature need not exclude the character of the commodity form, it must also explore aspects of literature relevant to a more complex concept of capitalist economic life.

The pertinent account of the relationship between literature and economy can only have to do with the basic structural characteristics of literature and, as noted, not with particular contents, biographical affiliations, and the like.

But those fundamental structural characteristics are precisely the building blocks of literary autonomy that have been discussed in the course of this book. In this sense, one can argue that the economic relevance of literature resides, for example, above all in the consequences of literacy: Economic development depends on the proliferation of literacy and — a separate but related claim — the distribution of literacy skills depends on some minimal dissemination of literature, if only in the sense of its importance in the educational processes of literacy acquisition.[5] This latter point is demonstrated by the fact that second-language acquisition and fictional literature reading remain tightly linked, despite efforts to separate them, and the same surely holds for first-language literacy: From the moment at which parents read stories to children, and then during the utilization of fiction in elementary school pedagogy, literacy acquisition proceeds through fiction. Of course, literacy is a much wider field than the reading of imaginative literature — it is reasonable to assume that the direct economic benefits of literacy have more to do with the ability to disseminate sorts of technical information — but imaginative literature nonetheless remains a core component, a sort of trace element within the culture that stands as a demonstration of the legitimacy of imagination. Socialization, which includes literacy acquisition, also typically passes through some extensive involvement with fiction, at least during childhood and adolescence, as reading skills and habits are acquired. The dissemination of literacy in general, including the ability to read material directly related to economic processes, depends on biographical learning processes that are deeply linked to phases in which reading imaginative literature is decisive.

Still, this pedagogical argument too is not genuinely about literature as such but only about literature as a vehicle for literacy; the economic significance of literature is therefore only indirect, if regarded solely in this light. To make a strong argument linking literature and economy, it is indispensable to proceed precisely from the one core and definitive aspect of literature, its standing as a formal structure of the imagination, the representation of the counterfactual, the possibility of which is accepted provisionally in the context of suspended disbelief. Imagination is linked to the facility with symbols inherent in language use, and it is precisely here that economic categories come into play. Imagination becomes the medium through which an excess or surplus to empirical reality can be envisioned and articulated. Because empirical reality in much of human history has typically been characterized by considerable material scarcity, literature allows for the invocation of abundance, although surely also in rhetorically powerful counterpoint to expressions of poverty and suffering. Literature is always about more than what exists empirically.

Yet the scope of the excess, which can be unlimited precisely because it is imaginary, can simultaneously threaten to overwhelm the real or, what amounts to nearly the same thing, it can slide into a sort of escapism in the face of actual scarcity and poverty. Literature attempts to manage this disruptively open character of the imagination through the sensuous category of taste, as well as the conceptual and minatory terms of judgment. The economics of literature are therefore not to be found primarily in the manner in which this or that work portrays the capitalist, the worker, or the merchant, but rather in the shifting configurations of imagined abundance, the subjectivity of taste, and the imperative of judgment. As long as there has been literature, there has been literary criticism as well to warn *caveat emptor* in face of imaginary excess. The core relationship of literature to economics is therefore in the articulation of psychological categories that allow for certain forms of economic behavior: the imagination of surplus, the caution of evaluation.

Discussing politics, as it emerges from literature, we noted the categorical tension between decisionism, which is the privilege of the powerful sovereign, and the liberal constitutional tendency toward a distribution or dispersion of the same power. A similar antinomy pervades modern economics, viewed from the literary side: the imagination of abundance, on the one hand, and, on the other, the imperative of selection. In the face of real-world scarcity as well as the potentially unlimited abundance implied by the imagination, literature imposes an economic choice on the reader, the need to choose among the surplus of imaginary possibilities. The literary text, the array of words on the page, allows for some indeterminacy in the sense that a reader may envision the contents of a given fiction in multiple ways. The reader selects among the possible understandings of the text in order to make sense of it, by opting, at least provisionally, for one imputed coherence, among the several that might be available. That structure of individual choice is at the basis of the category of taste, which arises through literature but which allows the reader to participate in economic choice more broadly. Economic choice is, ultimately, a selection, based in part on taste, among various options of consumption, unlike the political choice that entails a need for decisive action.

Imaginative literature therefore addresses the reader as an economic actor defined in two complementary ways: as the potentially entrepreneurial visionary who might creatively pursue the realization of the abundance present initially only in the imagination, and as the deliberative and selective consumer, sorting through multiple offerings with the help of taste and judgment and therefore potentially prepared for the complexity of market decisions. The economic categories inherent in literature, following from the standing of imagination, are therefore imaginative entrepreneurship (as visionary) and evaluation (as deliberative selection). These are furthermore dimensions of the capitalist economy that the reductionist model of commodity production largely ignores.

Literature, as political, appeals to the reader to make a choice in order to decide on action, but it also disperses that action by allowing for the multiplicity of readers who make up the public. Literature, as economic, appeals to the reader to deliberate and select, but it also invokes the imaginative creativity that is constitutive of any dynamic economic enterprise. In each case, literature as political and literature as economic, the categorical pairs represent sorts of internal corrections: The dispersion of power counteracts the centralizing will to act, and the practice of judgment reins in the free play of the imagination. The very openness of freedom — in political choice, economic vision, or poetic creation — is constantly accompanied by principles of caution and deliberation, indispensable components of any project to realize the contents of imagination, that is, the requisite realism necessary to transform a vision into a reality. Moreover, it is in literature, the privileged home of imagination, that the most dynamic categories of both politics and economics overlap. Political deeds and economic values are prefigured in aesthetic judgment. The engaged citizen and the innovative entrepreneur, our political and economic personae, are both the addressees of literature, strictly speaking. It is not literature *about* politics or *about* economics that is at stake here. Rather, in the very constitution of literature at its most poetic, the possibility of imaginative and innovative human action is elaborated, explored, and invoked: action in the public sphere of citizens, innovation in the pursuit of abundance. The distinctively Western institutions of political democracy and free-market capitalism are therefore intimately bound up with a third distinct institution of the West: autonomous literature. Its project is the amplification and focus of the human capacity for imagination, which has consequently come to pervade political and economic structures. Autonomous literature is foundational for the teleology of democracy and capitalism, as demonstrated by three examples, which display the interplay of imagination and economy at different points in the long development of economic history.

THE BOOK OF PSALMS is a foundational anthology for Western poetry. It is here that an emphatic notion of individual subjectivity is first articulated at length, and this same subjectivity eventually grows into the genuine topic of subsequent lyric poetry, just as much as it emerges as the central component in the Western elaboration of individualism. The volume is of course also a central source of Western liturgy. Poetry, in other words, contributes to the articulation of the categorical structure of individuality, which becomes the agent of social and cultural development.

Simultaneously, the psalms corroborate the hypotheses on literary history explored in this book, the relationship of literature to language acquisition, literacy, religion, and politics. The collection as a whole underscores the interplay between individuation and language, both through the repeated, if conventional, ascriptions of authorship (normally to David), that is, a paradigmatic representation of individual identity, and in the insistence on a definition of poetic praxis as incantatory, the recurring motif of "I sing." While incantation, as oral performance, stands at odds with the scriptural—written and therefore silent—character of the texts, the very standing of these texts as written, and not transcriptions of originally oral performances, is corroborated by the many instances of acrostic or alphabetic compositional practices. The fact that some psalms begin each verse with alphabetically ordered Hebrew letters would be lost on a mere listener of "song" but quite evident to a reader. The fact of literacy is demonstrable therefore on the basis of intratextual evidence (as it was in the Bellerophon incident in the *Iliad*). Thus Psalms is clearly not a relic of a primary orality, despite the incantatory self-characterization of the genre. Indeed, one can conjecture that the insistence on singing represents at most a memory of a preliterate oral performance. Furthermore, that the psalms also participate in structures of religious transcendence is equally clear and hardly needs elaboration; suffice it to say that through the very content of the direct relationship of individual to God, individuality itself acquires the heightened pathos that becomes defining for Western subjectivity. Nonetheless, at the same time, for all their message of individuality, the drama of the individual and his god, these texts also become preferred selections for collective prayer and therefore participate in the structure of community and public life. The oral performance of the written psalms, themselves marked by a memory of an erstwhile orality, is at the core of Western liturgy.

Beyond these categories discussed in earlier chapters — language (authorship), literacy (versus orality), religion (transcendence), and politics (public performance) — the goal here is to ferret out the economic categories within literature, which requires a closer examination of one particular text. Psalm 27 begins

> [A Psalm] of David.
> The Lord is my light and my salvation; whom shall I fear?
> The Lord is the stronghold of my life; of whom shall I be afraid?[6]

At the outset the poet places this classic expression of confidence in the infinite strength and security that the Lord provides as a foundation for the very possibility of individuality. Implicitly here, with the references to fear, and explicitly in the subsequent verses, the world emerges as a field of violent adversity, populated by military opponents, while it is God alone who affords protection. Thus in verse 6, the poet anticipates being lifted up above his enemies and, consequently, promises to "sing and make melody to the Lord."

Yet a transition in perspective immediately ensues in verse 7, suddenly with a direct address to God, who had appeared previously in the third person only. The poet now appeals to the divine addressee to "hear" and, suddenly, to "not hide" his face. This reversal of direction, as well as the chiasmic structure of sound and sight, moves the text from the initial section, the victory song, into a very different modality emphasizing an existential context of abandonment. Thus verses 9 and 10:

> Do not hide your face from me. Do not turn your servant away in anger, you
>   Who have been my help. Do not cast me off, do not forsake me,
>   O God of my salvation!
> If my father and mother forsake me, the Lord will take me up.

The author has been shaken, and his voice destabilized. It has lost its initially self-confident tone, as it shifts erratically between second and third person modes of expression. Furthermore, the initial triumphalism of the outset has dissipated and given way to a profound anxiety. It is no longer, or not only, external adversaries who threaten subjectivity but the very human condition of losing one's parents, and as much as verse 10 concludes with the affirmation of divine love, verse 9 gives expression to a deep underlying concern. The author quivers, oscillating between fear of godforsakenness and faith in redemption, while the consolation of the latter never fully expunges the panic of the former. What had commenced as triumph turns abruptly into a plea for security, since the initial threat, external military adversity, has given way to a much more profound condition of subjective abandonment. The psalm therefore concludes with the admonition to wait, in verse 14, "Wait for the Lord; be strong, and let your heart take courage; wait for the Lord!" The immediate abundance of divine protection in the first six verses has, in effect, been deferred in the second section until some undetermined future. Furthermore, the initial contrasts between military adversaries and God take on a considerably richer texture by verse 10, where the contrast is transformed into one between God and the psalmist's parents, cast now in the role once reserved for external opponents. The implication is that a radical individualism in the relationship to God is certain because he is not only more powerful than enemies, but also more steadfast even than one's parents. One should trust in him alone and in no one else, neither in military force nor parental love. This infinitely heightened individualism, consecrated by the divine sanction, goes hand in hand with the transformation of belief: from the objective certainty of the victory song into the subjectivized encouragement to faith inherent in the injunction to wait.

The goal here is not an exhaustive elaboration of the specific character of religious faith expressed in this core text of Western religion but rather, more narrowly, an exploration of one aspect of its standing as literature, the economic question. That heuristic distinction is not easy to maintain in practice, particularly in the light of the earlier arguments that faith, in the religions of transcendence, overlaps with the counterfactuality of fiction and, more broadly, imagination in the institution of literary autonomy. Western expectations for the work of art, and literature in particular, are informed by the emphatic sense of sacred scripture inseparable from notions of religion. This proximity of literature and religion, which makes distinguishing them so difficult, is perhaps particularly true for the psalms, which have become central to Jewish and Christian liturgy, that is, public expressions or celebrations of transcendence. Expressions of belief and suspensions of disbelief, faith and fiction, grow nearly congruent here. Needless to say, these reflections are quite at odds with those secularizing treatments of biblical texts as literature that disregard their sacred claims. On the contrary, the alternative assertion made here and argued at length in chapter 6 involves the manner in which the very category of literature is imbued with expectations of sacred transcendence, no matter how secular or seemingly irreligious its ostensible content may be. In the case at hand, we can also add the claim that Psalms is a key source, as genre history, for the tradition of Western lyric poetry.

For the argument on economic categories within literature, it should be noted that Psalm 27 is not an easy choice, with no obvious economic references, either to producers or markets. It is not about ancient peasants, tending flocks, nor is it comparable to the narrative of Jesus and the money changers in the Temple, which might equally lend itself to a topical, economic reading of ancient social ethics. Just as in the treatment of politics, the important point is not to find directly referential passages, that is, expressions of some economic program, but to derive the pertinent economic concepts from the standing of the imaginative text as such. For that reason, this text is a good choice.

Nonetheless, important elements point toward foundations of an economic discourse. Most prominently, economic categories of surplus are enacted in the very verse structure itself — admittedly not unique to this psalm but characteristic of the collection altogether — its iterative differentiation of imagery, "repetition with difference," characteristic of Lowth's "mystical allegories," in Milbank's treatment, as discussed in chapter 6. For example, pivoting around the experience of fear in the first verse, "light" and "salvation" are repeated but transformed into "stronghold of my life," a plausible but not obvious elaboration. The repetition of the same idea suggests a tight control of the imagery, indeed a sort of tropic parsimony, but this semantic severity in fact only serves to highlight the excess, the imaginative production of surplus as new material appears, in effect, always gratuitously. Thus, the expressed content that involves an abundance of confidence in the infinity of divine protection is accompanied by an abundance of material. This is a poetry that announces a need and then meets it: demand and supply. The dialectic of threat, or danger, and confidence in the course of the first six verses maps precisely onto these economic structures, and this duality, inherent in verse structure and the initial content, is repeated in the overall architecture of the poem, the suturing of the victory celebration in the first part with the subsequent lyric of anxious vulnerability in the second. The irony of the inversion is underscored, for example, through the rhetoric of seclusion: in verse 5, the Lord affords protection by "concealing" the poet,

Imagination and Economy

but in verse 9, after the peripatetic inversion of the rhetoric, the poet pleads that the Lord not "hide" his face.

In the context of the absolute threat of annihilation, an imminent reduction to nothingness, Psalm 27 imagines and expresses faith in an absolute abundance. However, in between abandonment to nothing and a divine embrace of infinite love, scarcity and excess, the poet chooses a cautious middle ground and seeks security. The imagination of surplus is therefore moderated by the more cautious principle of individual safety. This is precisely the dialectic of vision and taste explored in earlier arguments, and it is played out in the course of the poem. It is an expansive, even manic vision that pervades the praise poem of the first part, a genre that echoes with heroic battle, the warrior personality, and political deed, culminating in the name of the literary action: song. At this acme, the ecstatic effusion turns back on itself, seeking out a dimension of subjective interiority, where the search for protection turns into reclusive anxiety. The external threats of the opening — the menacing armies — are reshaped into the internal, subtle, and notionally more advanced and civilized threats of deception and mendacity. The epic world of heroic action gives way to the prosaic world of representation and exchange, the bourgeois sensibility of self and self-doubt — the doubt inscribed in the confusion of sight and sound in the transitional verses (6 – 8) and the destabilization of subject and object as evidenced in the shifting addressee.

Consider now the conclusion, which represents an alternative to the victory song of the beginning:

> Teach me your way, O Lord; and lead me on an even path because of my
>   enemies.
> Do not give me up to the will of my adversaries, for false
>   witnesses have risen against me, and they are breathing out violence.
> I believe that I shall see the goodness of the Lord in the land of the living.
> Wait for the Lord; be strong, and let your heart take courage; wait for
>   the Lord!

In terms of the expressed ethic of individuation, the transition from warrior to bourgeois culture is clear. The new goal becomes a very unheroic "teaching," finding a very bourgeois "even path," and the individual need to be able to judge truth and falsehood in a society of "false witnesses": *caveat emptor*. What follows is less political action, and certainly not soldierly prowess, but rather an ability to defer, to restrain oneself, to exercise self-control, and to wait. This substantive shift in ethics is mirrored by the transition in poetic language that is crucial, as the rhetoric slips from the visionary certitude in the counterfactual (or at least not empirically given) divine protection to humble expressions of pleading. The unbounded imagination is tamed by individuated judgment. Bourgeois prudence retracts the escape from adversity projected by imagination. It is therefore precisely from the phenomenon of fiction (or faith as fiction) that the dual substructure of bourgeois economics emerge. The aspiration to surplus is followed by a hesitant interiority, aggressive action elicits reflection, caution, and a pursuit of elusive truthfulness in a world of deceit.

IMAGINATIVE LITERATURE opens onto politics primarily through its necessary orientation toward a public, and hence a public sphere. It opens onto economics through the imaginative capacity to envision counterfactual abundance — and abundant possibilities — just as it encourages the cognitive capacity to limit the imaginative unreality through judgment, in order to facilitate realization. Literature necessarily involves the duality of unreality and realization, the free play of fantasy and the hard work of writing (and reading), imaginative invention and the restraining influence of taste, judgment, and convention. It is on this categorical level (rather than through an explicitly thematic agenda) that literature points toward an economy that combines visionary entrepreneurship and an ethics of caution. This combination is surely the underpinnings of capitalist institutions, on the same fundamental level that the orientation of literature toward a public of individual readers implies an autonomous literature in the Western project of liberal democracy.

Psalm 27, oscillating between triumphal abundance and anxious hesitation, warrior and mercantile ethics, very much involves the elaboration of core economic categories, even if the ancient economy is not directly thematized. The broader point at stake here is the implication of autonomous literature in the constitution of economic actors, which we now pursue in a very different sort of text, Molière's drama of 1665, *Dom Juan ou le festin de pierre*.

Hamlet concerns the presence of illusion — the appearance of the ghost, Hamlet's pretense of madness, and the play within the play. Believing in ghosts, he places his faith in the image and in the imagination. In contrast, *Dom Juan* explores the absence of faith, hence the faithlessness in love, the faithlessness to the creditor, and his faithlessness to God. For Molière,

Dom Juan is not primarily the positive embodiment of infinite seduction and eroticism, which he would become later for the romantics; rather, his amorous intrigues stand as one modality among several of his more fundamental refusals to believe. He is defined by this absence, a force of negativity: negating marriage, filial ties, and established faith. One misunderstands Molière's Dom Juan if Juan is treated as an incarnation of some full desire, unencumbered by restraints. On the contrary, it is nearly the opposite case, in the sense that he is given over to desire as absence, to a frantic and unceasing pursuit of satisfaction that always remains unachievable. This unachievable satisfaction informs the itinerant character of the play: from place to place, from encounter to encounter, a perpetual flight through very modern stations of despair in a pursuit of an always elusive happiness. Without the capacity to believe, he is forced to reduce the world to an empty accumulation of quantities, as he concedes, nearly absentmindedly, to his servant and interlocutor: "I believe that two and two make four, Sganarelle, and that four and four make eight." The claim is not merely a proto-enlightenment refusal of catechistic faith but a negation of all substantive relations as a consequence of a mathematical reduction of the world. Arithmetic is what he believes, and all that he believes. Dom Juan is an heir to Copernicus, but more importantly a predecessor of Goethe's Mephistopheles, negating everything, through an unstopping drive to deceive, to destroy, and to move on. The conclusion of the play, when the statue of the commander consigns him to the fires of hell, is therefore not only an interruption of his destructive trajectory by a divine judgment but also a consistent extension: one more escape from obligations into an ultimate absence.

For all the repetitions of Dom Juan's lack of faith, his continuous rejection of Sganarelle's admonitions and, especially, the discourse around his seduction of Dona Elvira (which necessarily elicits references to religion, since she had been a nun until she succumbed to his seduction), the play is not substantively about an individual dogmatic failing or a personal lapse. The implicit answer to the lack of faith is never a return to orthodox belief. Instead, *Dom Juan* registers and explores the disenchantment of the world in which all belief, belief as a cognitive-psychological possibility and not only religious belief, is in the midst of an unhalting process of disappearance. The matter goes far beyond the weakening of traditional Christian belief contents and instead concerns belief altogether. Sganarelle understands this and makes the point forcefully in the first, expository scene, when he characterizes his master to Gusman and thereby to the audience:

Mais, par précaution, je t'apprends, *inter nos*, que tu vois en Dom Juan, mon maître, le plus grand scélérat que la terre ait jamais porté, un enragé, un chien, un Diable, un Turc, un hérétique, qui ne croit ni Ciel, ni saint, ni Dieu, ni loup-garou, qui passe cette vie en véritable bête brute, en pourceau d'Epicure, en vrai Sardanapale, qui ferme l'oreille à toutes les remontrances chrétiennes, qu'on lui peut faire faire, et traite de billevesées tout ce que nous croyons. Tu me dis qu'il a épousé ta maîtresse: crois qu'il aurait plus fait pour contenter sa passion, et qu'avec elle il aurait encore épousé toi, son chien et son chat.

[But, just to prepare you for the worst, I tell you *inter nos* that the person you've known as Don Juan, my master, is the greatest scoundrel who ever walked the earth, a mad dog, a demon, a Turk, a heretic who doesn't believe in Heaven, or Hell, or werewolves even. He lives like a brute beast, an Epicurean swine, an absolute Sardanapalus, closing his ears to all the reproaches and treating all our noblest credences as nonsense. You mention that he has married your mistress; believe you me, he'd have done more than that if necessary. For the sake of his passion, he'd have married you too, And her dog and her cat to boot.][7]

Orthodox faith was still a powerful element in the culture of the seventeenth century, and Sganarelle's phrase concatenating God and the werewolf approached a scandalous sacrilege. It was therefore suppressed in early editions of the play in the 1680s. The implications of the characterization, far from celebrating a multicultural modernity in which all faiths are relativized, in fact constitute a devastating critique of modernity in general as hostile to faith. The absence of any particular faith, whether in God or in werewolves, is destructive; it enables a behavior that degrades marriage and renders Dona Elvira, Gusman's mistress, fully exchangeable with "her dog and her cat." Moreover, the speech includes rhetorical markers around the central description that highlight the substance of the transformation. For example, while Sganarelle refers to Dom Juan's "closing his ears," he himself addresses Gusman in confidence — *inter nos* — in a brief moment of sincerity that is unique, indeed socially atavistic in the play, a relic of an earlier social condition. All other conversations involve Dom Juan and his mendacity; but conversation, and even the possibility of speech in general, are undermined by the principle of faithlessness. Here, however, in the opening conversation between the servants, at the beginning of the play — and, in effect, for the last time — linguistic authenticity still prevails, since the regime of unlimited truthlessness, the "false witnesses" of the psalm, is about to commence.

All subsequent speech lacks the humanity, the care, and the truthfulness of Sganarelle's early dialogue with Gusman. This one expository instant sets a standard of care, against which later discussions can be measured and found lacking. Of course, there are the outbursts of honesty when Dom Juan's accusers denounce him, but he can never hear them, as we know from Sganarelle's characterization of his ability to close his ears. They are, in a sense, accusations *in absentia*, and never *inter nos*, since Dom Juan cannot register their severity or their ramifications. He is never truly present. What is perhaps more interesting, because less obvious, is that the presumed philosophical highpoint in act 3, scene 1 — when Dom Juan and Sganarelle find themselves at a distant site, in disguise — is itself a failed dialogue. It is the servant who inquires about his master's lack of faith; but the master consistently avoids any significant response. Even the arithmetic rejoinder, which may well be taken as an allegorical indication of a quantitative reduction of the world, has the standing of a throwaway remark. It is Sganarelle, after all, who from his first words in the play is seen pursuing an explicitly philosophical elaboration of the human condition, but Dom Juan refuses dialogue, the original genre of philosophy, and therefore philosophy as well. The problem of the play is not at all religion versus philosophy or religion versus the enlightenment. Instead, Dom Juan avoids religion as well as philosophy, and all sincere articulations of meaning. He is the incarnation of absolute insincerity, and he therefore cannot be insincerity's spokesman, for his speech would necessarily be inadequate.

It follows then that *Dom Juan*, as drama, is defined by the failure of speech, pursuant to the disappearance of faith. One result is the brilliant theater of the scene with Dom Juan's creditor, Dimanche (IV.3). Rather than avoiding him, as his servants suggest, Dom Juan receives him and overwhelms him with expressions of friendship and gratitude, never allowing the duped merchant an opportunity to say a word. Indeed, Dom Juan is even able to speak the truth, insisting to Dimanche that he is indeed his debtor, and underscoring that he hides this fact from no one. But this very speech act serves to prevent Dimanche from collecting on the debt. Even the very articulation of the truth becomes a vehicle for falsehood; faithlessness establishes a world of absolute deception in which right statements become wrong. In general, *Dom Juan* is not about the positive contents of philosophy — Sganarelle's references to Aristotle or Epicurus notwithstanding — or of economy, as in the examination of the aristocrat and the merchant, but about this disappearance of content altogether. All solid social relations, and their cultural corollaries, dissipate.

Among Dom Juan's serial encounters, two stand out as having particular architectural significance. Sganarelle frames the play: his discourse on tobacco, followed by the conversation with Gusman, opens the drama, and his outcry after his master's death, closes it. By foregrounding the servant, Molière has expanded the story of Dom Juan the sinner and placed it in a tradition that stretches from Quixote and Sancho Panza to Hegel's dialectic of master and servant. As a result of his degradation, the subordinate achieves a superior insight, and this binary structure is compounded by the theatrical tradition of the Pierrot and the comic standing of the lower classes on the aristocratic stage. The tensions within this tradition that erupt a century later in Beaumarchais's *Mariage de Figaro* are already evident in *Dom Juan*. Thus Sganarelle is introduced at the outset as the carrier of the authentic understanding of his master, while the master's dependence on his servant becomes increasingly clear.

Yet the social inversion inherent in the superiority of the servant is less telling than the peripatetic trajectory traced by Sganarelle himself between his first appearance and his last. His initial speech presents a utopia of repose, satisfaction, and human solidarity, especially in relation to Gusman. The praise of tobacco shows the servant at rest, contemplating happiness as both a personal and a social condition. The habit of sharing tobacco becomes allegorical of a social civility, an echo of the sharing among friends invoked at the end of *Phaedrus*. Tobacco is a drug, but one that cultivates virtue. This pharmacological project anticipates his reappearance in the middle of the play, in the "philosophical scene" of act 3, scene 1, in the costume of a doctor. Sganarelle is the ultimate servant in that he wants to cure the ills of the world and make life better, in contrast to his master, who can think only of the moment, while always fleeing into the future. If Dom Juan's depravity can be measured against any intratextual norm, it is surely the model of goodness presented by Sganarelle at the beginning of the play, confirming the superiority of the servant over the aristocrat.

Yet in the course of the play, Sganarelle plummets from this ethic of generosity to the self-interested cry for his wages at the play's end. Dom Juan has been pulled into hell, but Sganarelle's response is neither empathetic mourning nor God-fearing acceptance. Instead, he displays an egoism bemoaning his own fate alone, oblivious to his surroundings except to the extent that he is himself disadvantaged:

Ah! Mes gages, mes gages! Voilà par sa mort un chacun satisfait: Ciel offensé, lois violées, filles séduites, familles déshonorées, parents outragés, femmes mises à mal, maris poussées à bout, tout le monde est content. Il n'y a que moi seul de malheureux. Mes gages, mes gages, mes gages!

[Oh! My back wages! What about my wages! My master's death gives satisfaction to everyone: the Heaven he offended, the girls he ruined, the families he dishonored, the laws he broke, the parents he outraged, the wives he led astray, the husbands he drove to despair — they're all well pleased. I'm the only one who's unhappy. Alas, my wages! My wages! Who'll pay my wages?"][8]

The utopia of the beginning speech, in which tobacco cured the ills of society by uniting humanity, has turned sour. Everyone is satisfied now except the servant, the self-conscious figure of perpetual exclusion. The erstwhile generosity has been reduced to an insistence on wages, while Sganarelle's concluding list of all those satisfied by Dom Juan's condemnation is the rhetorical echo of his earlier description of Dom Juan's disbelief. If before he described how Dom Juan disbelieved everything, from God to werewolf, in order to be able to marry anything, even dogs or cats, now Sganarelle complains that everyone is satisfied, both heaven and earth. Sganarelle himself, however, remains the outsider, reduced to reclaiming his lost wages but thereby also losing his initial pretense to universality. Sganarelle is a victim of the world of faithlessness not only because Dom Juan's infernal departure may have cheated him of fair compensation, but also because he loses the personal quality he displayed during the normative utopia of the tobacco speech. Sganarelle the servant therefore falls from the opening height of generosity to the moral degradation of an absolute selfishness.

Dom Juan's second crucial encounter is with the statue itself, whose equality of standing is inscribed in the full title of the drama: *Dom Juan ou le festin de Pierre* — Dom Juan or the feast of stone. While Sganarelle tries to heal the world and save Dom Juan, the statue is the agent of judgment, whose stony presence puts an end to the frivolous escapades, the cavalier's movable feast. Sganarelle gives expression to the vision of absolute satisfaction and harmony, but the statue indicates the world of petrification and lack: the very lack of the life that it, as a work of art, represents and recalls. That the statue is intended to have an aesthetic standing is indicated by the admiration that Dom Juan directs to the mausoleum as a "superb edifice" described by all as marvelous (III.5). Yet here the contrast with *Hamlet* is particularly important. The experience of the ghost of the Danish king initiates a chain of encounters with the problem of appearance that point to the mediated relationship between aesthetic appearance and political deed. In contrast, neither viewing the mausoleum nor the interaction with the statue, the homologue of *Hamlet*'s ghost, initiates a similar transition in Dom Juan, impervious to any cognitive gain through aesthetic experience. If the audience can know that the statue implicitly carries the capacity for menacing judgment, indeed even though Sganarelle clearly knows as much, Dom Juan himself remains closed to this insight. Absolute faithlessness defines an aesthetic incapacity: He can observe the mausoleum, he can taunt the statue, but he cannot understand its significance.

Dom Juan ou le festin de pierre constructs the aesthetic object, the statue, with a double character: It recalls the fullness of life but it is also a *memento mori*, reminding the viewer of death, as it finally serves directly as the vehicle of capital punishment. Aesthetic autonomy does not only generate the category of judgment in the sense of criticism directed at the work of art or literature. Rather, the autonomous work itself is a judgment on the life of the recipient. Molière's statue therefore anticipates another statue, Rilke's "archaic torso of Apollo" and its message to "change your life."[9] Thus two principles are inherent in the statue: the urgency of judgment as well as the capacity to recollect and to imagine an experiential fullness. The work of art is both critical and anamnestic. Yet it is precisely this dialectic of fullness and absence that corresponds to Sganarelle's itinerary between generosity and wages, universal inclusion and his own melancholy exclusion. These categories define the economic discourse embedded in the play, the simultaneity of a vision of abundance, linked to the facility for imagination and the obligation of judgment.

In Molière's *Dom Juan*, the motivation for the murder of the commandant is unclear, and there is certainly no discussion of Dom Juan having seduced his daughter. While this variation of the traditional plot tends to weaken the relationship to the statue, which loses some of the psychological motivation in other versions, it also amplifies the standing of Dom Louis — the father of Dom Juan, not the father of one the victims — as the voice of judgment. In Psalm 27, the parents of the poet have abandoned him; in *Dom Juan*, it is the father who delivers the most trenchant condemnation of his son, even though the father too, later, will also be deceived by Dom Juan's capacity for simulation. Hamlet feigned madness in order to clear the way to action and to carry out a judgment on his father's killer; Dom Juan counterfeits conversions in order to evade judgment but can only postpone it. In both cases, a dialectic of imagination and judgment is played out on a fundamental level, albeit in quite distinct configurations. These distinctions aside, the play exemplifies how literature participates in the process of social development through the work of imagination by constantly generating counterfactual conditions that might be realized, but it also circumscribes these imaginary desiderata by demonstrating the absolute necessity of judgment. This constellation of utopian innovation and analytic caution defines the underlying economic categories embedded in literary imagination.

AUTONOMOUS LITERATURE, as a differentiated institution of Western society, contributes to the dissemination of capitalist behavior not because of any tendentious message, nor because of the represented economics, nor even primarily as commodified products for the publishing industry, but because the basic categories that constitute literature — imagination, taste, and judgment — are themselves indispensable sources for capitalist psychology: the drive to imagine, coupled to a facility for evaluation. In Psalm 27 and in *Dom Juan*, these categorical consequences of literary autonomy are elaborated in quite distinct historical settings: in the former, the dynamics of the ancient economy were played out in the transition between heroic warrior values and bourgeois, privatized ethics; in the latter, the social tensions of the *ancien régime* are exposed, facing the problems of modernity and the disappearance of substantive relations. In a third and closing example, Kafka's story "The Judgment," the questions of imagination and judgment are staged once more, at a different historical moment, an era of successful liberal capitalism, in which family life is challenged by growing competition, capital concentration, social unrest, and the destabilization of the individual in the context of an emerging mass society.

Kafka wrote "The Judgment" in a single burst of creative energy during the night of September 22 – 23, 1912; it marks his transition to a period of vigorous productivity, with many of his best-known works, such as "The Metamorphosis," following quickly. Among the various hypothetical textual sources for "The Judgment," the most intriguing, corroborating the argument made here in chapter 6, involves the Jewish liturgy for the Day of Atonement, which fell on that date; hence perhaps Kafka's focus on questions of judgment. In this light, a connection becomes apparent between a core element of religious transcendence and a centerpiece of literary modernism.

At this point, however, our primary concern lies elsewhere, in economics, not in religion. "The Judgment" is so fascinating because of its account of a reversal of fortune that is equally inexorable and, superficially at least, inexplicable. We find Georg at the outset in a setting of comfort and repose, a fully secure world, but very quickly this stability unravels and, just pages later, he jumps off a bridge. The father's accusations, on which the narrative appears to pivot, do not seem to support the sentence he pronounces, death by drowning, and one therefore returns to the opening passages to try to find some anticipatory indication of the dramatic events that follow. Georg, we discover, is not only a young businessman but also a writer. He is seated at his writing desk, where he has just finished a letter to a friend. It is soon revealed that he has a habit of filling his correspondence with banalities, in order to avoid serious matters, and that he is finishing this particular letter in a less-than-attentive state of mind. Indeed, throughout the story, Georg's frequently smug self-understanding as a caring and attentive person is undercut by evidence of his distraction and inattention. Unless one were to conjecture that the father's judgment is without grounds at all, it is this lack of attention, and in particular Georg's inattentiveness as a writer, that plausibly accounts for his imputed culpability.

Georg's inattention recalls Dom Juan and his inability to engage in substantive conversation with Sganarelle (just as Georg's efforts to manipulate the letter's addressee resemble Dom Juan's handling of Dimanche). That these two distant texts both proceed from the fact of an attention deficit suggests a constitutive problem of literature. Precisely because of its imaginative character, literature may be predisposed to concern itself with inattention, or better, an absentmindedness indicating a separation from the facticity of empirical existence. The comparative advantage of literature, its capacity to entertain counterfactuals, thus returns, thematically, as a problem. Lost in imagination, staring blankly out the window, Georg the writer loses contact with the specificities of his life-world, as underscored soon after by evidence of the disregard he has shown his father. The father's judgment is, ultimately, a response to this unworldliness. Such restrictive judgment functions as the correction to the excess of imagination: the price of poetic freedom, indicating that freedom, more generally, implies certain consequences and is therefore, in itself, not absolutely free. It is interesting that Dom Juan and Georg respond with precisely the same gesture to the condemnation articulated by their respective fathers. Thus Dom Juan: "Monsieur, si vous étiez assis, vous en seriez mieux pour parler" (IV.4). [Sir, if you were seated, you would talk more comfortably]. Similarly Georg, "I'll put you to bed now for a little, I'm sure you need to rest."[10] Their parallel efforts to seat their fathers amount to attempts to unseat them, to overthrow their authority by lowering them, into chairs or into graves: a gestural parricide. The affinity between the two narratives is heightened, insofar as Georg's father condemns him for amorous escapades, as does Dom Louis; and for the disregard for his mother's memory, like Dom Louis's eloquent invocation of the standing of the family's ancestors.

While one can maintain the parallel between Georg and Dom Juan to the extent that the imaginative excess of the sons is, in both cases, subject to fatherly condemnation, the similarity does not go much further. Dom Louis speaks the truth to his son, even though even he, the father, is subsequently deceived by Dom Juan's capacity for feigned remorse. In contrast, despite the strength and apparent integrity of the paternal verdict in "The Judgment," the text undermines the father just as much as it exposes the flaws in Georg's self-confidence. The accusations that he hurls at his son are typically grounded in references to facts always qualified by expressions of doubt; an example is his frequent use of "perhaps." Moreover, the accusations are sometimes self-contradictory, such as the suggestion that Georg's plans to marry are both too late and too early. As much as Kafka's representation of family argument captures the problem of the ambiguity, inconsistency and multiplicity of motivation, it also demonstrates the inadequacy of a certain deliberative rationality. Both Georg and his father attempt to judge — Georg judges his friend in Russia, while the father judges Georg — with clear and logical arguments, but in fact the very structures of the arguments are so consistently flawed as to suggest that logical judgment may be impossible in general. But it is not judgment itself that is impossible, only a judgment that aspires to internal consistency and logic. In other words, to the phenomenon of imaginative counterfactuality, which is constitutive of any literary fiction, judgment is a necessary corollary, but Kafka suggests that it is illusory to imagine that this judgment, or any other, can lay claim to an unassailable accuracy or to a truth higher than the fiction. "The Judgment," which appeared at first to be a story about young Georg's reversal of fortune, turns out indeed to have a peripatetic character, but it is about the reversal of judgment on the phenomenon of judgment itself: It cannot be avoided, but it may be internally incoherent. This is not to suggest that judgment is hopelessly flawed. Rather, the point is that judgment is necessary even though it is always fallible. To expect infallibility spirals backward quickly into oppressive behavior and unlivable conditions: hence the verdict.

The truth of "The Judgment" lies neither with Georg's initial musing reverie nor with the patriarchal severity of condemnation but in their antinomic entwinement. Judgment is an inescapable corollary to imagination, but it is also inescapably erroneous, in the sense that no judgment can achieve an absolute truthfulness. The process remains open, and a reversal of judgment is always possible, which points to the constant inconclusiveness inherent in the reading experience. Precisely this phenomenon is staged in Kafka's text. Although the father condemns his son to death, and we read of Georg hanging off the bridge and letting himself drop, the text in fact does not report his death. Rather, at that very moment an "unending stream of traffic" crosses the bridge, but that traffic is also, erotically, "intercourse" [Verkehr], leaving unresolved whether Georg's death is drowned out by the traffic or, alternatively, redeemed by the power of love, especially in light of the chain of christological markers in the text itself, leading to the inconclusive conclusion.[11]

This open end sheds light on the central theme of the "The Judgment." Georg's inattention is part of the problem at the outset, but so is the specific act of writing that he commits: He has "ended" the letter. Any such definitive conclusion may be as little possible in literature as it is in life, where reconsideration and new beginnings always remain possible. Thus the end of the letter reported at the beginning of the story contrasts with the unending character of the traffic in the final sentence. The text points therefore to the openness of freedom inherent in the world. In a social-historical sense, of course, one can attempt a location of "The Judgment," parallel to contextualizations of the psalm in the ancient economy and Dom Juan in the early modernity of absolutism: "The Judgment" explores the possibilities of individuality in the era of social revolution and mass conformism at the end of the age of laissez-faire liberalism. It insists on the desideratum of autonomous individuality despite the pressures to which it is subjected. Beyond this contextual determination, however, "The Judgment" provides a further permutation on the foundational dialectic of imagination and judgment in the economy of literature. As problematic as any judgment may be, be it Georg's judgment on his friend, the father's judgment on Georg, or the text's judgment on the problem of judgment itself, it is impossible to read literature and not judge. The judging may be more or less subtle, more or less informed or literate, but every act of reading initiates an evaluative response. Every act of reading implies a reader who becomes a judge. Just as it is impossible to read without judgment, it is equally impossible to read for a norm of positivist accuracy, whether a text "gets a description right." On the contrary, reading literature means suspending disbelief, refraining from posing the questions of accuracy, such as Phaedrus' pathological concern for locational precision (this sort of query might be directed at reportage or nonfictional essays but not at autonomous literature), and therefore engaging with the imagination — or, rather, the reader's imaginative engagement with the imaginative language of the author. In other words, literature is that particular social habit that simultaneously cultivates the antithetical capacities for imagination and judgment, counterfactual vision and deliberative evaluation. It follows that literature, as autonomous and imaginative, and by virtue of these basic characteristics (rather than by any particular authorial predispositions) enhances the central virtues of a free economy: imaginative vision and evaluative judgment.

The itinerary from Psalm 27 to *Dom Juan* and "The Judgment" traces a long historical path. On one level, individual works of literature may of course be taken as somehow representative of their respective contexts, in particular the underlying economic categories. More important than such particular, contextualizing claims, though, is the evidence that demonstrates a continuity associated with the very constitution of imaginative literature altogether. Because of its particular relations to the cognitive psychology of imagination, which is itself tied to the symbolic character of language, literature is predisposed to engage and articulate certain concerns. It stages imaginative abundance — surpassing empirical reality — and, at the same time, it subjects that imaginary content to scrutiny, in the forms of choice, taste, and judgment. Imagination is the counterfactual correction to any given reality, typically characterized by scarcity; but judgment is the secondary correction on imaginative excess, even though it is equally the case that the imagination resists this containment. In the end, the economic categories inherent in literature are innovative expansion and deliberative choice, both of which are foundational to capitalism, albeit not in the narrow sense of "commodity production." Literature is the institutionalized, linguistic appeal to discriminating individuals who can evaluate and to entrepreneurial risk takers who have the will to imagine. The reading experience accelerates the recipient's acquisition of these psychological capacities.

In the developmental course of human history, and above all in the dynamic history of the West, literature is not a mirror in the sense of a superfluous double to a notionally already complete and real existence. The tenacity with which particular cultures generate, protect, and disseminate literature speaks against any allegation of such superfluity, as does the significance literature can assume, particularly in times of adversity. The origins of art lie in the harsh conditions of the Ice Age; literature has subsequently flourished despite poverty and even in dissident resistance to extreme, sadistic oppression. These facts of literary life point to a functional necessity of literature in social development, rather than to some incidental or ornamental standing. The metaphor of mirror might, however, be acceptable in a different sense than a merely supplementary reproduction of the given. Literature encourages humanity's own self-knowledge, increasing its cognitive capacities and underscoring, in particular, the very possibility of selfhood, individuality, and with it imagination and innovation. Innovation in the course of social history depends on the imaginative capacity of individuals to transform the conditions of their existence by pursuing qualitatively new goals. Such imagination is embedded in the ability to think symbolically, and therefore to give consideration to that which is missing, to the counterfactual and to goals not yet achieved. Such symbolic usage is at the core of language and, therefore, our being human. Literature is therefore the particularly human practice, institutionalized in generic conventions, educational systems, and reading habits, that amplifies our imaginative capacity and, hence, our abilities to make choices, envision innovation, and weigh options. The crucible of imagination, literature imbues humanity with the cognitive facility to challenge empirically the given conditions of existence, and therefore to pursue social development through those institutions with which freedom can best flourish.

NOTES

Why Literature Matters

1. Émile Zola, quoted in Pierre Bourdieu, *The Rules of Art: Genesis and Structure of the Literary Field*, trans. Susan Emanuel (Stanford, Calif.: Stanford University Press, 1996), 128.

2. Walter Benjamin, "Theses on the Philosophy of History," in *Illuminations*, trans. Harry Zohn (New York: Schocken Books, 1969), 253–64.

3. Merlin Donald, *Origins of the Modern Mind: Three Stages in the Evolution of Culture and Cognition* (Cambridge, Mass.: Harvard University Press, 1991).

4. Steven Mithen, *The Prehistory of the Mind: The Cognitive Origins of Art and Science* (London: Thames and Hudson, 1996).

5. William Noble and Iain Davidson, *Human Evolution, Language, and Mind: A Psychological and Archeological Inquiry* (Cambridge, U.K.: Cambridge University Press, 1996).

6. Franz Kafka, "The Metamorphosis" and "Report to an Academy," in *The Complete Stories*, ed. Nahum N. Glatzer (New York: Schocken, 1971).

7. Alphonse de Lamartine, "Pensées des morts," in *Anthologie de la poésie française*, ed. Georges Pompidou (Paris: Hachette, 1961), 242–43.

8. Walter J. Ong, *Orality and Literacy: The Technologizing of the Word* (New York: Routledge, 1982); Eric A. Havelock, *The Muse Learns to Write: Reflections on Orality and Literacy from Antiquity to the Present* (New Haven, Conn.: Yale University Press, 1986) and *Preface to Plato* (Cambridge, Mass.: Harvard University Press, 1963); Jack Goody and Ian Watt, "Consequences of Literacy," in *Perspectives on Literacy*, ed. Eugene R. Kintgen, Barry M. Knoll, and Mike Rose (Carbondale: Southern Illinois University Press, 1988), 3–27.

9. Ong, *Orality and Literacy*.

10. Donald, *Origins of the Modern Mind*; Sylvia Scribner and Michael Cole, "Unpacking Literacy," in *Perspectives on Literacy*, ed. Eugene R. Kintgen, Barry, M. Knoll, and Mike Rose, 57–70 (Carbondale: Southern Illinois University Press, 1988).

11. Siegfried Grosse, trans., *Das Nibelugenlied*. Karl Bartsch and Helmut de Boor (Stuttgart: Reclam, 1997); *La Chanson de Roland*; Derek Walcott, *Omeros* (New York: Farrar, Straus and Giroux, 1990); Havelock, *Muse Learns to Write*.

12. Havelock, *Preface to Plato*, 61–86.

13. Bertolt Brecht, "Hollywood Quatrain," in *Gedichte*, vol. 4 in *Gesammelte Werke*, ed. Suhrkamp Verlag with Elisabeth Hauptmann (Frankfurt: Suhrkamp, 1967).

14. John Milbank, *The Word Made Strange: Theology, Language, Culture* (Oxford, U.K.: Blackwell, 1997); Catherine Pickstock, *After Writing: On the Liturgical Consummation of Philosophy* (Oxford, U.K.: Blackwell, 1998).

Introduction

1. To speak of a neo-Marxism, while technically legitimate, would nevertheless be confusing. That term more commonly refers to the variants of Marxist cultural criticism that circulated in the mid-twentieth century, particularly during and after the 1960s. The critical theory of the Frankfurt School plays a large role in that process, but that particular current was typically a defender of literature and aesthetic autonomy against more emphatically deterministic radicals. Indeed, there is a tension within Marxist literary criticism, with origins in the 1840s, between defenders of a high culture—such as Marx himself—and more consistently politicizing critics who have treated art at best as a vehicle to convey a topical political message. Marx's own appreciation of works of art independent of the artist or writer's political leanings indicates an understanding of the emancipatory character of the autonomous work, although his stance might well face a criticism from the Left, antithetical to bourgeois art appreciation. In this sense—but a century and a half later and in a very different cultural setting—contemporary cultural radicalism displays a strongly antiaesthetic predisposition, either directing an ideological suspicion toward works of art, deemed to act unavoidably as expressions of existing power structures, or dissolving those works into a generalized domain of culture, thereby robbing them of any aesthetic distinctiveness. The scholarly literature is enormous. Compare Hal Foster, ed., *The Anti-aesthetic: Essays in Postmodern Culture* (New York: New Press, 1998); Helga Gallas, *Marxistische Literaturtheorie: Kontroversen im Bund proletarisch-revolutionärer Schriftsteller* (Neuwied, Ger.: Luchterhand, 1971); Peter Uwe Hohendahl, ed., *A History of German Literary Criticism, 1739–1980* (Lincoln: University of Nebraska Press, 1988); Fredric Jameson, *Marxism and Form: Twentieth-Century Dialectical Theories of Literature* (Princeton, N.J.: Princeton University Press, 1971); Martin Jay, *The Dialectical Imagination: A History of the Frankfurt School and the Institute of Social Research, 1923–1950* (Berkeley: University of California Press, 1973); and Eugene Lunn, *Marxism and Modernism: An Historical Study of Lukács, Brecht, Benjamin, and Adorno* (Berkeley: University of California Press, 1982).

2. Thus, no twentieth-century critic was a more stalwart defender of aesthetic autonomy than Theodor W. Adorno, and yet none insisted more vociferously on the hidden or, as he sometimes puts it, "subterranean" reverberations between the work of art and society. Hence his famous designation of lyric verse as a *geschichtsphiloso-*

phische Sonnenuhr, a philosophical sundial of history, somehow indicating — albeit negatively, in the mode of a sundial's shadow — the temporal and categorical constitution of the social condition. However one understands the precise functioning of that metaphorical sundial, there is no doubt that, for Adorno, the poem, or more generally, the successful work of art, has this indicative capacity — the capacity to designate its historical moment and therefore to articulate its criticism — due precisely to the distinctiveness of art, its autonomy. In other words, his critical vision rests on the dialectical paradox that the proximity of art and society, the societal character of the aesthetic, is premised on their separation. See Adorno's "On Lyric Poetry and Society," in Adorno, *Notes on Literature*, trans. Shierry Weber Nicholson (New York: Columbia University Press, 1991), vol. 1, 46.

3. Eric Havelock underscores this Greek definition of oral poetry as a vessel of historical knowledge — past, present, and future in its temporality — in the sense, however, of a social encyclopedia, the repository of tribal wisdom. It is, in other words, precisely not aesthetic, in his view, because it is historical. That sharp categorical distinction, however, reflects the definitions of the era of New Criticism: Historical material is necessarily extrinsic, perhaps even opposed to artistic substance. In contrast, the argument in this book is that it is precisely the aesthetic character of the work that permits it to achieve a larger historical vision. Because it is imaginative, that is — not, in Havelock's sense, encyclopedic — it surpasses the limits of the present moment and extends into memory and aspiration. Moreover, Havelock argues for the historical knowledge presumably embedded in oral performance as part of his claim about the orality of the epics; in contrast, I claim that it is writing that increases the memory function of literature. Unlike Havelock, who sees literature as effectively superfluous, particularly since writing permits more accurate record-keeping in historiography and more logical thinking in philosophy, I argue that writing enhances the objective character of imaginative literature by allowing for a greater elaboration of tradition. See Havelock, *The Muse Learns to Write: Reflections on Orality and Literacy from Antiquity to the Present* (New Haven, Conn.: Yale University Press, 1986), 19, 80–81.

4. It is telling to find even the leading new historicist scholar Stephen Greenblatt complaining that professional literary criticism today has lost a sense of the specific character of literature: "My profession has become so oddly diffident and even phobic about literary power, so suspicious and tense, that it risks losing sight of — or at least failing to articulate — the whole reason anyone bothers with the enterprise in the first place" *Hamlet in Purgatory* (Princeton, N.J.: Princeton University Press, 2001), 46. In contrast, he purports to pursue the aesthetic experience, "to let the feeling of this vividness [of Hamlet's ghost] wash over me, and I wanted to understand how it was achieved" (4). Nonetheless, his specifically new historicist solution involves deferring literary analysis and minimizing the engagement with the literary work, replaced by lengthy and erudite expositions on reformation theology. If he avoids the conclusion that the play is a direct expression of a theological

position, the weight of the analysis nonetheless suggests that the border between the aesthetic field and the extra-aesthetic, in this case, dogmatic dispute, has been considerably leveled. It follows quite logically that he insists, "What we call ideology, then, Renaissance England called poetry" (46).

5. Moreover, the impact of the ethnographic turn not only reduces the specific aesthetic aspect of the work, it also diminishes the specifically political perspective, insofar as questions of the state — as one possible way to approach politics — are dissolved into generalizing cultural claims. Thus Pecora notes how Geertz's analysis of violence in Bali systematically excludes discussions of the political regime. See Vincent P. Pecora, "The Limits of Local Knowledge," in *The New Historicism*, ed. A. Haram Veeser (New York: Routledge, 1989), 243–76.

6. See James Clifford, Introduction to *Writing Culture: The Poetics and Politics of Ethnography*, ed. James Clifford and George E. Marcus (Berkeley: University of California Press, 1986), 8–12. On the "timeless present" of primary orality, see Havelock, *Muse Learns to Write*, 106.

7. "In contemporary society and culture — postindustrial society, postmodern culture — the question of the legitimation of knowledge is formulated in different terms. The grand narrative has lost its credibility, regardless of what mode of unification it uses, regardless of whether it is a speculative narrative or a narrative of emancipation." Jean-François Lyotard, *The Postmodern Condition* (Minneapolis: University of Minnesota Press, 1984), 37.

8. See Pierre Clastres, *Society against the State: The Leader as Servant and the Humane Uses of Power among the Indians of the Americas*, trans. Robert Hurley (New York: Urizen Books, 1977).

1. Periodization and the Canon

1. The term belongs to Hans Robert Jauss in his *Toward an Aesthetic of Reception*, trans. Timothy Bahti (Minneapolis: University of Minnesota Press, 1981). For a sober assessment of the confusion inherent in the project of establishing a horizon, see Robert D. Hume, *Reconstructing Contexts: The Aims and Principles of Archaeo-Historicism* (Oxford, U.K.: Oxford University Press, 1999), 18–25.

2. Karl Marx, *Grundrisse: Introduction to the Critique of Political Economy*, trans. Martin Nicolaus (New York: Vintage Books, 1973), 111.

3. Ibid.

4. Walter Benjamin, "Theses on the Philosophy of History," in *Illuminations*, trans. Harry Zohn (New York: Schocken Books, 1969), 253–64.

5. Leopold von Ranke, *The Theory and Practice of History*, ed. Georg G. Iggers and Konrad von Moltke (Indianapolis: Bobbs-Merrill, 1973), 137.

6. Benjamin's progressive anti-Hegelian historiography is foreshadowed in an early essay by Heinrich Heine, "Verschiedenartig Geschichtsauffassung," in *Werke*, ed. Helmut Schanze (Frankfurt: Insel, 1968), vol. 4, 33–35.

7. Benjamin, "Theses on the Philosophy of History," 257–58.

8. Thus he suggests that working-class radicalism once had a dimension of memory, in the sense of an effort to avenge past suffering, with "the task of liberation in the name of generations of the downtrodden. This conviction, which had a brief resurgence in the Spartacist group, has always been objectionable to Social Democrats. Within three decades they managed virtually to erase the name of Blanqui, though it had been the rallying sound that had reverberated through the preceding century." The reference to the past is lost in the rush to become progressive. Ibid., 260.

9. W. E. B. Du Bois, *The Souls of Black Folk* (New York: New American Library, 1969), 139.

2. Human Origins and Literary Beginnings

1. Thomas Goddard Bergin and Max Harold Fisch, trans., *The New Science of Giambattista Vico*, 3d ed. (Ithaca, N.Y.: Cornell University Press, 1968), 71. Cited in Stephen Greenblatt, *Hamlet in Purgatory* (Princeton, N.J.: Princeton University Press, 2001), 46.

2. See Katie Trumpener, *Bardic Nationalism: The Romantic Novel and the British Empire* (Princeton, N.J.: Princeton University Press, 1997).

3. Merlin Donald, *Origins of the Modern Mind: Three Stages in the Evolution of Culture and Cognition* (Cambridge, Mass.: Harvard University Press, 1991), 114.

4. Ibid., 115.

5. Ibid., 136.

6. Ibid., 164.

7. Ibid., 171.

8. Ibid., 189.

9. Ibid., 223.

10. Eric A. Havelock, *Preface to Plato* (Cambridge, Mass.: Harvard University Press, 1963), 61–86.

11. Noam Chomsky, *The Logical Structure of Linguistic Theory* (Chicago: University of Chicago Press, 1975).

12. Donald, 235.

13. Roy Harris, *The Origin of Writing* (London: Duckworth, 1986), cited in Donald, 279.

14. Donald, 272.

15. Ibid., 343.

16. Steven Mithen, *The Prehistory of the Mind: The Cognitive Origins of Art and Science* (London: Thames and Hudson, 1996), 42–50.

17. Ibid., 50–51.

18. Ibid., 55–56.

19. Susan Carey and Elizabeth Spelke, "Domain-Specific Knowledge and Concep-

tual Change," in *Mapping the Mind: Domain Specificity in Cognition and Cultures,* ed. Lawrence A. Hirschfeld and Susan A. Gelman (Cambridge, U.K.: Cambridge University Press, 1994), 184; cited in Mithen, 58.

20. Annette Karmiloff-Smith, "Précis of *Beyond Modularity: A Developmental Perspective on Cognitive Science," Behavioralism and Brain Sciences* 17 (1994): 706; cited in Mithen, 59.

21. Mithen, 59. See Dan Sperber, "The Modularity of Thought and the Epidemiology of Representation," in *Mapping the Mind,* ed. Hirschfeld and Gelman, 39 – 67.

22. "The crossing to Australia was . . . probably delayed for many hundreds of millennia because it demanded a highly developed symbolic tradition capable of placing sufficient trust in the conscious judgment of signs to accept the risks of sailing to an unseen destination." R.G. Bednarik, "Replicating the First Known Sea Travel by Humans: The Lower Pleistocene Crossing of the Lomboc Strait," *Human Evolution* 16 (2001): 230.

23. Mithen, 159.

24. Ibid., 168.

25.William Noble and Iain Davidson, *Human Evolution, Language, and Mind: A Psychological and Archeological Inquiry* (Cambridge, U.K.: Cambridge University Press, 1996), 13.

26. Ibid., 14, 15.

27. Ibid., 21, 141.

28. Ibid., 68.

29. Ibid., 21.

30. Ibid., 221.

31. Ibid., 223.

32. See Christopher S. Henshilwood, F. D'Errico, C. W. Marean, R. G. Milo, and R. Yates, "An Early Bone Tool Industry from the Middle Stone Age at Blombos Cave, South Africa: Implications for the Origins of Modern Human Behavior, *Journal of Human Evolution* 41, 6 (Dec. 2001): 631 – 78; Richard Stone, "Mammoth Hunters Put Hopes on Ice," *Science* 12 (Jan. 2001): 230 – 31.

33. Noble and Davidson, 226.

34. Jack Goody, *The Power of the Written Tradition* (Washington, D.C.: Smithsonian Institution Press, 2000), 23 – 24.

35. Albert Bates Lord, *The Singer of Tales* (Cambridge, Mass.: Harvard University Press, 1960); Adam Parry, ed., *The Making of Homeric Verse: The Collected Papers of Milman Parry* (New York: Oxford University Press, 1987).

36. Donald, *Origins,* 25 – 45.

37. Walter J. Ong, *Orality and Literacy: The Technologizing of the Word* (New York: Routledge, 1982), 155 – 16.

38. See Hartmut Binder, ed., *Kafka-Handbuch* (Stuttgart: Alfred Kröner, 1979), vol. 1, 37, 212, 241, 248, 251, and 252. See also James Rolleston, ed., *A Companion to the Works of Franz Kafka* (Rochester, N.Y.: Camden House, 2002).

39. Binder, vol. 2, 232, et passim.

40. Kafka, "The Metamorphosis," in *The Complete Stories*, ed. Nahum N. Glatzer (New York: Schocken, 1971), 89.

41. Ibid., 103, 104.

42. Alphonse de Lamartine, "Pensées des morts," in *Anthologie de la poésie française*, ed. Georges Pompidou (Paris: Hachette, 1961), 242–43.

43. Pierre Bourdieu, *The Rules of Art: Genesis and Structure of the Literary Field*, trans. Susan Emanuel (Stanford, Calif.: Stanford University Press, 1996), 155.

44. Consider, for example, Adorno's comment on the nonsemanticity of the lexeme "gar" in the poem by Stephan George discussed in "Lyric Poetry and Society," in *Notes on Literature*, trans. Shierry Weber Nicholson (New York: Columbia University Press, 1991), vol. 1, 53.

45. On Jane Goodall, see Noble and Davidson, 8.

3. Writing and Heroism

1. Pierre Bourdieu, *The Rules of Art: Genesis and Structure of the Literary Field*, trans. Susan Emanuel (Stanford, Calif.: Stanford University Press, 1996), 59.

2. Ibid.

3. Ibid., 104.

4. Ibid., 107.

5. Walter J. Ong, *Orality and Literacy: The Technologizing of the Word* (New York: Routledge, 1982), 12–13.

6. Jack Goody, *The Power of the Written Tradition* (Washington, D.C.: Smithsonian Institution Press, 2000), 27. See also Ruth Finnegan, *Oral Poetry: Its Nature, Significance, and Social Context* (Cambridge, U.K.: Cambridge University Press, 1977).

7. Charles O. Frake, "Did Literacy Cause the Great Cognitive Divide?" *American Ethnologist* 10 (1983): 368–71. Thus Ong: "Goody has convincingly shown how shifts hitherto labeled as shifts from magic to science, or from so-called 'prelogical' to the more and more 'rational' state of consciousness, or from Lévi-Strauss's 'savage' mind to domesticated thought, can be more economically and cogently explained as shifts from orality to various stages of literacy." *Orality and Literacy*, 29. For Goody's response to the postmodern and deconstructive denial of a divide, see *Power of the Written Tradition*, 30.

8. Denise Schmandt-Besserat, "The Earliest Precursors of Writing," *Scientific American* 238, 6 (1978): 50–59.

9. *The Epic of Gilgamesh: A New Translation*, trans. Andrew George (London: Penguin, 1999), 1.

10. According to Goody, and supported by Finnegan, epic writing was less dependent on oral material than previously thought, particularly less so than in Parry's account. "When we look at the societies where the classical epics flourished, these were all ones with writing. . . . In the area that has been the largest source of com-

positions from oral cultures, Africa, there is remarkably little legend or epic. . . . We find some epics in the warrior groups of the Saharan fringe . . . but these works are obviously influenced by the traditions of written Muslim culture coming from the Mediterranean." Goody, *Power of the Written Tradition*, 70.

11. Kathleen Gough, "Implication of Literacy in Traditional China and India," in *Perspectives on Literacy*, ed. Eugene R. Kintgen, Barry M. Knoll, and Mike Rose (Carbondale: Southern Illinois University Press, 1988), 44–56.

12. Merlin Donald, *Origins of the Modern Mind: Three Stages in the Evolution of Culture and Cognition* (Cambridge, Mass.: Harvard University Press, 1991), 308–9.

13. Ong, *Orality and Literacy*, 31–32, 71, 81; compare 162. Here the argument concerns the specificity of the oral as opposed to the written, and the latter is assumed to inform standard expectations about literature. Elsewhere, Ong dwells on the same point from another perspective, the distinctiveness of the written sign, as opposed to the oral: "By removing words from the world of sound where they had first had their origin in active human interchange and relegating them definitively to visual surface, and by otherwise exploiting visual space for the management of knowledge, print encouraged human beings to think of their own interior convictions and unconscious resources as more and more thing-like, impersonal and religiously neutral. Print encouraged the mind to sense that its possessions were held in some sort of inert mental space." Ong, *Orality and Literacy*, 131–32.

14. Eric A. Havelock, *Preface to Plato* (Cambridge, Mass.: Harvard University Press, 1963), 134–44.

15. Donald notes the tension between verbal and mimetic representation, particularly in theater, by citing examples from Aristophanes in *Origins of the Modern Mind*, 223.

16. Garrett Stewart, *Reading Voices: Literature and the Phonotext* (Berkeley: University of California Press, 1991).

17. For example, Harvey J. Graff, "The Legacies of Literacy," 86–87, and Jack Goody and Ian Watt, "Consequences of Literacy," 27, both in *Perspectives on Literacy*, ed. Eugene R. Kintgen, Barry M. Knoll, and Mike Rose (Carbondale: Southern Illinois University Press, 1988).

18. Ong, *Orality and Literacy*, 75.

19. M. T. Clanchy, *From Memory to Written Record: England, 1066–1307* (Cambridge, Mass.: Harvard University Press, 1979).

20. See Ong on novel readings in *Orality and Literacy*, 149.

21. This thesis that writing contributes to speech (as much as imaginative literature contributes to the social capacity for imagination and innovation) stands at odds with cultural-critical accounts of the novel as a vehicle of silence and alienation. Benjamin, in particular, contrasts the story as an oral genre and therefore the site of community wisdom with the novel, which is associated, pejoratively, with privacy and individuation. The pessimistic historical vision highlights a cultural loss: "The art of storytelling is coming to an end. Less and less frequently do we

encounter people with the ability to tell a tale properly. . . . It is as if something that seemed inalienable to us, the securest among our possessions, were taken from us: the ability to exchange experiences." He goes on to map this transformation onto a generic displacement: "The earliest symptom of a process whose end is the decline of storytelling is the rise of the novel at the beginning of modern times. What distinguishes the novel from the story (and from the epic in the narrower sense) is the essential dependence on the book. The dissemination of the novel became possible only with the invention of printing." Walter Benjamin, "The Storyteller," in Benjamin, *Illuminations* (New York: Schocken, 1969), 83, 87. Benjamin comes very close to Ong's account: Orality and community are contrasted with print and individuation. Indeed, even the individuation of the aesthetic object, signaled by the aesthetic-theoretical term *incommensurable*, is associated with a modernity of differentiation. Benjamin's collectivist predisposition is carried through consistently. The problematic is a defining characteristic for the modernism of the novel, where postindividual and collectivist elements compete with individuality and differentiation. Compare my *Rise of the Modern German Novel: Crisis and Charisma* (Cambridge, Mass.: Harvard University Press, 1986).

22. Ong, *Orality and Literacy*, 81–82.

23. By defining literature as writing, I do not preclude recognizing an oral literature within literate cultures, but it typically is a phenomenon that presumes literacy in one form or another; Ong calls this "secondary orality," and it ranges from the oral performance of poetry memorized from written texts to vernacular forms of performance, for example, stand-up comedians. On secondary orality, see Ong, *Orality and Literacy*, 135–36.

24. This is precisely the issue addressed in the reading of Homer provided by Max Horkheimer and Theodor Adorno in *Dialectic of Enlightenment*, trans. John Cumming (New York: Seabury Press, 1972), 43–80.

25. "Marsilies fait porter un livre avant: / La lei i fut Mahum e Tervagan." *Les Textes de la Chanson de Roland*, ed. Raoul Mortier (Paris: Éditions de la Geste Francor, 1940), vol. 1, 18 (*laisse* 47). "A book was brought by King Marsile's command: / Laws of Mohammed and Tervagant, his gods." *The Song of Roland*, trans. Patricia Terry (Indianapolis: Bobbs-Merrill, 1965), 26.

26. *Textes de la Chanson de Roland*, vol. 1, 42 (*laisse* 111); *Song of Roland*, 57.

27. *Textes de la Chanson de Roland*, vol. 1, 48 (*laisse* 127); *Song of Roland*, 57.

4. Literacy and Autonomy

1. Sylvia Scribner and Michael Cole, "Unpacking Literacy," in *Perspectives on Literacy*, ed. Eugene R. Kintgen, Barry M. Knoll, and Mike Rose (Carbondale: Southern Illinois University Press, 1988), 70.

2. Eric A. Havelock, *Preface to Plato* (Cambridge, Mass.: Harvard University Press, 1963), 60.

3. Havelock, *The Muse Learns to Write: Reflections on Orality and Literacy from Antiquity to the Present* (New Haven, Conn.: Yale University Press, 1986), 68.

4. Ibid., 69.

5. Ibid., 71.

6. Jack Goody and Ian Watt, "Consequences of Literacy," in *Perspectives on Literacy*, ed. Eugene R. Kintgen, Barry M. Knoll, and Mike Rose (Carbondale: Southern Illinois University Press, 1988), 4.

7. Hence Goody's comment: "The fact that virtually the only store of information is in the memories of men and women means that it is always susceptible to homeostatic transformation, to selective forgetting and remembering. There are, of course, techniques for preserving special kinds of information. But unless deliberately directed, memory bends to other interests, tending to set aside what does not fit. This feature of oral storage and transmission constitutes one aspect of the relatively homogeneous character of such cultures, in which uncomfortable dissonances tend to get overridden by the healing powers of oblivion while memory works with those experiences that link with others." Thus we know from written colonial records how orally transmitted knowledge regarding genealogies and territorial claims can change over time, despite the belief that oral performance accurately conveys cultural knowledge. Instead, oral transmission of knowledge allows for selective forgetting, adjustment to immediate needs and pressures, and a constant masking of current knowledge production with the aura of a mythic past. Goody, *The Power of the Written Tradition* (Washington, D.C.: Smithsonian Institution Press, 2000), 44–45.

8. "A language of action rather than reflection appears to be a prerequisite for oral memorization." Havelock, *Muse Learns to Write*, 76. Compare Walter J. Ong, *Orality and Literacy: The Technologizing of the Word* (New York: Routledge, 1982), 144.

9. Ong, *Orality and Literacy*, 102.

10. Ibid., 31–32.

11. Ibid., 162.

12. Denise Schmandt-Besserat, "The Earliest Precursors of Writing," *Scientific American* 238, 6 (1978): 50–59.

13. Goody, *Power of the Written Tradition*, 33–34.

14. Ong, *Orality and Literacy*, 102.

15. Walter Benjamin, "Goethes Wahlverwandtschaften," in *Gesammelte Schriften*, vol. 1, ed. Rolf Tiedemann and Hermann Schweppenhäuser (Frankfurt: Suhrkamp, 1974), 125–27.

5. The Epic and the Individual

1. Walter J. Ong, *Orality and Literacy. The Technologizing of the Word* (New York: Routledge, 1982), 13–14; quote, 158.

2. Derek Walcott, *Omeros* (New York: Farrar, Straus and Giroux, 1990), 5.

3. Ibid., 6.

4. Ibid., 8.

5. Franz Kafka, "In the Penal Colony," in *The Complete Stories*, ed. Nahum N. Glatzer (New York: Schocken, 1971), 149.

6. Siegfried Grosse, trans., *Das Nibelungenlied*, ed. Karl Bartsch and Helmut de Boor (Stuttgart: Reclam, 1997), 5; Arthur T. Hatto, trans., *The Nibelungenlied* (Baltimore: Penguin, 1965), 17.

7. Raoul Mortier, ed., *Les Textes de la Chanson de Roland* (Paris: Éditions de la Geste Francor, 1940), vol. 1, 112–13 (*laisse* 291); Patricia Terry, trans., *The Song of Roland* (Indianapolis: Bobbs-Merrill, 1965), 145–46.

8. Ong, *Orality and Literacy*, 78–79.

9. Jack Goody, *The Power of the Written Tradition* (Washington, D.C.: Smithsonian Institution Press, 2000), 24.

10. Alphonse de Lamartine, "Pensées des morts," in *Anthologie de la poésie française*, ed. Georges Pompidou (Paris: Hachette, 1961), 243.

11. Not only does writing introduce individuation and privacy, but also it was with primary orality that a more authentic reception of the world was possible. "In a primary oral culture, where the world has existence only in sound, with no reference whatsoever to any visually perceptible text, and no awareness even of the possibility of such a text, the phenomenology of sound enters deeply into human beings' feel for existence, as processed by the spoken word." Ong, *Orality and Literacy*, 73. By the end of the book, Ong qualifies this tendency to idealize the oral: "Orality is not an ideal, and never was. To approach it positively is not to advocate it as a permanent state for any culture. Literacy opens possibilities to the word and to human existence unimaginable without writing. Oral cultures today value their oral traditions and agonize over the loss of these traditions, but I have never encountered or heard of an oral culture that does not want to achieve literacy as soon as possible" (175).

12. Compare Goody, *Power of the Written Tradition*, 79.

13. Thomas Mann, *Reflections of a Nonpolitical Man*, trans. Walter D. Morris (New York: Ungar, 1983).

14. Compare Goody, *Power of the Written Tradition*, 82.

15. "Homer deserves praise for many reasons, but above all because he alone among poets is not ignorant of what he should do in his own person. The poet in person should say as little as possible; that is not what makes him an imitator. Other poets perform in person throughout, and imitate little and seldom; but after a brief preamble Homer introduces a man or woman or some other character and none of them are characterless: they have character." Aristotle, *Poetics*, trans. Malcolm Heath, sec. 10.4 (New York: Penguin, 1996), 40.

16. Ong, *Orality and Literacy*, 148.

17. Bertolt Brecht, "The Modern Theater Is the Epic Theater: Notes on the Opera *Aufstieg und Fall der Stadt Mahagonny*," in *Brecht on Theatre*, ed. and trans. John

Willett (London: Methuen, 1974), 37. Compare Peter Szondi, *Theory of Modern Drama*, trans. Michael Hays (Minneapolis: University of Minnesota Press, 1987), 69–73.

18. Goody, *Power of the Written Tradition*, 24; compare Eric A. Havelock, *The Muse Learns to Write: Reflections on Orality and Literacy from Antiquity to the Present* (New Haven, Conn.: Yale University Press, 1986), 68.

19. Marguérite Duras, *Écrire* (Paris: Gallimard, 1993), 17.

20. Jack Goody and Ian Watt, "Consequences of Literacy," in *Perspectives on Literacy*, ed. Eugene R. Kintgen, Barry M. Knoll, and Mike Rose (Carbondale: Southern Illinois University Press, 1988), 19.

21. Plato, "The Republic," in *The Works of Plato*, ed. Irwin Edman (New York: Modern Library, 1928), 327.

6. Religion and Writing

1. See Karl Jaspers, *Socrates, Buddha, Confucius, Jesus: The Paradigmatic Individuals*, ed. Hannah Arendt (New York: Harcourt, Brace, 1957).

2. Plato, "Phaedrus," in *The Works of Plato*, ed. Irwin Edman (New York: Modern Library, 1928), 329. Compare T. G. Rosenmeyer, "Plato's Prayer to Pan (*Phaedrus*, 279b8–c3)," *Hermes* 90 (1962): 34–44.

3. In this discussion I follow Catherine Pickstock, *After Writing: On the Liturgical Consummation of Philosophy* (Oxford, U.K.: Blackwell, 1998), 3–46.

4. Ibid., 31, 32.

5. Max Horkheimer and Theodor Adorno in *Dialectic of Enlightenment*, trans. John Cumming (New York: Seabury Press, 1972), 79–89.

6. Arthur T. Hatto, trans., *The Nibelungenlied* (Baltimore: Penguin, 1965), 291.

7. Michael Curschmann, "Dichter *alter maere*. Zur Prologstrophe des Nibelungenliedes im Spannungs feld von mündlicher Erzähltradition und laikaler Schriftkultur," in *Grundlagen des Verstehens in mittelalterlicher Literatur: Literarische Werke und ihr historischer Erkenntniswert*, ed. Gerhard Hahn and Hedda Rogalzki (Stuttgart: Kröner, 1992), 55–71.

8. Pickstock comments, "expressions of ontological and vocal crisis can be situated within a traditional medieval poetic commonplace known as *dorveille,* a psychological term describing the peculiar psycho-physical and spiritual depression suffered by bardic narrators, who typically complain of bodily exhaustion, restlessness, social withdrawal, or hypnotic suspension, an ontological diminution linked with the sin of *acedia* — a psychic deterioration or apathy which fears its own vocal erasure into silence." *After Writing*, 215; see also 215, n. 118.

9. Ibid., 214, 215.

10. Kathleen Gough, "Implication of Literacy in Traditional China and India," in *Perspectives on Literacy*, ed. Eugene R. Kintgen, Barry M. Knoll, and Mike Rose (Carbondale: Southern Illinois University Press, 1988), 44–56.

11. Samuel Taylor Coleridge, *Collected Works*, ed. Kathleen Coburn (Princeton, N.J.: Princeton University Press, 1969), vol. 6, 29–30; Blaise Pascal, *Oeuvres complètes*, ed. Michel Le Guern (Paris: Éditions Gallimard, 2000), vol. 2, 544.

12. John Milbank, *The Word Made Strange: Theology, Language, Culture* (Oxford, U.K.: Blackwell, 1997), 124.

13. Hannah Arendt, *The Human Condition* (Chicago: University of Chicago Press, 1958), 167–74.

14. Pickstock, *After Writing*, 221.

15. Milbank, *Word Made Strange*, 62.

16. Henri de Lubac, *Scripture in the Tradition* (New York: Herder and Herder, 2000), xx.

17. See Barbara Herrnstein-Smith, "Contingencies of Value," in *Canons*, ed. Robert von Hallberg (Chicago: University of Chicago Press, 1983), 5–40, and Herbert Lindenberger, *The History in Literature: On Value, Genre, Institutions* (New York: Columbia University Press, 1990).

18. Robert Alter, *Canon and Creativity: Modern Writing and the Authority of Scripture* (New Haven, Conn.: Yale University Press, 2000), 59–60.

19. Pickstock, *After Writing*, 220–52.

20. "Everything told in Scripture actually occurred in visible reality, but the account that stems from that reality does not have its end in itself; it must all yet be accomplished and it is in fact accomplished daily in us, through the mystery of spiritual understanding. Then alone — but this, to be sure, is a direction which is recommended rather than an end which is ever reached — will Scripture exist for us in all its fullness; then alone will we possess its 'truth.'" De Lubac, *Scripture in the Tradition*, 88. In other words, the allegorical historicization, the relation of past to present and future, is not only a matter of the outward events, but has implications for the very character of the temporality experienced by the subject. In this sense, de Lubac cites L. Boyer: The Bible is "not a dead word, imprisoned in the past, but a living word immediately addressed to the man of today . . ., a word which affects him, since it is for him that it was uttered and remains uttered." Cited in de Lubac, *Scripture in the Tradition*, 73.

21. Milbank, *Word Made Strange*, 95.

22. Pickstock, *After Writing*, 54.

23. John Milbank, "The Last of the Last: Theology, Authority and Democracy," *Telos* 123 (Spring 2002), 17.

24. Bertolt Brecht, *Gedichte*, vol. 4 in *Gesammelte Werke*, ed. Suhrkamp Verlag with Elisabeth Hauptmann (Frankfurt: Suhrkamp, 1967), 848. Translation is mine.

25. De Lubac, *Scripture in the Tradition*, 88.

26. Milbank, *Word Made Strange*, 65, 66.

27. Milbank cites Lowth: "Sometimes the principal or figurative idea is exhibited to the attentive eye with a constant and equal light, and sometimes it unexpectedly

glares upon us, and breaks forth with sudden and astonishing coruscations, like a flash of lightning bursting from the clouds. But the mode or form of this figure which possesses the most beauty and elegance is, when the two images equally conspicuous run, as it were, parallel through the whole poem, mutually illustrating and correspondent to each other. We may then perceive the vast disparity of the two images, and yet the continued harmony and agreement that subsists between them, the amazing resemblance as between near relations, in every feature and lineament, and the accurate analogy which is preserved, so that either may pass for the original whence the other was copied. New light is reflected upon the diction, and a degree of dignity and importance is added to the sentiments, whilst they gradually rise from humble to more elevated objects; from human to divine, till at length the great subject of the poem is placed in the most conspicuous light, and the composition attains the highest point of sublimity." Ibid., 69.

28. De Lubac, *Scripture in the Tradition*, 163.

29. Milbank, *Word Made Strange*, 106–7.

30. Compare James Carroll, *Constantine's Sword: The Church and the Jews, a History* (Boston: Houghton Mifflin, 2001).

31. De Lubac, *Scripture in the Tradition*, 163.

32. Ibid., 172.

7. The Democracy of Literature

1. Thomas Mann, "A Brother," in *Death in Venice, Tonio Kröger, and Other Writings*, ed. Frederick A. Lubich (New York: Continuum, 1999), 297–302.

2. Compare Lee Baxandall and Stefan Morawski, eds., *Marx and Engels on Literature and Art* (St. Louis: Telos Press, 1973), 199–28. In contrast, for Sartre the mediocrity of tendentious literature is not of concern: "Doubtless, the engaged writer can be mediocre; he can even be conscious of being so; but as one cannot write without the intention of succeeding perfectly, the modesty with which he envisages his work should not divert him from constructing it *as if* it were to have the greatest celebrity. He should never say to himself, 'Bah! I'll be lucky if I have three thousand readers,' but rather, 'What would happen if everybody read what I wrote?'" Jean-Paul Sartre, *What Is Literature?* trans. Bernard Frechtman (New York: Philosophical Library, 1949), 23.

3. On this point see Peter Uwe Hohendahl, *Building a National Literature: The Case of Germany 1830–1870*, trans. Renate Baron Franciscono (Ithaca, N.Y.: Cornell University Press, 1989).

4. "The failure of the protest novel lies in its rejection of life, the human being, the denial of his beauty, dread, power, in its insistence that it is his categorization alone which is real and which cannot be transcended." James Baldwin, "Everybody's Protest Novel," in *Collected Essays*, ed. Toni Morrison (New York: Literary Classics of the United States, 1998), 18.

5. Sartre, *What Is Literature?* 24.

6. On decisionism, see Carl Schmidt, *The Crisis of Parliamentary Democracy*, trans. Ellen Kennedy (Cambridge, Mass.: MIT Press, 1988); on the dispersion of power, see Raymond Aron, *Introduction à la philosophie politique: démocratie et révolution* (Paris: Éditions de Fallois, 1997).

7. See Hannah Arendt, *The Human Condition* (Chicago: University of Chicago Press, 1958), esp. 40, 45, 93.

8. On the tension between democracy and liberalism, see Schmitt, *Crisis of Parliamentary Democracy*, 22–32.

9. On the relationship between literary discussion and the emergence of the public sphere in modern Europe, see Jürgen Habermas, *The Structural Transformation of the Public Sphere: An Inquiry into a Category of Bourgeois Society*, trans. Thomas Burger with assistance from Frederick Lawrence (Cambridge, Mass.: MIT Press, 1989). See also Robert C. Holub, *Jürgen Habermas: Critic in the Public Sphere* (New York: Routledge, 1991), and Richard Sennett, *The Fall of Public Man* (New York: Knopf, 1977).

10. Edmund Burke, *Reflections on the Revolution in France* (New York: Penguin, 1986), 110.

11. On the contrasting absence of this distinction between religion and politics in Islam, see Luciano Pellicani, "Islam and the West," *Telos* 121 (Fall 2001): 86–112.

12. "Sovereign is he who decides on the exception." Carl Schmitt, *Political Theology: Four Chapters on the Concept of the Sovereign*, trans. George Schwab (Cambridge, Mass.: MIT Press, 1985), 5.

13. Sartre, *What Is Literature?* 64.

14. Citations from *Hamlet*, ed. Ann Thompson and Neil Taylor (London: Arden Shakespeare, 2006). Here page 148, but henceforth act, scene, and verse are given in the text.

15. Although Stephen Greenblatt emphasizes the theological, rather than the political issues, he does draw attention to the vital relationship between the appearance of the ghost in *Hamlet* and questions of imagination and a literary aesthetic. Stephen Greenblatt, *Hamlet in Purgatory* (Princeton, N.J.: Princeton University Press, 2001), esp. 205–57.

16. "The French revolution, Fichte's philosophy, and Goethe's *Meister* are the greatest tendencies of the age. Whoever is offended by this juxtaposition, whoever cannot take any revolution seriously that isn't noisy and materialistic, hasn't yet achieved a lofty, broad perspective on the history of mankind. Even in our shabby histories of civilization, which usually resemble a collection of variants accompanied by a running commentary for which the original classical text has been lost; even there many a little book, almost unnoticed by the noisy rabble at the time, plays a greater role than anything they did." "Athenäum," Fragment #216 in Friedrich Schlegel, *Lucinde and the Fragments*, trans. Peter Firchow (Minneapolis: University of Minnesota Press, 1971), 190.

17. Johann Wolfgang Goethe, *Wilhelm Meister's Apprenticeship*, ed. and trans. Eric A. Blackall with Victor Lange (Princeton, N.J.: Princeton University Press, 1989), vol. 9, 175. Page numbers for subsequent citations to this volume are given in the text.

8. Imagination and Economy

1. Peter Szondi, *Die Theorie des bürgerlichen Trauerspiels im achtzehnten Jahrhundert: Der Kaufmann, der Hausvater, und der Hofmeister*, ed. Gert Matenklott (Frankfurt: Suhrkamp, 1973).

2. "The novel searches for the German people where they will be found showing their industriousness, that is, at their work." Michael Kienzle, *Der Erfolgsroman: Zur Kritik seiner poetischen Ökonomie bei Gustav Freytag und Eugenie Marlitt* (Stuttgart: Metzler, 1975), 12. See also Theodor Fontante, review of *Soll und Haben*, in *Literarische Essays und Studien*, ed. Kurt Schreinert (Munich: Nymphenburger, 1963), vol. 21, pt. 1, 214–30; and my *Rise of the Modern German Novel: Crisis and Charisma* (Cambridge, Mass.: Harvard University Press, 1986), 79–104.

3. Pierre Bourdieu, *The Rules of Art: Genesis and Structure of the Literary Field*, trans. Susan Emanuel (Stanford, Calif.: Stanford University Press, 1996).

4. Mark W. Rectanus, *Culture Incorporated: Museums, Artists, and Corporate Sponsorships* (Minneapolis: University of Minnesota Press, 2002).

5. Carlo M. Cipolla, *Literacy and Development in the West* (Baltimore: Penguin, 1969).

6. Cited from *The New Oxford Annotated Bible*, ed. Bruce M. Meltzer and Roland E. Murphy (New York: Oxford University Press, 1994), 694–95.

7. Jean-Baptiste Molière, *Dom Juan ou le festin de Pierre*, in *Théâtre complet*, ed. Pierre Malandain (Paris: Imprimerie Nationale, 1997), vol. 3, 19; and *Don Juan*, trans. Richard Wilbur (San Diego: Harcourt, 2001), 9–10.

8. Molière, *Théâtre complet*, vol. 3, 87, and *Don Juan*, 146.

9. Rainer Maria Rilke, "Archäischer Torso Apollos," in *Werke in drei Bänden*, ed. Rilke Archive with Ruth Sieber-Rilke (Frankfurt: Insel, 1966), vol. 1, 313.

10. Franz Kafka, *The Complete Stories*, ed. Nahum N. Glatzer (New York: Schocken, 1971), 83.

11. Ibid., 88. See also Stanley Corngold, "The Hermeneutics of 'The Judgement,'" in *The Problem of the Judgement: Eleven Approaches to Kafka's Story*, ed. Angel Flores (New York: Gordian Press, 1977), 40.

BIBLIOGRAPHY

Adorno, Theodor W. *Notes on Literature*. Trans. Shierry Weber Nicholson. New York: Columbia University Press, 1991.

Aitchinson, Jean. *The Seeds of Speech: Language Origin and Evolution*. Cambridge, U.K.: Cambridge University Press, 2000.

Alter, Robert. *Canon and Creativity: Modern Writing and the Authority of Scripture*. New Haven, Conn.: Yale University Press, 2000.

Arendt, Hannah. *The Human Condition*. Chicago: University of Chicago Press, 1958.

Aristotle. *Poetics*. Trans. Malcolm Heath. New York: Penguin, 1996.

Aron, Raymond. *Introduction à la philosophie politique: démocratie et révolution*. Paris: Éditions de Fallois, 1997.

Auerbach, Erich. *Mimesis: The Representation of Reality in Western Literature*. Trans. Willard R. Trask. Princeton, N.J.: Princeton University Press, 2003.

Baldwin, James. "Everybody's Protest Novel." In *Collected Essays*, edited by Toni Morrison, 11–18. New York: Library of America, 1998.

Baudrillard, Jean. *The Mirror of Production*. St. Louis: Telos Press, 1975.

Baxandall, Lee, and Stefan Morawski, eds. *Marx and Engels on Literature and Art*. St. Louis: Telos Press, 1973.

Bednarik, R. G. "Replicating the First Known Sea Travel by Humans: The Lower Pleistocene Crossing of the Lombok Strait." *Human Evolution* 16 (2001): 229–42.

Benjamin, Walter. "Goethes Wahlverwandtschaften." In *Gesammelte Schriften*, vol. 1, edited by Rolf Tiedemann and Hermann Schweppenhäuser, 125–27. Frankfurt: Suhrkamp, 1974.

———. *Illuminations*. Trans. Harry Zohn. New York: Schocken Books, 1969.

Berman, Russell. *Rise of the Modern German Novel: Crisis and Charisma*. Cambridge, Mass.: Harvard University Press, 1986.

Binder, Hartmut. *Kafka-Handbuch*. Stuttgart: Alfred Kröner, 1979.

Bourdieu, Pierre. *The Rules of Art: Genesis and Structure of the Literary Field*. Trans. Susan Emanuel. Stanford, Calif.: Stanford University Press, 1996.

Brecht, Bertolt. *Brecht on Theatre*. Ed. and trans. John Willet. London: Methuen, 1974.

———. *Gedichte*. Vol. 4 in *Gesammelte Werke*. Ed. Suhrkamp Verlag with Elisabeth Hauptmann. Frankfurt: Suhrkamp, 1967.

Carey, Susan, and Elizabeth Spelke. "Domain-Specific Knowledge and Conceptual Change." In *Mapping the Mind: Domain Specificity in Cognition and Culture*, edited by Lawrence A. Hirschfeld and Susan A. Gelman, 169–200. Cambridge, U.K.: Cambridge University Press, 1994.

Carroll, James. *Constantine's Sword: The Church and the Jews, a History*. Boston: Houghton Mifflin, 2001.

Cavalli-Sforza, Luigi Luca. *Genes, Peoples, and Languages*. Trans. Mark Seielstad. Berkeley: University of California Press, 2001.

Chartier, Roger. *Culture écrite et société: l'ordre des livres (XIVe–XVIIIe siècle)*. Paris: Albin Michel, 1996.

Chomsky, Noam. *The Logical Structure of Linguistic Theory*. Chicago: University of Chicago Press, 1975.

Cipolla, Carlo M. *Literacy and Development in the West*. Baltimore: Penguin, 1969.

Clanchy, M. T. *From Memory to Written Record: England 1066–1307*. Cambridge, Mass.: Harvard University Press, 1979.

Clastres, Pierre. *Society against the State: The Leader as Servant and the Humane Uses of Power among the Indians of the Americas*. Trans. Robert Hurley. New York: Urizen Books, 1977.

Clifford, James. Introduction to *Writing Culture: The Poetics and Politics of Ethnography*, edited by James Clifford and George E. Marcus. Berkeley: University of California Press, 1986.

———, and George E. Marcus, eds. *Writing Culture: The Poetics and Politics of Ethnography*. Berkeley: University of California Press, 1986.

Corngold, Stanley. "The Hermeneutics of 'The Judgment.'" In *The Problem of the Judgment: Eleven Approaches to Kafka's Story*, edited by Angel Flores, 39–62 (New York: Gordian Press, 1977).

Coser, Lewis A., Charles Kadushin, and Walter W. Powell. *Books: The Culture and Commerce of Publishing*. New York: Basic Books, 1982.

Curschmann, Michael. "Dichter *alter maere*: Zur Prologstrophe des Nibelungenliedes im Spannungsfeld von mündlicher Erzähltradition und laikaler Schriftkultur." In *Grundlagen des Verstehens Mittelalterlicher Literatur: Literarische Texte und ihr historischer Erkenntniswert*, edited by Gerhard Hahn and Hedda Ragotzky, 55–71. Stuttgart: Kröner, 1992.

de Lubac, Henri. *Scripture in the Tradition*. New York: Herder and Herder, 2001.

———. *Surnaturel: Études historiques*. Paris: Desclée de Brouwer, 1991.

Donald, Merlin. *Origins of the Modern Mind: Three Stages in the Evolution of Culture and Cognition*. Cambridge, Mass.: Harvard University Press, 1991.

Du Bois, W. E. B. *The Souls of Black Folk*. New York: New American Library, 1969.

Duras, Marguerite. *Écrire*. Paris: Gallimard, 1993.

Finnegan, Ruth H. *Oral Poetry: Its Nature, Significance, and Social Context*. Cambridge, U.K.: Cambridge University Press, 1977.

Flores, Angel, ed. *The Problem of the Judgement: Eleven Approaches to Kafka's Story*. New York: Gordian, 1977.

Fontane, Theodor. Review of *Soll und Haben*. In *Literarische Essays und Studien*, edited by Kurt Schreinert, 2,1: 214–30 (Munich: Nymphenburger, 1963).

Foster, Hal, ed. *The Anti-aesthetic: Essays on Postmodern Culture*. New York: New Press, 1998.

Frake, Charles O. "Did Literacy Cause the Great Cognitive Divide?" *American Ethnologist* 10 (1983): 368–71.

Gallas, Helga. *Marxistische Literaturtheorie: Kontroversen im Bund proletarisch-revolutionärer Schriftsteller*. Neuwied, Ger.: Luchterhand, 1971.

George, Andrew, trans. *The Epic of Gilgamesh: A New Translation*. London: Penguin, 2000.

Goethe, Johann Wolfgang. *Werke*. Ed. Erich Trunz. Munich: Beck, 1968.

———. *Wilhelm Meister's Apprenticeship*. Ed. and trans. Eric A. Blackall, in cooperation with Victor Lange. Princeton, N.J.: Princeton University Press, 1989.

Goody, Jack. *The Interface between the Written and the Oral*. Cambridge, U.K.: Cambridge University Press, 1987.

———. *The Power of the Written Tradition*. Washington, D.C.: Smithsonian Institution Press, 2000.

———, and Ian Watt. "Consequences of Literacy." In *Perspectives on Literacy*, edited by Eugene R. Kintgen, Barry M. Kroll, and Mike Rose, 3–27. Carbondale: Southern Illinois University Press, 1988.

Gough, Kathleen. "Implications of Literacy in Traditional China and India." In *Perspectives on Literacy*, edited by Eugene R. Kintgen, Barry M. Kroll, and Mike Rose, 44–56. Carbondale: Southern Illinois University Press, 1988.

Graff, Harvey J. "The Legacies of Literacy." In *Perspectives on Literacy*, edited by Eugene R. Kintgen, Barry M. Kroll, and Mike Rose, 82–91. Carbondale: Southern Illinois University Press, 1988.

Greenblatt, Stephen. *Hamlet in Purgatory*. Princeton, N.J.: Princeton University Press, 2001.

Grosse, Siegfried, trans. *Das Nibelungenlied*. Ed. Karl Bartsch and Helmut de Boor. Stuttgart: Reclam, 1997.

Habermas, Jürgen. *The Structural Transformation of the Public Sphere: An Inquiry into a Category of Bourgeois Society*. Trans. Thomas Burger with assistance from Frederick Lawrence. Cambridge, Mass.: MIT Press, 1989.

Hahn, Gerhard, and Hedda Ragotzky, eds. *Grundlagen des Verstehens mittelalterlicher Literatur: Literarische Texte und ihr historischer Erkenntniswert*. Stuttgart: Kröner, 1992.

Harris, Wendell V. "Canonicity." *PMLA* 106 (1991): 110–21.

Hatto, Arthur T., trans. *The Nibelungenlied*. Baltimore: Penguin, 1965.

Havelock, Eric A. *The Muse Learns to Write: Reflections on Orality and Literacy from Antiquity to the Present.* New Haven, Conn.: Yale University Press, 1986.

———. *Preface to Plato.* Cambridge, Mass.: Harvard University Press, 1963.

Heine, Heinrich. *Werke.* Ed. Helmut Schanze. Frankfurt: Insel, 1968.

Herrnstein-Smith, Barbara. "Contingencies of Value." In *Canons,* edited by Robert von Hallberg, 5–40. Chicago: University of Chicago Press, 1984.

Hirschfeld, Lawrence A., and Susan A. Gelman, eds. *Mapping the Mind: Domain Specificity in Cognition and Culture.* Cambridge, U.K.: Cambridge University Press, 1994.

Hohendahl, Peter Uwe. *Building a National Literature: The Case of Germany, 1830–1870.* Trans. Renate Baron Franciscono. Ithaca, N.Y.: Cornell University Press, 1989.

———, ed. *A History of German Literary Criticism, 1739–1980.* Lincoln: University of Nebraska Press, 1988.

Holub, Robert C. *Jürgen Habermas: Critic in the Public Sphere.* New York: Routledge, 1991.

Horkheimer, Max, and Theodor W. Adorno. *Dialectic of Enlightenment.* Trans. John Cumming. New York: Seabury Press, 1972.

Hume, Robert D. *Reconstructing Contexts: The Aims and Principles of Archaeo-Historicism.* Oxford, U.K.: Oxford University Press, 1999.

Jameson, Fredric. *Marxism and Form: Twentieth-Century Dialectical Theories of Literature.* Princeton, N.J.: Princeton University Press, 1971.

Jaspers, Karl. *Socrates, Buddha, Confucius, Jesus: The Paradigmatic Individuals.* Ed. Hannah Arendt. New York: Harcourt Brace, 1957.

Jauss, Hans Robert. *Toward an Aesthetic of Reception.* Trans. Timothy Bahti. Minneapolis: University of Minnesota Press, 1981.

Jay, Martin. *The Dialectical Imagination: A History of the Frankfurt School and the Institute of Social Research, 1923–1950.* Berkeley: University of California Press, 1973.

Kafka, Franz. *The Complete Stories.* Ed. Nahum N. Glatzer. New York: Schocken, 1971.

Karmiloff-Smith, Annette. *Beyond Modularity: A Developmental Perspective on Cognitive Science.* Cambridge, Mass.: MIT Press, 1992.

———. "Precis of *Beyond Modularity: A Developmental Perspective on Cognitive Science.*" *Behavioral and Brain Sciences* 17 (1994): 693–745.

Kienzle, Michael. *Der Erfolgsroman: Zur Kritik seiner poetischen Ökonomie bei Gustav Freytag und Eugenie Marlitt.* Stuttgart: Metzler, 1975.

Kintgen, Eugene R., Barry M. Kroll, and Mike Rose, eds. *Perspectives on Literacy.* Carbondale: Southern Illinois University Press, 1988.

Lindenberger, Herbert. *The History in Literature: On Value, Genre, Institutions.* New York: Columbia University Press, 1990.

Lord, Albert Bates. *The Singer of Tales.* Cambridge, Mass.: Harvard University Press, 1960.

Lunn, Eugene. *Marxism and Modernism: An Historical Study of Lukács, Brecht, Benjamin, and Adorno.* Berkeley: University of California Press, 1982.

Lyotard, Jean-François. *The Postmodern Condition: A Report on Knowledge.* Trans. Geoff Bennington and Brian Massumi. Minneapolis: University of Minnesota Press, 1984.

Mann, Thomas. "A Brother." In *Death in Venice, Tonio Kröger, and Other Writings,* edited by Frederick A. Lubich, 297–302. New York: Continuum, 1999.

Marx, Karl. *Grundrisse: Foundations of the Critique of Political Economy.* Trans. Martin Nicolaus. New York: Random House, 1973.

Metzger, Bruce M., and Roland E. Murphy. *New Oxford Annotated Bible.* New York: Oxford University Press, 1994.

Milbank, John. "The Last of the Last: Theology, Authority, and Democracy." *Telos* 123 (Spring 2002): 17.

———. *The Word Made Strange: Theology, Language, Culture.* Oxford, U.K.: Blackwell, 1997.

———, Catherine Pickstock, and Graham Ward, eds. *Radical Orthodoxy: A New Theology.* London: Routledge, 1999.

Mithen, Steven. *The Prehistory of the Mind: The Cognitive Origins of Art, Religion, and Science.* London: Thames and Hudson, 1996.

Molière, Jean Baptiste. *Dom Juan.* Trans. Richard Wilbur. San Diego: Harcourt, 2001.

———. *Dom Juan ou le festin de Pierre.* In *Théâtre Complet,* edited by Pierre Malandain. Paris. Imprimerie Nationale, 1997.

Mortier, Raoul, ed. *Les Textes de la Chanson de Roland.* Paris: Éditions de la Geste Francot, 1940.

Noble, William, and Iain Davidson. *Human Evolution, Language, and Mind: A Psychological and Archeological Inquiry.* Cambridge, U.K.: Cambridge University Press, 1996.

Ong, Walter J. *Orality and Literacy: The Technologizing of the Word.* New York: Routledge, 1982.

Parkinson, Richard, and Stephen Quirke. *Papyrus.* Austin: University of Texas Press, 1995.

Parry, Adam, ed. *The Making of Homeric Verse: The Collected Papers of Milman Parry.* New York: Oxford University Press, 1987.

Pecora, Vincent P. "The Limits of Local Knowledge." In *The New Historicism,* edited by H. Aram Veeser, 243–76. New York: Routledge, 1989.

Pellicani, Luciano. "Islam and the West." *Telos* 121 (Fall 2001): 86–112.

Pickstock, Catherine. *After Writing: On the Liturgical Consummation of Philosophy.* Oxford, U.K.: Blackwell, 1998.

Plato. *The Works of Plato,* edited by Irwin Edman. New York: Modern Library, 1928.

Pompidou, Georges. *Anthologie de la poésie française.* Paris: Hachette, 1961.

Rectanus, Mark W. *Culture Incorporated: Museums, Artists, and Corporate Sponsorships.* Minneapolis: University of Minnesota Press, 2002.

Rilke, Rainer Maria. *Werke in drei Bänden.* 3 vols. Frankfurt: Insel, 1966.

Rolleston, James, ed. *A Companion to the Works of Franz Kafka.* Rochester, N.Y.: Camden House, 2002.

Rosenmeyer, T. G. "Plato's Prayer to Pan (*Phaedrus*, 279b8 – c3)." *Hermes* 90 (1962): 34 – 44.

Sartre, Jean-Paul. *What Is Literature?* Trans. Bernard Frechtman. New York: Philosophical Library, 1949.

Schlegel, Friedrich. *Philosophical Fragments.* Trans. Peter Firchow. Minneapolis: University of Minnesota Press, 1991.

Schmandt-Besserat, Denise. "The Earliest Precursor of Writing." *Scientific American* 238, no. 6 (1978): 50 – 59.

Schmitt, Carl. *The Crisis of Parliamentary Democracy.* Trans. Ellen Kennedy. Cambridge, Mass.: MIT Press, 1988.

———. *Political Theology: Four Chapters on the Concept of Sovereignty.* Trans. George Schwab. Cambridge, Mass.: MIT Press, 1986.

Scribner, Sylvia, and Michael Cole. "Unpacking Literacy." In *Perspectives on Literacy,* edited by Eugene R. Kintgen, Barry M. Kroll, and Mike Rose, 57 – 70. Carbondale: Southern Illinois University Press, 1988.

Sennett, Richard. *The Fall of Public Man.* New York: Knopf, 1976.

Shakespeare, William. *Hamlet,* edited by Ann Thompson and Neil Taylor. London: Arden Shakespeare, 2006.

Sperber, Dan. "The Modularity of Thought and the Epidemiology of Representations." In *Mapping the Mind: Domain Specificity in Cognition and Culture,* edited by Lawrence A. Hirschman and Susan A. Gelman, 39 – 67. Cambridge, U.K.: Cambridge University Press, 1994.

Steiner, George. *Real Presences: Is There Anything in What We Say?* Boston: Faber and Faber, 1989.

Stewart, Garrett. *Reading Voices: Literature and the Phonotext.* Berkeley: University of California Press, 1990.

Szondi, Peter. *Die Theorie des bürgerlichen Trauerspiels im achtzehnten Jahrhundert: Der Kaufmann, der Hausvater, und der Hofmeister.* Ed. Gert Matenklott. Frankfurt: Suhrkamp, 1973.

———. *Theory of the Modern Drama.* Trans. Michael Hays. Minneapolis: University of Minnesota Press, 1987.

Terry, Patricia, trans.. *The Song of Roland.* Indianapolis: Bobbs-Merrill, 1965.

Trumpener, Katie. *Bardic Nationalism: The Romantic Novel and the British Empire.* Princeton, N.J.: Princeton University Press, 1997.

Veeser, H. Aram., ed. *The New Historicism.* New York: Routledge, 1989.

Vico, Giambattista. *The New Science of Giambattista Vico,* 3d ed. [1744]. Trans. Thomas Goddard Bergin. Ithaca, N.Y.: Cornell University Press, 1968.

Vidal-Naquet, Pierre. *Le monde d'Homère.* Paris: Perrin, 2000.

Walcott, Derek. *Omeros.* New York: Farrar, Straus and Giroux, 1990.

INDEX

behavior: adaptations, 23, 26; economic and literary categories, 187; and exogenous factors, 67; and intelligence, 36; and language acquisition, 74; and language use, 39, 40, 45; at oral performance, 89; prelinguistic, 31; and stone-throwing, 41; symbolic, 57

Benjamin, Walter: and auratic art, 161; *Jetztzeit*, 18, 22; messianism, 147; mortification, 99; *Theses on the Philosophy of History*, 15–19

betrayal, 89, 99, 114–15

bildungsroman, 173, 175, 181

Blombos, South Africa, 42

Bloom, Harold, 138

book burnings, 99

Bourdieu, Pierre: on autonomy, 56, 61; on creativity, 62; on Zola, 182

Brecht, Bertolt, 11; and canonicity, 140–41; and engagement, 164; and epic theater, 114; his "Hollywood Quatrain," 139–42; and Lamartine, 152–58; and transcendence, 156

bureaucracy, 163

Bürgerliches Trauerspiel, 181

burial sites, 37; and art, 93; and understanding mortality, 38, 45

Burke, Edmund, 165

canonicity, 19, 22, 136; for Brecht, 140–41; in literary competition, 56; and religion, 143; and revisionism, 21

Carey, Susan, 36

cave paintings: 37, 42; and durability, 70; fixed locations of, 97; as information, 70; as memory prompts, 94

Céline, Louis-Ferdinand: and fascism, 164; and language, 57; *Voyage au bout de la nuit*, 166

censorship, 129; as self-censorship, 96

Cervantes, Miguel de, 50

Chanson de Roland: competition with

chronicles, 89; conclusion of, 125–26; fiction and history, 111; limits of heroism, 106–07, 114; and writing, 80

Chomsky, Noam, 32, 35

Christianity, 125; and allegory, 146; and betrayal, 81; and exegesis, 137; and Islam in *Chanson de Roland*, 80; and literature, 72; missionary, 46; in relation to the state, 166

cinema, 72, 98

Clancy, M. T., 72

Cole, Michael, 85–86

Coleridge, Samuel, 128, 130

commerce: commercialization, 184; and culture, 183

commodity aesthetics, 182–83

communication: informational, 31; and intention, 45; nonverbal, 30; pointing, 41; and symbols, 38, 44

comparative literature, 119, 128

competition: of authors, 138, 184; in epic, 107–08, 116; interspecies, 31, 67; of literature and the arts, 78; between literature and politics, 108, 111–12; of literature and wealth production, 68; between oral and written, 72; with prior writing, 48, 56; in society, 82, 86; among written texts, 80, 95

consciousness, 28; antimythological, 103; archaic, 30; closed, 32; episodic, 30; and evolution, 29, 39; and intentionality, 39; and literacy, 112; persistence of early formations, 84; semanticity in, 40; and symbols, 41; and writing, 85, 89, 108

consumer selection, 187

context, 20, 22; avoiding reduction to, 99; cultural, 101; of Dante, 48–49; inadequacy of, 127; of language acquisition, 44; and literature, 205; narrow, 48 counterfactuals: as comparative advantage of literature, 202; in fiction and faith, 130; and imagination, 45; and judgment, 203; literary, 149; in literary imagination, 143; representation of, 186; and suspension of disbelief, 143

creation: as linguistic, 138; and newness, 132

creativity: and compromise, 184; epilogic, 135; and facts, 138; Judeo-Christian account of, 133, 182; and poesis, 131; poetics of, 140; production of, 62; in religion, 143; and social order, 44

critical theory, 180

cultural relativism, 135

Dante, 32–33, 48–49

Darwin, 47; and Kafka, 49

Davidson, Iain, 39–44; on colonization of Australia, 37

De Lubac, Henri, 134; on exegesis, 146; and historical truth, 147; on history and transcendence, 142

decisionism, 163, 187

degradation: and loss of particularity, 53

dehominization, 52

democracy, 23; and autonomy, 178; and imagination, 167; of literary community, 96; of literary contents, 56; and literature, 152, 160; revolutions and 167; and writing, 75

demodularization, 43; and language, 38

dereliction, 133, 134

Derrida, Jacques, 121

determinism: and literary history, 134; technological, 76, 78

developmentalism, 123

disenchantment, 195

dispersion of power, 163, 187

Dom Juan, 194–201; and *Hamlet*, 199–200; and Mephistopheles, 195

Donald, Merlin: and Darwin, 30; his evolutionary account, 84; on gesture and mimetic expression, 94; on language and literature, 43; on language as revolutionary system, 30, 32; on mimesis, 31; on mimetic and mythic culture, 37, 72; *Origins of the Modern Mind*, 28–35; on Spencer and Dante, 32–33; and technology, 41

drama: and community, 164; and oral performance, 73; as written, 113

Du Bois, W. E. B, *Souls of Black Folk*, 21–22

Dubos, Jean-Baptiste, 145

durability: and evanescence, 99; of visual artifacts, 95; and writing, 70, 95

Duras, Marguerite, 115–16

economy: agricultural, 67; ancient, 192, 194; capitalistic, 23, 182, 188, 201, 205; consumer judgment, 187, 205; deliberative evaluation, 205; development and literacy, 83; and entrepreneur, 187–88, 194; of excess, 187; of innovation and caution, 201; and literature, 180–83, 185, 192

electronic media, 66, 119

Eliot, T. S., 162

emancipation, 21; and alienation, 133; in critical theory, 180; and phenomenology of literature, 167; redemptive, 146

engagement, 164

entrepreneurship: in literature, 194; vision of, 187

epic, 19; and adversarial writer, 123; agonistic structure of, 108; betrayal in, 89; and derivation of, 120; as didactic, 87; etymology of, 101; and failure, 114; foundational, 97; and heroism, 89, 92, 193; and historical thinking, 103; and historiography, 81; and individuals, 80–81; length of, 97; as national, 105; as oral or written, 103; and orality, 68, 73; its plot structure, 112–13; as record of violence, 109; and violence, 148; and writing, 92, 99, 113, 130

epigonality: aesthetic, 146; in epics, 107, 114; of Greek time, 132; in writing, 138

epilogic aesthetics, 146

ethics of reading, 160

evanescence: of materiality, 99; in writing, 115

evolution: 23, 28; and adaptation, 28; in archeology and psychology, 35; cultural and rhyme, 56; and innovation, 32; and language, 41, 45, 51; and motor skills, 41; and progress, 52; as response to environment, 31–32; and symbols, 29; theory of, 84

faith: of Charlemagne in Chanson de Roland, 125; for Coleridge and Pascal, 128; and faithlessness, in Dom Juan, 195; and fiction, 127, 128, 130, 143, 148; fideistic argument, 144; and modernization, 130; and reason, for Milbank, 138; and suspension of disbelief, 143, 148, 191; as waiting, 191

fiction: and faith, 127, 130; versus historiography, 111; and mendacity, 140; and modernization, 130

Flaubert, Gustav: and autonomy, 56; on corruption and commercialism, 69; his critical adversariality, 89, 116; integrity as writer, 82; letter to George Sand, 61; and social criticism, 61

Fontane, Theodor, Effi Briest, 150

freedom: and autonomy, 92; and caution, 188; as creativity, 159; through

formal integrity, 115; of gift, 131; and institutions, 206; literary and individual, 78, 167; in market economy, 182; in praxis, 133; and resignation, 52; and slavery, 133; of speech, 129; in Wilhelm Meister, 178

Freud, Sigmund, 50

Freytag, Gustav, Soll und Haben, 181

genre: dedifferentiation of, 76, 77; history of, 101–12; and religious legacy, 143; social restrictions in tragedy, 79

George, Stefan, 57

gesture calls: and human speech, 40; and language, 45

Gilgamesh, 67, 79; hero as writer, 102, 109, 123–24; and literature and politics, 165; and Ong's critique of writing, 103; the tablets, 89

glaciation, 40, 67, 206

Goethe, Johann Wolfgang von: and individualism, 175; Wilhelm Meister's Apprenticeship, 172–78

Goodall, Jane, 57

Goody, Jack: on deleterious impact of writing, 89–90, 117; on the epic, 64, 79, 93; on literacy and development, 67, 88; on narrative, 89; on oral performance, 46, 109; on spread of literacy, 68

Gutenberg, Johannes, 119

Hamann, Johann Georg, 145–46

Hamlet: as appeal to action, 168–69; and appearance and essence, 169; capacity to act, 171, 178; German reception, 168

Harris, Roy, 33

Havelock, Eric, 68; and binary of orality and literacy, 123; on encyclopedic function of epics, 32, 76, 111; on Milman Parry, 88; orality of Homeric epic, 86; and rhyme in oral culture, 55

Heine, Heinrich, 110

hermeneutics of suspicion, 136

hermeticism, 57

hero: the author as, 62; battling death, 58, 115; and conformism, 115; and the epic, 78–79, 103; in modernity, 109; in *Nibelungenlied*, 106; relation to autonomy, 79; relation to early literacy, 109; resistance to regression, 102

historical materialism 17–18, 22

historical writing, 151

historicism: 16, 20, 22; as reductionistic, 160

history of literature, 19, 23, 25; and altriciality, 43; foundations of, 127; and human origins, 26, 44; and language acquisition, 43; and literacy, 83; national, 25; and speech, 73; technological, 66, 120; and world religions, 128; and writing, 63, 119

Hoffmann E. T. A., 50

Hohenstein-Stadel, 37, 38, 49

homeostasis: as adjustment, 88–89; and conformity, 104, 124, 149; as editing, 96; impact of writing, 115, 167, 182; for Ong, 90, 109; and orality, 89, 92, 108

Homer, 19, 46; affective transformation from Achilles to Odysseus, 103; Aristotle's judgments, 73, 113; Bellerophon episode in *Iliad*, 89; border with animals, 50; and cognitive psychology, 35–36; compared to Herodotus, 77, 111; compared to Isaiah, 144; compared to Jeremiah, 125; dating of epics, 93; encyclopedic role, 32; Hominization, 23, 26, 27, 28; in Kafka, 51, 52; and language, 29; as literary topic, 52; Marx on, 48, 67; mnemonic verse, 94; his objectivity,

126; Parry's study of, 86; as preliterate, 79; reception of, 48, 160; stages of, 30; and tools, 57; use of epithets, 132; on violence, 124

human origins, 23, 25, 27

humanities, 23, 25, 47; and the market, 184; and politics, 161; and prehistory, 45; and social sciences, 33; treatment of individual cases, 50

idolatry, 100, 132–33

imagination, 23; and action, 172; and displacement, 96; and faith, 138, 143; and judgments, 194, 200, 201, 202, 204; and language, 43; and psychology, 205; relation to taste, 187; and surplus, 186, 193

incantatory poetry, 189

incarnation of the Word, 134

individual, 23; adversarial and entrepreneurial, 92; and conformism, 62; as ethic, 193; and faith, 191; in Kafka's "The Judgment," 203; for Lamartine, 157; in literature, 157; in Psalms, 189; and solidarity, 148; in *Wilhelm Meister*, 173, 177

innovation, 29; artistic, 33; and creativity, 131; and critique of idolatry, 132–33; and imagination, 206; in language, 30; models of, 58; in Olduwan culture, 37; for orality studies, 87

irony: of inversion, 192; and literature, 97; in *Wilhelm Meister*, 174, 177; in writing, 108

Judaism: 125; relationship of the Church to, 146

judgment, 11; adversarial, 61; in Kafka, 201–05; relation to imagination, 194; on the recipient, 200; and social criticism, 82

Kafka, Franz: context of, 48–49; his cultural pessimism, 52; and Darwin, 49; "In the Penal Colony," 105; "The Judgment," 201–05; and logical problem, 51; "The Metamorphosis," 52–54, 135; and Molière, 202–03; reception of, 97; "Report to an Academy," 49–52

Kahlschlagliteratur, 139

Karmiloff-Smith, Annette, 36

Klee, Paul, 18–19

La Fontaine, Jean de, 50

Lamartine, Alphonse de: compared to Brecht, 152–58; on death, 58; and language, 57; *Pensées des Morts*, 54–55; on position of author, 109; use of rhyme, 55–57

language: acquisition, 23, 26, 28, 31, 32, 39; alphabetic, 33; anatomical preconditions, 39, 41; and animals, 49; and the arts, 31; as behavior adaptation, 34–35; and encephalization, 41; and evolution, 39, 41, 45; and gesture calls, 40; in hominization, 50; and innovation, 32; as interior monologue, 53; and literature, 27, 31, 33, 54; and modular specialization, 38; and myth, 32; numbers of, 33; particularity of, 155; in prehistoric culture, 29, 38–39; relation to imagination, 43, 45; relation to mindedness, 39; revitalization of, 57; as revolutionary system, 30; role of cross-generational relationships, 44; scientific, 31; as shaped, 57; technology history of, 67

liberal arts, 116

literacy: and criticism, 167; critique of, 123; and democratization, 96; development of, 62; in Greece, India, and China, 68; in the *Iliad*, 89; as impov-

ershiment, 90; for Ong, 90; and orality, 65; psychological ramifications of, 86; relation to economic development, 186; restricted, 62; and social environment, 86; and temporality, 90–91; Vai, 85–86; as visual, 95

literariness: in human condition, 27; and language, 57; and politics, 159; relation to religion, 142

literary history: and altriciality, 44; and economic categories, 185; and evidence, 27; and language acquisition, 54; relation to human origins, 58–59; and religion, 120, 122; role of technology in, 108

literature: and action, 171; and altriciality, 43; and the arts, 78; as artifact, 78; and autonomy, 82; and capitalism, 201; and circulation of ideas, 161; and cultural memory, 55; and democracy, 160, 166–67; and economy, 180, 181–82, 185, 188, 205; and faith, 143; and formal imperative, 58, 96; as grammatological or symbolic, 76, 78; and heroism, 82; high and low, 57; as historical document, 150; and inattention, 202, 204; incongruity of, 84; and language, 32, 43; and letters, 76; and literacy, 186; and media history, 81; and myth, 85; openness of, 148; between orality and visuality, 73; origin of 26, 27; as Orphic, 58; and politics, 79, 106, 152, 159, 162, 185, 188; redemptive, 135; relation to philosophy, 88; and religion, 143, 148, 191; in social development, 206; as social network, 44; totalitarian, 160; transcendence in, 191; and visual culture, 64

liturgy, 117; in Kafka's, "The Judgment," 201; and myth, 123; of Psalms, 190; and solidarity, 124

Lord, A. B., 46
Lowth, Robert: on Hebrew poetry, 144–48; mystical allegories, 192
Luther, Martin: relationship to the text, 137; translation of Bible, 140

Maccabean moment, 146
Mann, Thomas: "Brother Hitler," 151; *The Magic Mountain*, 133
Mariage de Figaro, 198
Marx, Karl: and Greek mythology, 12–15, 16, 18, 109; on Homer, 48, 67; on tendentious literature, 153
Marxism, 17, 66, 67, 185
mathematical reduction, 137, 195
Mélodrame, 180
memorization and recitation practices, 94
memory: impact of writing, 117; in literature, 85; in primary orality, 46; and recitation, 94
Midrash, 137, 145
migration, 40, 41, 45
Milbank, John: on Aristotle, 131; on faith and reason, 138; on Johann Georg Hamann, 145–46; on Robert Lowth, 144–48, 192
mimesis: and culture, 30, 31; and language, 51
Mithen, Steven, 35–39, 66, 79; language and literature, 43; on technology, 41
modularity, 35, 36
Molière, Jean Baptise: *Dom Juan*, 194–201; and Kafka, 202–03; and Rilke, 200
mourning: in *Chanson de Roland*, 107; in epics, 125–26; and religion, 148
movable type, 66, 119
myth: and criticism, 97; and culture, 31–32; and science, 32, 85; and theory, 34

narrative: as chain of events, 28; heroic, 78; and myth, 32, 84; in oral cultures, 93; veracity of, 51
natural science, 47, 85
Neanderthals, 29, 31; competition with, 41; culture, 37
Neruda, Pablo, 48–49
New Criticism, 91
Nibelungenlied: conclusion of, 125; condemnation of violence, 104; retrospective opening, 105
Nietzsche, Friedrich, 14; and Kafka, 49; and rebarbarization, 57
Noble, William, 39–44; on colonization of Australia, 37
Norris, Frank, 180
novel: chapter divisions of, 113; and democracy, 79; of education, 44, 173, 175, 181; and privacy, 164; readings of, 73, 94; subtlety in, 108

Olduwan culture, 36–37, 39
Ong, Walter J.: contrasts epic and novel, 108; and Corinthians, 72; critique of literacy, 89–90; deleterious impact of writing, 117; on Greek drama, 113; on evanescence, 69; on homeostasis, 90, 108; on literary history, 76; on oral performance, 63–64, 76; phenomenological account, 92; and Plato, 123; visuality, 95, 98; on writing, 66, 74
oral performance: and cultural continuity, 47, 87–88; as encyclopedic, 76; genres of, 64; and literacy, 46–47, 65, 94; and literature, 63; and material artifacts, 47; and memory, 69–70, 87, 88
orality, 33, 34; and culture, 46; evanescence of, 70; and indeterminacy, 126; in literature, 72; and mortality, 90; in narrative and epic, 97; primary,

44, 93, 108; secondary, 47, 94, 113; and
transition to literacy, 74; and visual
arts, 70
Orwell, George, 50
Ossian, 47
Ovid, *Metamorphoses*, 135

paper, 66, 119
Parry, Milman, 46, 79, 86
Pascal, Blaise, 128
patronage, 134
periodization, 11–15, 18, 19, 20, 21
Phaedrus: identity and difference, 122;
and precision, 205. *See also* Plato
philosophy: and literature, 88; and
writing, 77
Pickstock, Catherine, 121–23, 126–27;
on Peter Ramus, 137; on temporality, 136
Plato: and differentiation of knowledge,
77; on poetry in *The Republic*, 84,
117; and Socrates' prayer, 127; on
writing in *Phaedrus*, 117–18, 120–23
Pleonasm: in Hebrew poetry, 144; and
Midrash, 145
plot, 112
poesis, 135
poetry: and death, 58; and language, 56;
lyric, 73; and Psalms, 191; readings
of, 73; symbolist, 57
pointing, 41, 56
politics: and autonomy, 161; and choice,
152, 164; for *Gilgamesh*, 165; and
literature, 106, 108, 111–12, 159, 162,
185, 188; Thomas Mann on literature
and politics, 112; and scholarship,
159; and temporality, 165. *See also*
democracy
portability: as challenge, 167; and literature, 95–96; of sculptures, 70
postmodernism, 77, 150–51

Pound, Ezra: *The Cantos*, 158; and economic doctrine, 180–81
praise poem, 89, 102; and orality, 99; in
Psalm 27, 193
Praxis, 131
prayer: and Psalms, 189–90; of
Socrates, 121–23
primates, 30
print, 90
promise: for Brecht, 142; of happiness,
134, 148; of redemption, 136–37
propaganda, 164
Psalm 27, 190–94
Psalms, 189
public sphere: and individuals, 179; and
literature, 185, 194

radical orthodoxy, 138
Ramus, Peter, 137
Ranke, Leopold von, 15, 19
readers: ability to return to text, 98;
affect of, 126; appeal to, 157; and author, 159; and choice, 187; as citizens,
158, 165; and imagination, 148; and
irritation, 51; and mass audience, 44;
subjectivity of, 82
reception history, 100
record keeping, 34
redemption: dialectic of, 133; faith in,
191; in religion and literature, 130, 135;
of the Word, 134;
regression: psychological, 50; tales of,
53
religion, 20; of eternal life, 58; in literary
history, 127; and literature, 191; and
metaphoricity, 146; prehistoric, 45
rhyme: abandonment of, 56; in Lamartine, 55–56; and meter, 69–70; in oral
performance, 93; and speech, 56; and
transmission, 55
Roman rite, 136

romanticism, 27, 47, 116; and author-ship, 93; on commercialization, 184; and *Dom Juan*, 195; of Lamartine, 157; and literature and death, 58; and medievalism, 106

rotation press, 66

Rousseau, Jean-Jacques: on Bellero-phon in *Illiad*, 79; and language, 27

sacred texts, 78, 120, 128

Sartre, Jean-Paul, 162, 163; on anti-Semitism and the novel, 167; on en-gagement, 164

scarcity, 186–87

Schlegel, Friedrich, 172

Schmandt-Besserat, Denise, 93

scholarship: and politics, 159; and writ-ing, 73

schooling: and language acquisition, 44; for Vai people, 85

Scribner, Sylvia: on the literacy transi-tion, 85–86

scripture, 58

sculptures and portability, 94

secularization, 130

self-consciousness, 29, 36

semantics: and absence, 58; and con-sciousness, 40; and reference, 57; and rhyme, 56

Shakespeare, 11, 149–50; *Hamlet*, 168–72; *Merchant of Venice*, 180

social sciences, 23, 33, 47, 50

Socrates: in *Clouds*, 31; and myth, 34. *See also* Plato

solidarity, 198

Sonderweg, 176

Spelke, Elizabeth, 36

Sperber, Dan, 36

Spiegelman, Art, 50

state: building, 67; and individuality, 165

Stendhal (Marie-Henri Beyle), *Lucien Leuwen*, 150

suffering, 133

surplus, 193

suspension of disbelief, 143, 148, 167

symbol, 27, 30; and adult-child inter-action, 41; alphabetic, 96; capacity for, 43; communicative, 44; dynamic use of, 29; epistemology of, 93; and imagination, 45; and innovation, 32, 41; prehistoric, 37; sign and refer-ent, 38; and tools, 57; visual, 34, 46; and writing systems, 33; written and phonetic, 76

talking animals, 49–51

taste: and imagination, 187; and vision, 193

technology: and change, 29; and fire, 41; and literature, 108, 119; sea-faring, 40; of writing, 97–98

temporality: developmental, 23; epig-onic, 102; external and internal, 23; and literacy, 90–91; of literature, 48; for literature and politics, 165; post-modern, 136; retrospective, 105; and transcendence, 139–40; of writing, 98

Tendenzliteratur, 153

Torah, 134

tradition, 20, 26; in Brecht, 141–42; suppression of, 21; transmission of, 87

transcendence: and the hero, 126; spiri-tual, 120

tyranny, 163

Vai literacy, 85–86

Vico, Giambattista, *New Science*, 25

violence: in the epic, 103, 108, 109; Hamlet's judgment on, 172; and modernity, 109; in *Phaedrus*, 122–23; prayer as corrective, 123; and religion, 127; in spiritual revolution, 125; and writing, 124

Voltaire, 129

Walcott, Derek, *Omeros*, 102–04

Watt, Ian: on dissemination of literacy, 68; on literacy and development, 67, 88; on negative consequences of writing, 89–90

Weber, Max: and Protestant ethic, 142

western culture: and autonomous art, 179; and individuality, 62, 83; and literature, 205; and religion, 120, 142, 191; and suffering, 133; and teleology, 33; and writing, 68

Wilhelm Meister: and American Revolution, 172–73, 176–77, 178; and aristocracy, 181; and irony, 174, 177; letter to Werner, 174; and subjectivity, 176

Wright, Richard, *Native Son*, 150, 162

writing: and accuracy, 122, 126; acquisition of, 83; and adversariality, 82; as agonistic, 111; alphabetic, 46; as cognitive specialization, 77; and content, 155; and decisions, 166; and demythologization, 34; and durability, 70, 90; and part of great divide, 65; Greek, 34; and heroism, 103–04, 109; as hybrid of visual and oral, 98, 115; and imagination, 75; impact on literature, 65; inattention, 182; and institutions, 86; integrity of texts, 89, 93; and interiority, 121; Korean, 65; lack of, 68; and length of work, 97; and memory, 34; in modernity, 73; and mortality, 58, 99; and nationality, 155; relation to orality, 63, 189; origins of, 62–63, 65; and passivity, 68; Phoenician, 34; and politics, 109; precursors of, 93; prehistoric symbols, 37; as protest against violence, 124; as record, 26, 66, 76; and regret, 104; and rhyme, 55; role in state building, 69; and scholarship, 63; and solitude, 115–16; "in the soul," 117, 120; of Soviet dissidents, 160; and speech in drama, 114; subsequentiality, 48; suspicion of, 72; technologies, 23, 66, 74; and text criticism, 70, 77, 90, 97; and theory, 33, 84; and visuality, 71, 94–95

Zola, Emile: on autonomy and money, 182